COACHING TENNIS SUCCESSFULLY

United States Tennis Association

Ron Woods
USTA

Mike Hoctor
Astronaut High School

Rebecca Desmond
Downingtown Senior High School

Human Kinetics

Library of Congress Cataloging-in-Publication Data

United States Tennis Association.
   Coaching tennis successfully / United States Tennis Association ;
Ron Woods, Mike Hoctor, Rebecca Desmond.
     p.   cm.
   Includes index.
   ISBN 0-87322-461-2
   1. Tennis--Coaching. I. Woods, Ron, 1943 Nov. 6- II. Hoctor,
Mike. III. Desmond, Rebecca. IV. Title.
GV1002.9.C63U55 1995
796.342'07'7--dc20   94-41682
                                                  CIP

ISBN: 0-87322-461-2

Developmental Editor: Jan Colarusso Seeley; **Assistant Editors:** Karen Grieves, Karen Bojda, Dawn Roselund, Ann Greenseth; **Copyeditor:** John Wentworth; **Proofreader:** Jim Burns; **Indexer:** Barbara E. Cohen; **Typesetter:** Ruby Zimmerman; **Text Design and Layout:** Robert M. Reuther; **Cover Designer:** Keith Blomberg; **Photographer (cover):** Dave Black; **Interior Photos:** USTA/Lance Jeffrey, Russ Adams Productions, Inc., Rebecca Desmond, Scott Roman, and Scott Rowan; **Interior Art:** Studio 2D, Paul To; **Printer:** United Graphics

Printed in the United States of America   10 9 8 7 6 5 4

Human Kinetics
Web site: http:/www.humankinetics.com/

United States: Human Kinetics, P.O. Box 5076, Champaign, IL 61825-5076
1-800-747-4457
e-mail: humank@hkusa.com

Canada: Human Kinetics, 475 Devonshire Road, Unit 100, Windsor, ON N8Y 2L5
1-800-465-7301 (in Canada only)
e-mail: humank@hkcanada.com

Europe: Human Kinetics, P.O. Box IW14, Leeds LS16 6TR, United Kingdom
+44 (0)113-278 1708
e-mail: humank@hkeurope.com

Australia: Human Kinetics, 57A Price Avenue, Lower Mitcham, South Australia 5062
(08) 82771555
e-mail: humank@hkaustralia.com

New Zealand: Human Kinetics, P.O. Box 105-231, Auckland Central
09-523-3462
e-mail: humank@hknewz.com

Contents

Foreword

This book, *Coaching Tennis Successfully*, is the only book of its kind. It is a comprehensive manual on coaching, particularly in team situations. I have been fortunate to be on high school, college, and Davis Cup teams, and my coaches knew much of this material, but at every level the information presented here would have helped to make these coaches even more effective. The experience of being on a tennis team, especially at the junior high or high school level, is not only tremendously important in preparing a young person to meet the challenges of tennis competition but also the challenges of life.

I recommend this book to any coach who wants to be more effective and would like some suggestions on developing a coaching philosophy, planning for the season, working on on-court skills, and preparing for and evaluating match play. This book can be a very practical guide in helping you, as a coach, to be the best you can be.

The many anecdotes illustrating the important points presented in this book are real-life examples of both positive experiences and mistakes made along the way. The book is written in a form that is easy to understand and put into practice.

In addition, *Coaching Tennis Successfully* is also up-to-date in the areas of sport science and technique, so you can relate the information to today's game and to the players who are excelling.

I wish you the best of luck as you develop your own coaching style. You have a crucial role in influencing the lives of the young people with whom you work.

Stan Smith
Hall of Fame Professional Tennis Player
Associate Director,
USTA Player Development

Acknowledgments

The organization and preparation of the material in this book could not have been accomplished without the professional expertise of USTA staff member Linda P. Jusiewicz. Paul Roetert and Lew Brewer also freely shared their expertise in sport science and coaching methodology. Lynne Rolley, Nick Saviano, Tom Gullikson, and Stan Smith helped by contributing their combined coaching wisdom, which guided the sections on strategy and technique. The USTA proudly acknowledges the contributions of each of these members of our professional staff for player development.

Introduction

The United States Tennis Association owns and operates the U.S. Open Championships, which helps provide revenue to promote and develop the sport of tennis. Among our over 500,000 members are a significant number of high school coaches, players on school teams, and parents of those players. This book is designed to help all involved in competitive school tennis enjoy the experience and to help all players become the best they can be.

The material presented here reflects the cutting edge of tennis coaching today by our USTA national coaching staff as well as our sport science staff of experts. We have blended the ideas with the practical experiences of highly successful coaches who, over many years, have produced championship high school tennis teams for both boys and girls. If you coach a tennis team—be it an Olympic, college, or high school team or kids' junior team tennis—you'll find much helpful advice within these pages.

The first part of the book sets the stage and lays the foundation for your coaching style and philosophy, offers advice on critical interpersonal communication skills, and tackles the difficult issues of motivating your players while developing their mental toughness. These are the fundamental principles in coaching young people that truly define success over the long term.

Part II deals with planning for both the overall season and each practice in an organized, efficient way. Instruction from this section will save you time and effort that can be better spent doing what you really love—working with young people.

The nuts and bolts of on-court coaching are presented in the third section. Teaching tennis skills and strategies are blended together so that players can learn more quickly and use what they learn in match play. Concepts are accented by practical on-court drills explained and displayed in diagram form.

Preparing players for competitive match play is covered in Part IV, including tips on scouting opponents and conducting prematch practices. The coach's role during matches is discussed along with important advice for helping players deal with a win or a loss after a match.

The concluding section deals with the coach's role in the evaluation of players and the program. The orderly approach includes asking the right questions; assessing needed improvements in personnel, facilities, or equipment; and building a plan for future success.

All of us who have contributed to this book recognize the thousands of dedicated tennis coaches, like you, across our land who are devoted to helping young people enjoy Tennis—The Sport for a Lifetime. We hope our suggestions help you just as we have learned from our coaches and, especially, our players.

Part I

Coaching Foundation

Chapter 1

Developing a Tennis Coaching Philosophy

I remember that late fall drive in 1969 as if it were yesterday. I was traveling the back roads, alone, pondering my response to a question posed by our high school athletic director earlier in the day. Specifically, he had asked me, "Would you consider coaching boys' and girls' tennis in the spring?"

As a second-year teacher just getting used to the rigors of classroom teaching, I didn't find the thought of adding coaching responsibilities to the end of the school day too appealing. Before I gave our athletic director an answer, I needed some time alone to consider the positives and negatives of becoming a high school tennis coach.

On the plus side were three important factors: First, I love sports and coaching in general; all the heroes of my youth were athletes or coaches. Second, I love to work with high school students, as I enjoy interacting with teenagers and helping them develop. Third, I had a general athletic background, including a couple of years of playing high school football and basketball; where tennis was concerned, I was the proverbial weekend warrior.

On the negative side were three equally strong reasons I feared I might not be a successful coach: Number one, I had no high school or college competitive playing experience. Two, I had no training to teach tennis. And three, I was young at the time and intimidated by the thought of being a head coach in any sport.

After weighing the pluses and minuses, I finally threw caution to the wind and accepted the offer to become a tennis coach. Time has proven that I made the right decision.

In my 25 years of coaching I have enjoyed—and continue to enjoy—rich, rewarding experiences that I don't believe I'd have had in any other profession. I've had the privilege of watching all three of my sons mature on the court as I coached them. I've experienced triumphs and defeats, relationships and rivalries, teaching and learning. And above all, I've had the pleasure of seeing the players progress from our program to lead very successful lives. These are the compensations a coach treasures above and beyond any monetary considerations.

Building a Coaching Foundation

Development of a coaching philosophy, like learning, is an essential and continuous process. It begins the first day you decide to become a coach and ends only if you shut yourself off to new ideas and new experiences. As coaches we never have all the answers. Be willing to give new coaching techniques a try!

Tennis Coach Versus Tennis Pro

Most high school tennis coaches must learn to work in harmony with the local tennis teaching professionals. A player's teaching pro may be the best resource for developing individual stroke production. However, most teaching pros work with one player at a time during private lessons. As a high school tennis coach you don't have this luxury—you may have 8 to 12 players to attend to at one time. Plus, during a typical high school tennis season, there simply isn't time to focus on stroke development. As the high school coach, you should emphasize tactics and strategies while molding the individuals into a team. Stress the "team first" attitude that all successful sports teams exhibit. Even a novice tennis coach with a background in team sports can work in harmony with a teaching pro. You may choose to let the pro develop your players' strokes as you introduce effective strategies and the concept of playing tennis in a team setting.

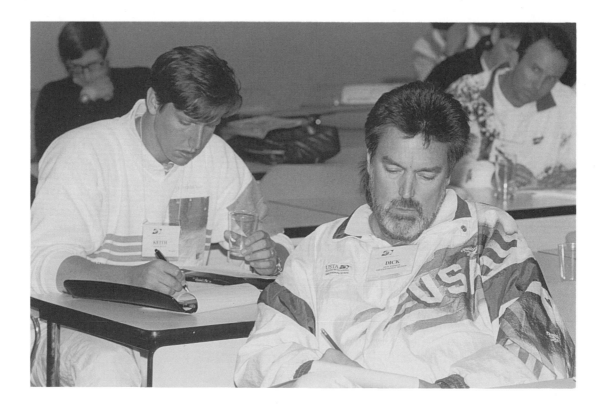

Nonteaching Coaches

Many high school tennis coaches are not members of the faculty. Some are teaching pros; others are interested tennis enthusiasts recruited from the community to coach tennis. Regardless of your qualifications to coach tennis, remember to incorporate the "big picture" into your coaching. To do this, you'll need to get to know the administration and staff of the high school you represent. Your tennis team is an extension of the entire high school's athletic program, so you should establish a coaching philosophy consistent with that of the other school sports. Introduce yourself to fellow coaches at the school, as you may be sharing some of the same athletes. Attend athletic functions so that you are a visible member of the coaching staff.

Be Eager To Learn

All successful coaches borrow bits and pieces of their coaching philosophy from other coaches. The sport or level of play doesn't really matter. Our school's successful football coach, Bill Shields, reads books by tennis coaches and coaches of many other sports. Similarly, I have read books by football coaches and coaches of other sports and incorporated some of their successful techniques into my coaching philosophy. You see, after we take away our Xs and Os, we're really all doing the same thing: teaching our players skills to use throughout their lives as they compete and strive to better themselves. So it's only natural that we learn from one another about how to be successful.

Seek out courses, clinics, publications, and videos. The United States Tennis Association and the two recognized professional tennis teachers' organizations (the United States Professional Tennis Association and the United States Professional Tennis Registry) offer clinics throughout the year. Every clinic I've attended has provided me with information that I've put to use on the court.

Your state high school coaching organization may run clinics specific to each sport. Find out when they are offered and be there! As tennis chairman for Florida's coaches' association (FACA), I've organized clinics all over our state for the past 5 years. More and more coaches are recognizing that there's no better place than these clinics to hear and share ideas about our profession.

Excellent magazines, instructional books, and videos about tennis, coaching, and conditioning are widely available. The fact that you are reading this book shows that you are sufficiently interested. Try to develop (or expand) your own tennis coaching library.

If you are a "hands-on" learner, ask other coaches for permission to attend their practices (most college or high school coaches will consider this a compliment). There's no better place to pick up drills and general coaching tips. Also, use your local teaching pro as a resource for helping you and your players gain additional playing skills.

Take advantage of all of these learning opportunities—even if you're an old veteran like me. The more you know, the better able you'll be to keep current and to develop the best possible coaching philosophy—the foundation for every successful coach.

Learn From Coaches You Respect

In its 20-year history, Astronaut High School in Titusville, Florida, has produced such nationally recognized athletes as NFL All-Pros Wilber Marshall and Cris Collinsworth. The excellent coaches of these athletes have taught me some valuable lessons.

Our former athletic director and track coach, Nick Gailey, who is now in the Florida Coaches Hall of Fame, showed me the importance of keeping athletes focused on and working toward goals. Our present athletic director and current Florida Athletic Coaches Association president, Jay Donnelly (who served as Astronaut's football coach for its first 15 years), made clear to me the need for good organizational skills. Most important, Norman Holmes, a tennis-teaching legend on the central east coast of Florida, taught me the art of teaching and coaching tennis skills. Through Norm's sessions I learned the fundamentals of coaching and stroke production management. I progressed from a weekend player to a novice instructor and coach, eager to apply my new knowledge. But I was in for a surprise when I tried to apply the lessons I learned from Norm. What worked for him didn't work for me, although I tried to copy everything I had seen him do so successfully.

🎾 LEARNING FROM A MASTER

As a rookie coach, I took my players on the hour-long trip each week. Our destination? The tennis court/classroom where Norman Holmes worked his magic. Norman gave my players private lessons while I stood by the net and soaked it all in. I marvelled at Norm's technique and delivery of important messages, one stroke after another. My players learned a lot—but I learned even more.

What I had failed to grasp was a simple but important fact about coaching: Although you can (and should) borrow ideas and methods, the delivery of those ideas and methods must be your own. My attempt to copy Norm's delivery of all his coaching knowledge didn't work for me because his delivery didn't suit my personal style. So, the lesson is: Learn what you can from your coaching models, but don't try to *be* them. Instead incorporate what you learn into your personal coaching style and delivery.

Tennis Coaching Styles

Different situations on the practice court and during match play require coaches to react to players in different ways. Sometimes a firm hand is called for, whereas other times a reassuring pat on the back will get the job done. Above all, keeping your lines of communication open with players is the key to success.

During the formative years of my coaching career, I tried to lean more toward the authoritarian approach. My word was law, or so I thought. Looking back at this point in my coaching career I now realize that my tough approach allowed me to hide my lack of coaching experience. If my players weren't allowed to question me or have any input, how could I ever be wrong? Well, I was wrong—plenty. And probably my biggest error was ever using this authoritarian style of coaching in the first place. It just didn't feel right to me or my players.

🎾 LOSING THE BATTLE

During my second year as a coach I tried to dictate the importance of tennis to my players. Most of my inexperienced players were trying tennis for the first time. One of my cardinal rules at the time was never to be late to practice for any reason. Ten minutes into practice one day a late arrival prompted me to vent my ire. Without asking the player why he was late, I "got in his face," my purpose being to make him an example. His response was to walk away, get in his car, and leave. Later I learned that he had been making up a test, and even after I apologized for my shortsightedness, he never returned to the team. My authoritarian tirade cost me a potential member of the team. The player in question was a freshman who subsequently went out for track and had a great career as a track athlete.

High school players look at tennis as an extracurricular activity, and they expect to have fun. When they are coached by someone who uses predominantly an authoritarian style, they usually aren't going to have fun. And, most likely, the coach will either have to be a little less authoritarian or spend a lot of time trying to convince players to stay on the team.

The opposite of this authoritarian style is an approach that treats players like buddies. Forget the discipline—just let everyone do his or her own thing. Unfortunately, I see this approach too often in high school tennis coaching. This permissive style of coaching can lead to disaster. Players may not want a know-it-all coach, but they do want, and need, direction. A coach who sits idly watching as players' discipline and learning suffer simply isn't doing the job. The term "tennis chaperone" comes to mind, and such a stereotype of a high school tennis coach hurts all of us.

In many situations and with most players, the approach that works best for me and a lot of other coaches is the *cooperative* style. This isn't a combination of the other two styles but is in fact a third style.

Cooperative style coaching allows for very firm discipline, but only when discipline is necessary. When discipline is applied, the players understand why. A cooperative approach allows you to get close enough to your players so that they feel they can talk to you about almost anything. And when they know you will listen to their suggestions, they are much more receptive to yours.

A COOPERATIVE EXCHANGE

Philippe Signore, an exchange student from France, entered our tennis program in 1984. Philippe was small but had a competitive fire that endeared him to everyone in our program.

As our number one player, Philippe led us to consecutive district titles. After graduation, Philippe signed a tennis scholarship at the University of Tennessee at Chattanooga, where he worked his way up to number one during his senior year, winning a Southern Conference individual and team championship for UTC in the process.

Philippe is now working on a doctorate in physics at the University of Florida. These are his recollections of the 2 years he spent in our tennis program:

> Coach was the boss, but he was also a friend on and off the court. I remember the only loss of my senior year. It was at home against a much younger opponent whom I felt I should have beaten. Naturally I was extremely upset at myself for losing. The only words that coach offered me for the rest of the day were about how to beat their doubles team. He never mentioned my performance, the opponent, or anything related to my singles match. We clinched the match with a win in my doubles, but I went home still highly upset and finally went to bed.
>
> It was only the next day that coach raised the subject of my defeat. I remember being so focused on his words. He spoke in simple terms, a total of five sentences. He concluded by giving me two tactics to use the next time I'd play that opponent. I kept these two pieces of advice as I'd have kept a brand-new expensive watch.
>
> I played the guy again in the semifinals of the district tournament. Applying coach's strategy, I won the match. It turned out to be the deciding point in our team's come-from-behind district championship.

Philippe came along after I had coached for 15 years. Early in my coaching career I wouldn't have been able to leave him alone after a loss that was so devastating to him and our team. As soon as he left the court, I probably would have chastised him for playing such a stupid match. Florida high school rules then did not allow me to talk to Philippe during the match to set him straight. But by that time in my career, I knew that the best thing I could do for the team (first) and Philippe (second) was to focus on getting him ready to play doubles. And that approach probably helped the team win that day.

Coaching Priorities

The first priority of tennis is to make it the enjoyable extracurricular activity for players that it is meant to be. Young people now have more ways to spend their time than ever before. Your program will be able to compete for their time and interest only if they think that being a player in your program is important and fun.

Assistant coaches, parents, and others who directly influence your players during the course of a season must be schooled in your coaching priorities. If the players are getting mixed messages from people they respect when they are not with you, your coaching priorities will likely lose their effect.

I introduce my coaching philosophy to parents at a meeting for parents and players at the beginning of every season. During this potluck dinner I introduce myself to each parent of our new players. I follow this with an introduction of the team members, a brief summation of what we hope to accomplish during the tennis season, and an explanation of the ways we will try to achieve our goals. Every parent and player gets to know me and becomes familiar with my coaching priorities. We follow up this meeting by giving parents a copy of the player's handbook, which contains the team's goals, a schedule, and important dates. An end-of-the-season awards dinner brings closure to the season and informs everyone what we will do in the off-season.

Assistant coaches are usually former players familiar with the program's philosophy. However, occasionally an assistant or parent will undermine your coaching philosophy with a player. Talk to this person immediately and tactfully come to an understanding. When everyone that influences your players is on the same coaching wavelength, your players will prosper and grow.

Making Tennis Fun

The athletes of today still want most of the same things they've always wanted: direction, discipline, an opportunity to play, and a chance to compete. Tennis can provide young people all of these things and more.

At the same time, tennis, like other sports, can burn out young players by placing them in highly structured, competitive programs too early. Therefore, strive to provide structure without suffocating your players. Give them proper instruction and guidelines, but also allow them to have some say in day-to-day activities. I start every year with the same statement to my players: "This is a voluntary activity. It is not compulsory, like school. This is your team and it will move in whatever direction you feel is appropriate." This statement sets the tone. The lines of communication are always open, and I am receptive to new ideas coming from the players.

Perhaps you don't feel confident enough to take the cooperative approach to coaching. I understand that. It wasn't easy for me to loosen the reins either. But I encourage you to try. You'll be surprised how capable your players are at making good decisions and how much better they feel when they can help control the team's direction.

 LESSONS LEARNED

Last fall I ran into one of my former players who had returned from college to attend one of our school's football games. Jon Sloan had played for me from 1985 to 1988, starring on four consecutive district championship teams. He was good enough to play college tennis but chose not to.

I asked Jon if he played tennis at all these days. He said no, not competitively, just for fun. Then he thought for a moment and said, "Coach, tennis just seemed so important back in high school."

I asked Jon why competitive tennis wasn't important to him now. He replied that school-work allowed him only a few hours a week for tennis. He said,

> Coach, even though I wasn't the best student in high school, I'm doing really well with my grades now, and that's what is most important to me. But once I get my degree and have more time I'll be back out on the court more often.

Jon Sloan represents what high school athletics is all about. Our tennis program provided him with an opportunity to experience the joy of competition at a time in his life when nothing else seemed more important. Now he can play tennis for fun and apply his competitive tennis experiences on a much bigger court—the court of life.

DEVELOPING A TENNIS COACHING PHILOSOPHY 9

Jon Sloan is an example of what can happen when we help our players learn how to make their own good decisions. They can apply and develop those decision-making skills throughout their lives. As coaches we are the facilitators. The players are the participants. It's their game; let them play it.

Winning Versus Development

When coaches and players believe "as long as we win, everything is okay," the team's development suffers. After a victory, errors are often undetected or dismissed. After a loss, every little detail of poor play is dissected and criticized. The result is that players develop a false sense of security after a win. Conversely, after a loss the players' confidence takes a dramatic nosedive.

Instead of focusing on winning itself, stress to your players the importance of a winning *effort*. Encourage them to try working on their weaknesses against opponents they are beating handily. After a loss, praise their effort, even if they were badly overmatched. Every little step in the right direction makes them more complete players and people.

Staples of a Coaching Philosophy

Tennis coaching is not a static endeavor. The kids we work with change from year to year. The game changes with new trends and technology. Application of sport science and coaching methods are being constantly revised and upgraded.

Among all of these dynamics, a tennis coach must establish a set of overriding coaching principles that don't shift with the winds of change. These tenets provide the roots of consistent and continued excellence— the hallmark of every successful tennis program:

- Look for results, not excuses.
- Focus on performance, not winning (the challenge response).
- Improve gradually, through hard and fun practice.
- Respect your opponent.

I emphasize these principles to my players in some way each day at practice. It makes a difference.

Results, Not Excuses

Tennis has become a game of excuses: poor court conditions, a lucky opponent, lousy weather, an "off" day. Players often seem to think these excuses are legitimate reasons for performing poorly. But I've never known a successful person to make excuses, whether she or he be in sports, business, or any other worthwhile pursuit. As a coach, I feel an obligation to myself, our profession, my school, and my players to prepare my athletes for success. So, from day one, we focus only on those things that we can control— physical conditioning, attitude, mental and stroke production skills, match preparation, and a willingness to deal with whatever problems arise during a match.

If an opponent happens to have a career day against one of my players, all I expect— and always expect—is that my player not drop his level of effort or performance because of discouragement. If that proves not to be enough on this particular day, he can come to the net with his head held high, shake his opponent's hand, and congratulate him for playing better on that day. No complaints, no excuses. We simply start preparing for the next challenge.

The Challenge Response

What is the first question players are usually asked after a match? You know the answer: "Did you win?" Too often our focus is on the result of the match. With amateur players, and especially young, developing players, we should instead focus on performance. Following a match ask, "How did you play?" This kind of question makes a player think about what is most important: Not winning itself but striving to produce a winning effort.

Of course we want our players to win. But we know that they will achieve so much more—and have a better time doing it—if the results of their matches are secondary to their effort, attitude, and performance. Redirect your players' thoughts to performance goals that can be accomplished. The match may be lost 6-1, 6-1, but if the performance goal was to play longer points without making quick unforced errors from the baseline and this was accomplished, then your player was successful, regardless of the outcome of the match.

We ask our players to focus on realistic performance goals during a match as well as trying to overcome the obstacles their opponents throw at them. This mental game redirects their attention from winning to the challenge of the competitive situation.

We tell them to love the challenge and to be ready to respond to it. It's what we call the "challenge response." Players must have it if they are going to feel successful at the end of a match.

Gaining Ground Gradually

People in our society "want it all, right now." But immediate mastery is just not possible in a skill-building sport like tennis. Tennis is a game of plateaus; players often remain at a performance level for months without improvement. During this time they can often get discouraged and quit. Or they can practice diligently, work patiently on their weak areas, and progress to the next level.

Tennis is the ultimate teacher of perseverance. Young players must build on their stroke production daily and appreciate small, positive gains. The big wins and devastating losses even out; there are peaks and valleys in what is a very gradual ascent with many plateaus along the way. The patience, persistence, and skills your players can develop while making this climb will help them compete on and off the court.

Respect Your Opponent

The fourth principle, respect your opponent, is not optional—you demand it. Players must abide by a code of conduct that represents themselves and the program well and is consistent with tennis rules and proper behavior. Respect of school, tennis program, self, and opponents is essential. Players' behaviors will reflect their respect.

For example, players shouldn't put down an upcoming opponent. Nor should they brag about their own skills; their performance should do the talking. Tennis is a difficult enough game to play without carrying the excess baggage of a negative, arrogant attitude. By respecting every opponent, your players will be able to focus on the important things—playing hard, playing smart, and having fun. They will be free to enjoy the competition and play their best tennis.

Establishing Priorities

As important as team goals are, they take a back seat to more important priorities in each player's life. We ask our players to emphasize this order:

1. Family
2. Schoolwork
3. Team

Family

Positive interaction with the members of his or her own family is paramount to a player's success. All parents have to make sacrifices so that their child can enjoy interscholastic competition. By acknowledging these sacrifices, a player can assume her role in the family—a role of give and take, not one that places her needs as an athlete above all others in the family.

Schoolwork

Each player on your team should be a student first and an athlete second. Coaches need to remember that tennis is an extracurricular activity that should never supersede a player's academic priorities. Stress the importance of success in school, not just in athletics. Once a student athlete has developed balance between her academic endeavors and the tennis court, the result will be a better student and a better athlete.

Team

Our team-first attitude can be summed up in one sentence: dedication to the game, devotion to the team. We share these priorities with each player's parents before the season. If we see a player neglecting the first two priorities because of tennis, I ask the parents to support me in redirecting the player's attention. When each member of the team is the best person, scholar, and player he can be, we can ask no more.

Team Versus Individual

Because famous professional tennis players are sometimes perceived as self-centered and rarely thought of as team players, some people think of tennis as only an individual sport. This is unfortunate because tennis can be a terrific team sport.

No coach should let one player become more important than the team. This philosophy allows all players equal treatment and a chance to share individually in the group's success. The development of each player is still important. But our primary emphasis—from day one—is the team.

THAT TEAM FEELING

In 1990 our program experienced our ultimate triumph. We won the school's first ever Florida state team championship.

After the championship had been secured, our number one player, Eric Dobsha, and I embraced. Eric was a nationally ranked player who had won six national junior age division titles. His name is displayed on a permanent plaque in Kalamazoo, Michigan, at Stowe Tennis Stadium, the mecca of junior tennis. There he teamed with one of America's most promising junior players, Brian Dunn, and won the national 16-and-under doubles championship.

But with all of those individual titles in his pocket, here Eric stood, hugging me in jubilation after our team championship. He later said, "Coach, this feels better than any individual titles I've won."

Nothing compares with the camaraderie players share as teammates, working as a unit, knowing their success depends on one another. And no amount of personal pride gained from an individual achievement or award can match the shared feeling of accomplishment resulting from the team's priorities coming before any individual's.

Summary

The best ways to develop your own coaching philosophy while allowing your players and teams to reach their full potential are as follows:

- Be eager to learn; stay current by attending clinics, reading, and talking to fellow coaches.
- Develop a coaching foundation that fits your personal style.
- Make tennis fun for your players as they practice, providing structure during this special time in their lives.
- Be objective when you evaluate wins and losses; develop performance goals that allow players to focus on a winning effort more than the match outcome.
- Develop a coaching philosophy that encompasses respect of opponents and a focus on gradual improvement.
- Find ways to overcome obstacles rather than using them as excuses.

Chapter 2

Communicating
Your Approach

What determines whether a tennis coach does a good, mediocre, or poor job? After reading chapter 1 you might be inclined to say, "The difference is a positive coaching philosophy." Others would say that "previous playing experience" and "knowledge of the game" are the key factors. But if these were the chief determinants, why do former stars sometimes fail when they coach the sport they once excelled in?

Those of you who have coached for several years know how important communication skills are to succeeding in our profession. We can have a positive philosophy and be experts in tennis techniques, but these don't mean a thing unless we can effectively communicate them to our players.

In this chapter you'll find many specifics that will enable you to successfully communicate with players and also with parents, administrators, and the media.

Successful Communicators

The late Arthur Ashe, Jr. influenced the sports world, and especially tennis, through public appearances, countless works of charity, television commentary, and writing several books, including an anthology of the history of the black athlete. In his adult years Ashe was an effective spokesperson who prodded the tennis world to ensure opportunities for young African-Americans in tennis. The last years of his life were dedicated to raising public consciousness to the critical need for financial and moral support to combat AIDS. His life and his death were powerful influences on a generation, especially in the tennis world.

Arthur Ashe, like great coaches, found a way to get people to respond. Good communicators are not necessarily smooth talkers, but they do get their message across to all types of people.

YOU'RE NEVER TOO OLD

As tennis chairperson of District I of the Pennsylvania Interscholastic Athletic Association for 21 years, I come in contact with many coaches. They often ask, "Why do you still go to clinics and workshops?" Or they comment, "With your years of experience, you must know all there is to know about coaching."

I tell them that I always learn through talking with and observing other coaches. Knowing tennis skills and strategies is one thing; knowing how to best teach and communicate what I know is quite another. Even a veteran coach like me can learn new ways to get my ideas across.

Seven Keys to Effective Communication

Communicating effectively in a variety of situations will have a significant impact on your success as a coach. Situations that require skillful communicating include:

- Helping your players perform their best in important matches
- Dealing with aggressive parents who pressure you to move their child up in the team lineup
- Motivating players to work harder at improving a skill or their fitness level
- Consoling players after a difficult setback and encouraging them to put it behind them
- Rallying support for your team from the school community

Although the list could be expanded, it will be helpful to concentrate on the following seven keys to communicating effectively:

- Be real
- Listen first
- Use a two-way street
- Be honest
- Be caring
- Set an example
- Be consistent

Be Real

Just be who you are. Share this tip with your players, their parents, and the school community. Kids will learn a lot from adults like you if you let them. Use a style of communication that's natural and easy for you.

Share your life in a natural way with your players by talking about your family and work in conversation. Your taste in music or movies reveals a side of you, too. Other topics may include volunteer work that you do or even banter about your own tennis game, which helps your players form a more complete picture of you as a person.

Listen First

Communication starts with listening to players and parents and being sensitive to their hopes, goals, and attitudes about competitive tennis specifically and life in general. You'll find out how to motivate players, as they will tell you if you take the time to listen.

Someone once asked, "Who learns the most in a conversation between a wise man and a fool?" Of course, the answer is the wise man. The point is that even though we're older, more mature, and typically more knowledgeable than our players, communication still needs to start with us listening to others first!

Sometimes coaches get caught up in overcoaching and directing every move for their players. This is especially true of older coaches who often believe it is important to teach young people everything they know and thereby prevent the mistakes they made themselves as young athletes.

It is easy, too, to fall into the trap of listening to players by simply maintaining silence while they speak. The problem here is that the kids may not feel the understanding and empathy that you really are experiencing, or you may misunderstand their real problem.

Active listening is a skill that helps you communicate your interest and understanding to your players. While they talk, you show attention and involvement in their ideas with your eyes, nods of understanding, and patience as they complete their thought. Then you respond with probing questions to be sure you have grasped their meaning. Or you might reflect their comments back to them, in your own words to check your receiving skills. A conversation might take the following form:

Player: I can't believe how bad I'm playing. My serve really stinks.

Coach: It's natural to be nervous the day before an important match. I'd be worried if you were too cocky.

Player: But what about my serve? I'm just not hitting it well.

Coach: Your motion is fine, but remember to relax and put more spin on your first serve. Maybe you're trying for too many aces.

Player: Yeah, I've got to remember to take my time when I get anxious.

Coach: Now you've hit on the key. Remember to breathe deeply, bounce the ball a few times, and then let it go. You've got a real weapon with your serve when you slow the whole process down.

The coach is showing empathy for the player who is anxious about the match and manages to gently suggest some corrective action while expressing faith in the player to deal with the situation.

 BUILDING RAPPORT

When our program first began, we had a difficult time attracting quality athletes. The better athletes in our school preferred to play the higher profile sports. In the mid 1980s a freshman of considerable athletic repute entered our school. He played a major sport and dabbled at tennis. I liked him and we talked frequently during the fall of his freshman year whenever he needed someone to listen to him. However, we never discussed his athletic plans for the spring during tennis season. Before tennis began that spring he came to me and said, "Coach, I would really like to play tennis." I realized that the rapport we had built—because I listened to him rather than trying to influence him—was the primary reason he wanted to play tennis. He capped a great high school career by earning a tennis scholarship to college.

Use a Two-Way Street

Good communication goes two ways. Athlete-coach interchange can be spoken, written on paper, or transmitted by body language. Your role is to let players know you are accessible and open to an exchange of thoughts, feelings, and frustrations. At the same time, let them know that you expect them to communicate with you. Whenever they feel uncertain about team policies or their status on the team or confused about the direction of their tennis game, it is their responsibility to seek your counsel.

 A BREAKDOWN

Rick Addison, a freshman player, had been absent from practice and several matches because he was with his family on vacation. Team policy required that Rick make up the time he missed before he could compete again. The day before Rick's suspension was to end, he failed to show up for practice, nor did he show on any of the 5 days left in the season.

I learned from his teammates that Rick wasn't coming back to the team because he thought I had been unfair. He mentioned another player who had gone on vacation and been suspended for a fewer number of days. But what Rick didn't know was that the other player's suspension matched the amount of time he was absent on vacation, just as Rick's had.

Rick's misunderstanding and our lack of communication led to Rick quitting the team. If we had communicated better and cleared up the misinformation, he may have significantly contributed to the team in future years.

Be Honest

It's all in the eyes. People can tell when you're being straight with them by body language and eye contact. Get in the habit of saying what you mean and what you believe and then standing by your word. Because most matches and tournaments in junior and school tennis require the players and coaches to act as their own officials, temptations and opportunities for dishonest behavior are plentiful. Let players know by what you say and what you do that you value honesty above all else and expect them to do the same.

When you speak directly to a player, make eye contact, especially if you're delivering bad news, such as a demotion in the lineup. Help your player deal with the news objectively and rationally while communicating

your sensitivity for his disappointment with your eyes. Help him out by rehearsing how each of you will convey the news to teammates, friends, and parents. It may be just the consistently better performances of a teammate that prompted the move. Reassure the player that no changes are forever.

Be Caring

Show players you care about them, not just their tennis. Adolescence is a tough time of life marked by struggles for independence, a search for identity, and a yearning for social acceptance and popularity. Players need to know you're in their corner, concerned about their schoolwork, glad to meet their friends, eager to know their parents, and willing to share a part of yourself with them.

For coaches who don't teach at the school, this can be a challenge. You may need to spend some extra time after practices or use away trips as opportunities to really get to know your players. On match days, be available to chat with parents and friends of your players after the match is over. Introduce yourself, strike up a conversation, and say a few kind words about your player—they'll treasure your comments and relay them back to the player later.

 CARING FIRST

Jamie stood dejected with tears in his eyes after a particularly tough loss. He felt like he had let his teammates down. I knew he had played poorly and cost the team a chance at a championship. I also knew he had fought his heart out during the match. What galled me was that he had made the same tactical errors in judgment we had discussed throughout the season. Holding back my need to vent my frustrations, I walked up to him and put my arm around him. I reminded him that he had tried as hard as he could and that I was proud of his effort. When he looked up at me and we established eye contact, it was evident that my words were exactly what he needed to hear. From that match until the end of his career, Jamie would do anything I asked of him on court because he knew I cared about him first and the results of match play second.

Set an Example

Be the kind of person you'd like to have on your team. (This is not as easy as it sounds.) I've always felt that tennis teams reflect the style and substance of their coaches. Some schools have a reputation for poor line-calling, some for poor on-court manners, whereas other schools enjoy the highest respect from opponents. Over a period of years under the same coach (even though there are new players each year) a school team's reputation as poor sports suggests that the coach is likely responsible. Be sure you're setting the right example and insist on high standards of conduct both on and off the tennis court.

In the heat of battle in a tightly contested match, a coach's behavior will have a powerful impact on players from both teams, the opposing coach, and spectators. Because tennis matches are typically not controlled by officials, it is your job as a coach to set the tone of the competition as friendly but competitive, enforce the rules fairly for both teams as well as the spectators, and handle disputes calmly and rationally. Coaches who lose control of their emotions can hardly expect their young athletes to do better. Coaches who use inappropriate language, profanity, or taunting are tacitly telling players it's okay for them to do the same. Tell your players at the beginning of the season the goals you have for yourself as a coach. Ask them to help you achieve your goals just as they expect your help.

Be Consistent

Your credibility as a coach results from communication and behavior that is consistent from one player to the other and consistent from one time to the next. The kids at your school have a right to know what you expect of them on the tennis team and how they will be treated.

The secret to consistent coaching behavior is to have a sound coaching philosophy and principles to guide you in your decision making. Using your personal philosophy and coaching style as the guide for your interactions with players will produce a consistent pattern of behavior. The effect on your players will be a feeling of security and confidence in your coaching approach that is like a rudder in the sometimes rough seas of competitive sport.

Every player on the squad is important to the success of the team if you make it so. Act like it and your players will follow your lead. Treat players the same after wins and losses, let them know cheating will never be tolerated, expect their full attention at practices and matches, and insist that they compete as hard as they can in every match.

Communicating With Your Players

One of your primary goals should be to help your players become independent competitors, able to handle any situation effectively. To foster independence, allow players to make their own decisions and deal with the consequences, good or bad.

The challenges of competitive tennis require effective practice sessions to prepare for a match, adjustment to the opponent and the flow during the match, and an ability to evaluate and analyze the result after the match. What you say to your players before, during, and after matches is crucial to their development of independent analysis and adjustment to the challenges of competition.

Coaching Your Own Child

The key to coaching your own child is to separate your duties as a coach and a parent. On court treat your child as you do every other player on the team. Sometimes a coach will make things tougher for his or her own child than other players on the squad so that there is no appearance of favoritism. This is a mistake. Your child deserves the same treatment afforded every player on the team.

At home, become a parent and leave tennis back at the courts. Don't discuss tennis-related matters at home unless your child initiates it. Never suggest after-hours practice to improve a faulty serve or groundstroke. Remember—if the rest of the squad doesn't have to listen to you suggest unwanted evening practice sessions, why should your child? Above all, make your child feel comfortable that you accept her for who she is and that you don't expect more from her because you are the coach.

Communicating Before Matches

As coach of a team of players, you have the difficult task of dealing with each player in an individual way. Comments must be tailored to each one's style, personality, and mood. A sense of humor and prematch horseplay may be the antidote to counteract prematch jitters for some, whereas others react better to an objective review of the game plan.

If suggestions or reminders are in order, make them brief and limit them to no more than three. Longer lists of prematch hints will not be retained and are only a reflection of your nervousness and anxiety. As a secure coach, you know that everything has been done during the practice sessions in the weeks before, and last-minute cramming for a match is no more effective than the all-night vigil for a school exam.

A final remark to each player or the team as a group should be to encourage them to *have fun* and enjoy the competitive challenge. By your manner and spoken comments, you should exhibit a positive, supportive, and encouraging attitude no matter what the expected outcome of the match. Above all, convey the expectation that players will do the best they possibly can for that day.

ACCEPTING THE CONSEQUENCES

In the off-season the majority of the team decided to enter a junior tournament, and I accompanied them as sort of a chaperone and coach. The distance the tournament was from home required us to stay overnight in a motel. After dinner, we spent some time in a local mall and then returned to our rooms. About 1:00 AM I heard a noise outside of my motel room and went out to investigate. I was surprised to discover one of my female players trying to sneak back into her room. I informed her that we would talk about the consequences of this later. The next day she tired quickly in a match she was favored to win and was upset. When she exited the court, it would have been very easy to throw the previous night's escapade in her face as the reason she lost the match. Instead I waited until we returned home 2 days later to discuss the match with her. At that time I made it very clear that she, not I, was responsible for her prematch preparation. Understanding, without a lecture from me, that her lack of sleep contributed to the loss allowed her to deal with the consequences of her bad decision and learn from the experience.

Communicating During Matches

At some levels, absolutely no coaching is allowed. In many states, coaching is allowed after a set is completed. In other settings, the time of the changeover to the other side provides brief but frequent opportunities to coach.

Although coaching is allowed in a team setting, many players have experience in individual tournament play where coaching is not permitted. As a prudent coach, thoroughly discuss coaching during matches with each player well before the match so that you can agree on the timing and amount of coaching to be expected. Some players respond well to coaching and like the support of an objective observer—others are distracted by an interference and perform better when left alone.

When things are going well in a match, little coaching is necessary other than well-chosen remarks of encouragement and reminders to enjoy their good play. However, if trouble develops, you might find that a few key comments help refocus a wandering mind. Suggestions to be more aware of balance and positioning or attention to error margins can benefit the error-prone player. Suggestions for handling a particularly troublesome shot or opponent might also be welcome. The team concept of doubles often provides an opportunity for coaching. When you notice that doubles partners are seeing things from different perspectives, you may be able to help them plan and agree on the tactical adjustments they need to make.

Make it clear by your body language and gestures that you are on the side of your players and make suggestions in a non-threatening, uncritical way. Obviously most players are trying to do their best and will welcome a comment from a friend but likely ignore a critic.

Communicating After Matches

Immediately following the match your response should depend on the player and perhaps the outcome of the match. Some performers are ready to interact with a coach by the time they reach the sidelines; others need some time to be alone to work through the results of the struggle just ended. A pat on the back or an arm around the shoulder is likely to be the safest, most effective way for the coach to convey to the player that he is okay, win or lose. This is the time to rejoice in a good effort and reinforce things done well. It is *not* a time to point out errors or to ignore an athlete, regardless of the outcome.

ACCEPTING SOME BLAME FOR A LOSS

Once a match is completed, win or lose, the team meets as a group. When the team is successful, I make a point of giving them credit for the win. After this particular match, which turned out to be a bitter defeat, my opening statement was much different then usual. I told the team that if I had prepared them better for the match, they would have had a better chance of success. The next day when I talked to individuals about how they could have better accomplished their prematch performance goals, I had their undivided attention. They understood that we were all in this together.

As coach, your most significant task after a match is to give your players a sense of perspective. Let young people enjoy a good performance, as that is the primary reason to play. Soothe feelings of inadequacy and disappointment after poor performances and point out the process of development that is gradually proceeding. Shoulder some of the blame for unfulfilled dreams when appropriate and resolve together to persevere in the face of the challenge of competitive tennis.

Communicating With Parents

Because parents (or guardians) typically present as many communication challenges as players, make a special effort to share with them your expectations and your coaching

philosophy. You might do this through a preseason meeting.

Schedule the parents' meeting at the school and mail invitations about 2 weeks in advance. Be sure to invite both parents if they are living separately. Along with the invitation, highlight the topics you'll cover so parents will be interested in attending and can readily see how their interest and role may affect the success of their child in the sport.

Create a relaxed, pleasant, and friendly atmosphere and offer light refreshments at the end. Start and end the meeting on time, have an agenda prepared, and allow ample time for questions from the audience.

You can prevent many misunderstandings by committing key policies and procedures to writing and sharing them with parents and players. It may be a good idea to ask both players and parents to sign certain documents and return them to you to be sure they have read the contents and agree to follow the procedures described.

Here are some topics that you may want to include on the agenda:

- Motivational remarks and your coaching philosophy
- Goals for the season
- Team selection procedures

- Lineup selection criteria
- Practice policies and procedures
- Match procedure (including parent role)
- What parents can do at home to support player participation
- Relevant school policies
- The partnership between player, parent, and coach

Many parents of tournament players feel that their child gains nothing by attending a high school practice with inferior players. Clearly outline your attendance policy before the season begins, then communicate with the parent and compromise as necessary. Allow the player to miss practice once or twice a week to play better competition or receive a lesson from their teaching pro. But expect him to give something back to the high school practice by working with teammates the rest of the practice week.

Help parents understand that their children can gain something from the experience of team play at the high school level that isn't available in individual tournament play. Working as a member of a team, where the team's goals take precedence over individual goals, is a lesson that will make them more productive as working adults.

Communicate to parents that the best thing they can do for their children is to accept them as they are, win or lose. Parents need to be supportive, not critical, of their own children. If you see a parent's actions around the tennis court undermining your efforts to put the sport in proper perspective, talk to her or him immediately. Don't lecture on parenthood; just remind parents that every member of the supporting staff, from coach to team to parent, wants the same thing. Give parents a role that they can accomplish and still feel as if they are contributing to the success of their child and the team. That role would be supporting their child's effort (as well as their teammates') on court without being too critical.

Communicating With School Faculty

The athletic director (AD) is your key staff person and needs to be fully informed of every issue concerning your team. The rapport you establish with the AD will go a long way toward accomplishing the administrative and organizational tasks you'll need to operate efficiently. The athletic director helps in scheduling, transportation, and budget allocation. Communication with your AD about your program's goals and direction will determine your program's success.

Most administrators dislike surprises and want to be informed early regarding operation difficulties, behavior problems, or sensitive issues. Take the time to drop short notes or stop by regularly for a chat. Better yet, invite the AD to stop by a practice or a match so that you can compare notes. Our athletic director, Jay Donnelly, a tennis player himself, often attends our matches. This direct contact makes communicating the tennis program's direction and needs very simple.

Other members of the school faculty need your attention, too. Let them know you care and value the education they provide to the team members. Ask them to keep you informed if they anticipate academic problems and perhaps you can work together to head off danger.

Encourage players to invite their teachers to stop by matches and watch a bit. This will promote the student-faculty relationship and with luck generate new tennis enthusiasts from the faculty.

Many schools have a monitoring system to ensure that varsity athletes are making academic progress. Because suspension from the team can follow poor academic performance, it makes good sense for you to keep on top of players' school performances. At certain critical times, tutoring or makeup

tests may conflict with team practices and you'll have to adjust to the policies of your school.

Communicating With Team Supporters

Within the school family, everyone should be aware of the players on the team and the challenges you face throughout the season. You have to do some public relations work or enlist the aid of parents, a booster club, or a team manager/reporter. Use the public address system for announcements about team achievements, lobby for articles in the student newspaper, and establish a team bulletin board to announce team news.

At home matches, consider having team supporters keep score, or ask them to keep simple match-charting statistics. Have comfortable seating available and match scoretenders on every court and be sure that players put up the score when changing sides. Imagine attending a football or basketball game without a scoreboard . . . but tennis teams often ignore the issue and then lament the poor turnout of fans.

Communicating With the Media

If you want good media coverage, find out what you can do to make the job easy for reporters and make them look good. A preseason lunch is a good idea to exchange plans for the season and establish the procedures for reporting during the season.

Most newspaper reporters have the impossible task of covering multiple sports and lots of team results every day. Provide the results for each match in an easy-to-understand format and add some "juicy" match highlights that convey the flavor of an exciting team win, an heroic individual effort, or a disappointing loss.

It's a good idea for your team manager to drop off the results as soon as possible after a match to avoid newspaper deadline problems. Telephoning or faxing results may work too if time and travel distance are factors.

Coaches who whine about press coverage usually haven't taken the time to cultivate the media. Some coaches are notorious for sharing only news of great wins and ignoring or "forgetting to submit" news of poor performances. You've got to be fair, consistent, and open with the press if you expect the same from them. Encourage local reporters, including school paper reporters, to interview players before and after matches. This sends a message that it is their team, not the coach's, and they have the experience of the interview, which can be very educational.

🎾 HELPING THE MEDIA

Each year the local newspaper selects, with the help of the coaches, an all-star tennis team. One particular year, I was shocked that a very deserving player on our team was omitted. My first inclination was to call the reporter responsible and blast him for the oversight, regardless of the coaches' vote. My wife reminded me that the oversight was probably because rival coaches who voted for the team didn't know what my player's record had been that year. The next day I sat and wrote a letter to the newspaper. I complimented the newspaper for recognizing deserving tennis players each year and asked them if I could help them in the tedious selection process by collecting the records of every player in our district from the coaches before balloting. They thanked me and allowed me to do just that the next year.

Because tennis is both an individual and a team sport, sometimes the star players' performances overshadow the team's success. It's a good idea to prepare your players for press interviews, provide them with a checklist of do's and don'ts, and practice fielding some difficult questions. In fact, you should probably join them in trying to answer some difficult questions. A few tips you may want to remember and share with your players include the following:

• Develop some standard stock answers that convey enthusiasm and a positive outlook and emphasize these phrases with any reporter.

• Be alert for human interest stories or comments that can help a writer. For example, it's better for athletes and coaches to identify specific performers or types of music they enjoy rather than just saying "I enjoy music." Talk about your family, friends, hobbies, and school interests to present a more well-rounded impression.

• Stick to upbeat, encouraging words about your team, school, and community. And remember that none of your comments are really "off the record," so be as open as you can and then simply close the interview.

• Be careful about slang, jargon, or coachspeak. Try to put your thoughts in simple, convenient phrases.

• Convey your humility after a good team performance and spread the credit around to the team, assistant coaches, parents, or other key people.

Summary

Here are the keys we've described for communicating effectively:

- Good communicators are honest and genuine in their approach and start by listening to others first.
- The process of communication is two-way, with both sides expressing, listening, and responding.
- Coaches have to accept and utilize their natural position as role models for young athletes. Actions speak louder than words.
- Communicating before, during, and after matches is critical. The impact of the moment is heightened by the competition, so these times demand a special approach to young athletes.
- The school family, including administrators, teachers, students, and parents are crucial to team success. You have to spend time with each group to garner their support and understanding.
- The media is a special challenge. Promote your team players and build a tradition of openness and cooperation that will help your kids become hometown heroes.

Chapter 3

Motivating Players

One of the most frequent questions I'm asked at coaching conferences and workshops is "How do you get your players to listen to you? Kids these days are tough to handle." This question is a telltale sign that a coach is unsure how to motivate players.

Motivating competitive athletes is one of the crucial elements of successful coaching. It requires a keen understanding of young people and the pressures they face, particularly in the adolescent years, and a firm grasp of the techniques and tactics that have proved successful over time.

A high level of motivation results in athletes who are committed, energetic, and driven toward success. Motivated players can endure frustration, practice for hours, survive pressure, and rebound from disappointing performances. The trick to producing and sustaining high levels of motivation is to know what motivates adolescents.

Motivation is the result of people trying to fulfill their needs . . . and for young athletes the most important psychological needs are

- self-identity,
- peer approval,
- recognition, and
- perceived success.

If you understand these basic needs and how to help your players satisfy them, your players will be well motivated. The final section of the chapter discusses how to develop mental toughness in your players. Excellent technical skills and a sound understanding of tennis strategies will only carry your players so far. Mental toughness is the final component your players need to succeed in the competitive practice and match arenas. As you will learn in this chapter, goal setting is closely tied to motivation. Your players will want to develop goals for technique, fitness, and mental toughness.

Making Tennis Fun

You will probably not be shocked to learn that tennis or any other sport must be fun for players if they are to continue participation. In fact, young athletes say that lack of fun is a leading reason for dropping out of sport.

In a 1990 landmark study of about 10,000 high school students sponsored by the Athletic Footwear Association (AFA)[1], the 10 most important reasons for playing a sport are

1. to have fun,
2. to improve my skills,
3. to stay in shape,
4. to do something I'm good at,
5. for the excitement of competition,
6. to get exercise,
7. to play as part of a team,
8. for the challenge of competition,
9. to learn new skills, and
10. to win.

These results may surprise some coaches or parents who think winning is the key to having fun. In fact, kids rank winning no higher than tenth in importance.

 BATTER UP!

It was still 2 weeks until the first match, and practices were dragging. The players were tired of drilling and needed to have a little fun. Suddenly I arrived at a solution. I told the team to put their racquets down and follow me off the courts into the adjoining grassy area. Going to my car, I retrieved from my trunk a Wiffle ball and bat that my own children used. I told the team captains to choose sides because we were going to play an inning of Wiffle ball before we went back on court.

The competitive juices started flowing as soon as sides were picked and we began playing Wiffle ball. I pitched to both sides and we played one inning, with the promise that we could resume the game at a later date. When we returned to the courts, the atmosphere was totally different. The Wiffle ball break had rekindled the team, and tennis was fun again.

We'd all probably agree that having fun is important in sports but getting a handle on just what *fun* is may be difficult. When you spend some time with young athletes you learn that they are looking for a challenge to test their skill. If the challenge is pretty well matched to their skill and ability, sports are fun.

On the other hand, if the challenge is too great, kids get anxious. And a challenge that is too easy to achieve naturally produces boredom. Figure 3.1 shows my preference for striking a balance between challenge and skill. Your role as the coach is to make sure tennis is fun by adjusting the challenges your players face so that they are pushed to improve but experience success along the way.

Here are a few tips to make tennis fun:

• Treat each player as an individual and help her discover the needs she can satisfy by competing in tennis.

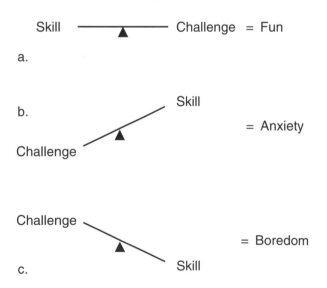

Figure 3.1 (a) When challenge is well matched with skill, sports are fun; (b) too great a challenge leads to anxiety; (c) whereas too easy a challenge leads to boredom.

---

[1]Martha E. Ewing & Vern Seefeldt (1990). *American Youth and Sports Participation.* Sponsored by Athletic Footwear Association (AFA), North Palm Beach, Florida 33408.

• Help every player set personal performance goals that ensure some success.

• Recognize player success through token awards, praise, and publicity.

• Make practices fun through frequent changes of activity, creative drills, and game simulations; let the players choose some activities.

• Make matches fun by encouraging your players, emphasizing personal improvement, and reducing pressure to win. Look for things you can reinforce after the match.

• Promote team spirit and let athletes enjoy the natural bonds that develop during a season's adventures. Help each player feel part of the team.

Recognizing Individual Differences

You can't simply treat all players the same and expect success. Instead, find out what motivates each player and use that information wisely. The most serious and intrinsically motivated athletes want to improve their skills and often use sports to discover their limits or to identify their strengths or weaknesses.

These players are often team leaders and can help influence team attitudes and behavior. You need to support their serious efforts, be sure their expectations are realistic (as they may tend to be overly ambitious), and be wary of the possibility of self-induced pressure to perform.

 CREATIVE COACHING SOLUTIONS

Scott seemed to always be indifferent to my coaching suggestions on court. Although he was a talented player, he needed help with parts of his game. But no matter how I suggested changes, he rebuffed me. Finally I hit on a solution. I asked Scott to help me teach a particular skill to JV players on our team. As we taught the skill, Scott and I interacted like we had never done before. We shared suggestions as to how to best teach the skill to these players. Scott now saw himself as an equal and from that day on listened to my coaching suggestions about his game. He didn't always agree, but he listened!

A significant percentage of players are more extrinsically motivated and may participate on your team to be part of a group, win approval of their peers, be popular, or receive trophies or awards. Once you realize what makes them click, use that information effectively. Help these players both achieve the recognition they crave and experience the benefits of inner satisfaction and pride in personal success.

Setting Goals

Perhaps nothing you do for your players is more significant regarding motivation than to help them learn to set effective and challenging but also realistic goals. Goal setting is a critical lifetime skill that is worth spending significant time on so your players master the process. Your players should write their goals down on paper, not just think about them.

It's probably a good idea in a sport like tennis to set individual player goals first and then develop team goals as a group. This sequence will ensure that each player has clarified her individual goals, and team goals can then be set not to conflict with these private goals. For example, players who want to improve their serves may set the goal of working on serving for 30 minutes at the end of every practice. If the team sets a team goal of running movement or fitness drills at the end of each day, there is a conflict. To keep motivation strong, it's best to try to accommodate the individual goals within the team goals.

BEING REALISTIC

From day one of our relationship, Justin made it clear to me that his long-term goal was a Division I collegiate tennis scholarship. I knew that his chances of attaining this goal were remote at best. However, I didn't want to dash a young man's dreams. So little by little I talked to him about constructing shorter term goals that were realistic. As he continued to work in our program for 2 years he realized that he was not meeting his short-term goals unless they were simplified. His skills improved, but not as fast as he imagined they would. Gradually, by making his short and intermediate goals more realistic, he softened his stance on his long-term goals. When he graduated, he did receive scholarship aid to a Division I college, but as a trainer's assistant, not a tennis player. He realized his long-term goal of remaining active in sports at the collegiate level and contributing to an athletic team.

Outcome Versus Performance Goals

Young athletes need to achieve success to increase their feelings of self-worth. Realistic, attainable goals help ensure the chance of success and directly affect motivation. Help your players define success in terms of their own performances and successes rather than by comparing their performances to others.

The main difference between outcome and performance goals is the amount of control your players have in achieving them. Outcome goals are those over which players have little direct control, such as winning a league title or defeating a particular player. The problem with outcome goals is that players can work hard and prepare well for competition and still lose a match on a particular day. Or your players may set unrealistic goals that include victories over better skilled players. The team that adopts goals like these is setting itself up for trouble.

Winning league, district, or state championships, compiling a specific record of wins or losses, or winning every close match are examples of goals that set the stage for failure (see Figure 3.2).

Figure 3.2   Unrealistic goals lead to failure.

**UNREALISTIC GOALS
CAN BE DANGEROUS**

As a young coach, I helped a team set the ambitious goals of going undefeated and winning the conference before the season. We all worked hard and in the first match of the season played a rival school and lost 5-4, the last match lost in a third-set tiebreaker. The next day, several players wanted to quit the team because we had lost our chance to reach our two main goals. It took a lot of convincing on my part to refocus their efforts and set new goals . . . but I never made that mistake again.

Performance goals, on the other hand, can be totally controlled by your players, and successful achievement of each goal is a powerful incentive to keep working. Some examples of realistic team performance goals are committing to get in excellent physical condition; playing smart, strategic tennis; emphasizing great teamwork in doubles; and helping every player on your team become a better player (see Figure 3.3).

Figure 3.3   Performance goals can be controlled by your players.

Categorizing Performance Goals

It's a good idea to have your players divide their goals into three main categories:

- Tennis technique
- Fitness
- Mental toughness

These three categories define the major areas for possible improvement and help organize thinking and planning. Many players (and some coaches) will ignore setting goals in one of these categories, thus handicapping the chance for overall improvement. The following are good examples of measurable goals:

- Technique goals should address racquet skills: "To hit 25 successful second serves with good spin and depth at the end of every practice."

- Fitness goals should be specific to particular individual weaknesses as shown by physical testing: "To increase the number of sit-ups and push-ups I can perform in 1 minute by 25% within the next 6 weeks."

- Mental toughness goals become increasingly important as the intensity of competition increases: "To maintain a strong, confident fighter image during matches even when things don't go my way."

Sequencing Goals

Preseason goals that apply to the upcoming season can be divided into four categories:

- Long-term goals
- Intermediate goals
- Short-term goals
- Now goals

Long-Term Goals

Young players need to have long-term goals—these are their dreams. Encourage and support their dream of someday playing professional tennis, earning a college scholarship, or defeating a former hero. But make sure your players don't get lost in their long-term goals. Although I encourage them to set long-term goals, I don't ask them to write them down and share them with me unless they want to. As much as possible, keep the players in the present by focusing on their shorter range goals that apply to the current year or the next 2 years.

Intermediate Goals

Intermediate goals are the stepping stones to achieving long-term goals. Many of the goals in this category apply to tactical or mental skills play or to team leadership (see Figure 3.4). Progress in this area may be the hardest for each player to realistically measure. Generally expect intermediate goals to take 6 months to a year to accomplish. Being able to hit a dependable topspin backhand passing shot could easily take a summer to learn and an entire season of play before a player owns the shot. Review intermediate goals at midseason and again at the end of the year. Praise your players during postmatch evaluations if they have made progress during match or ladder play on an intermediate goal.

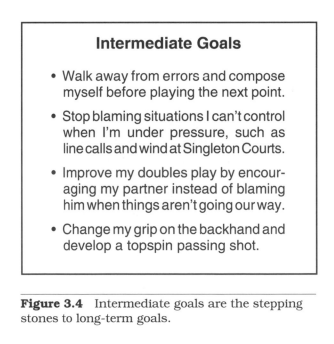

Intermediate Goals

- Walk away from errors and compose myself before playing the next point.

- Stop blaming situations I can't control when I'm under pressure, such as line calls and wind at Singleton Courts.

- Improve my doubles play by encouraging my partner instead of blaming him when things aren't going our way.

- Change my grip on the backhand and develop a topspin passing shot.

Figure 3.4 Intermediate goals are the stepping stones to long-term goals.

Although the high school season typically extends only 8 to 14 weeks, you should help your players think in terms of a whole year in planning goals. Even if they play other sports, it's reasonable to expect some skill or fitness improvement during the off-season. Just a few weeks of concentrated work on a specific weakness can make a huge difference before the next season rolls around.

Short-Term Goals

Short-term goals are the daily training commitments your players must make if they expect to improve at a steady rate. These goals usually focus on mechanical changes in stroke production or strategy in match play (see Figure 3.5). Once again, insist that short-term goals are performance based, not outcome based. These goals should be reviewed weekly by each player. If a player appears to be losing focus on her short-term goals, step in and remind her of the priorities she has set for herself. All it should take to achieve these goals is discipline and hard work. The best time for you and the player to assess short-term goals is when you work one-on-one with the player. A simple yet powerful short-term goal for high school players is to insist that they develop a specific game plan for each match they play, write it down, and with your help evaluate its effectiveness after the match.

Short-Term Goals

- Continue to work on changing my forehand grip to make it easier to slice approach shots.
- Come in when midcourt balls allow me to rather than hanging at the baseline during crucial points.
- Spend extra time on my backhand approach shot.
- Hit with more wrist snap on my second serve to create more spin.
- Prepare a specific game plan before each match I play and evaluate the plan after the match.

Figure 3.5 Meeting short-term goals helps players improve at a steady rate.

Now Goals

Now goals are used by every player every day at practice and should be personally evaluated at the end of each practice (see Figure 3.6). At least half of the now goals should be worded in terms that make them easy to measure, such as 80% of groundstrokes crosscourt or 100% effort and concentration during drills. Time management during practice will increase tremendously if you constantly remind players to work on their now goals during drills that apply.

Now Goals

- I will give 100% concentration and effort during drills in practice.
- I will not change the incoming ball's angle in drills from the baseline unless I can step inside the baseline.
- During two-ball drills I'll hit 80% of my groundstrokes crosscourt behind the service line.
- During passing shot drills, I will hit all of my backhands with topspin so that the ball doesn't float as much as when I hit underspin.
- During service placement drills I'll try to hit 90% of my second serves into all three placement areas with depth.

Figure 3.6 Now goals are used by players every day at practice.

Team Goals

Team goals should be set each season and follow the same principles and patterns as each player's individual goals. This is the time to set standards of performance that put the mark of excellence on players at your school and help establish a tradition and sense of pride.

Discuss team goals at the annual preseason meeting. Let the players discuss and agree on the goals with leadership from the seniors or team captains. Each year's team is a little different, and their goals will probably reflect some variations from past teams. Use a gentle guiding hand when they're stuck, but your best function is simply to record the goals for the group. Team goals are described in our preseason handout for every player to see.

You might suggest that players consider some overall team issues in these goals such as respecting each player and opposing players, helping teammates practice their weaknesses, calling lines fairly, following team rules, and supporting teammates during matches. Team goals help to focus your efforts on the important issues and create a group effort to achieve. Your players can spur each other on to greater efforts and encourage a sense of unity. If you do a good job of setting team goals, the difficult situations and decisions that occur during the season can be handled by a simple comparison to the team goals.

 BEING THE BEST YOU CAN BE

Our team sets team goals every year before the season begins. Most years these goals have a realistic chance of being met. This particular year the goals set by the team were dashed when the number one player was injured in an auto accident. For a week the realization that their dreams for the season were dashed pushed the team into a collective sense of self-pity. The spell was broken when the injured player returned to practice in a wheelchair. As a senior captain, the player took matters into his own hands at a players-only team meeting. The team members rededicated themselves to being the best they could be without their fallen compatriot. No championships were won, but until the end of the season that team worked harder and more unselfishly than any I had coached before.

A frequent problem on tennis teams is individual needs conflicting with team goals. For example, most teams expect every player to attend team practices, especially on days prior to tough matches. A typical team goal might be 100% attendance at such practices. But what if your star player also has a high national ranking in the country and a long-term relationship with his personal coach who is preparing him for summer tournament play? The coaching sessions with his personal coach may conflict with your team practices.

If you look at your team goals and see one that says "every player's personal development is important," then it may be clear that exceptions for a top player must be made to maintain his interest and motivation. Your team will benefit from having a talented and committed player who is there most of the time, and you will avoid making the player face the hard choice of an all-or-nothing commitment to the team.

Tennis teams are different from team sports like football or basketball in dealing with conflicts in individual and team goals. Most highly talented players compete in USTA sanctioned tournaments year-round and the high school season is just one component of

their competitive year. Consequently, having a personal coach is quite normal and you need to work together with that coach for the long-term welfare of the player.

Punishment and Rewards

Players have a right to know what behavior is expected of them to be part of the school team. Give them the chance to have pride in their own discipline as they adhere to high standards of behavior.

Rather than print a list of team rules that emphasize the negatives, use the team and individual goals as markers for both player achievement and behavior. If players are not progressing toward achieving their set goals, meet with them to refocus their priorities.

Because most adolescents are affected more by peer pressure than anything else, use such pressure in a positive way. Help your veteran players bring the rookies along and set the pace for team behavior. I have found that a few well-timed comments from an upperclassman will often whip the newcomers into line without any comment from me. Whether the issue is tardiness, on-court behavior, casualness during drills, or lack of effort in fitness activities, player sanctions are powerful influences on most players.

If necessary, take your cues from other athletic teams in your school to get a sense of the level of commitment you should require from your players. It might be smart to expect just a bit more of your players so they feel pride in a first-class program.

When players have violated school or team policy, they expect to be punished for the infraction. Here are a few suggestions based on years of experience:

• Separate infractions that are serious enough to inform parents and school officials from those that can be handled within the team.

• To be sure the issues are all clear, give players the opportunity to explain their behavior. Then ask them to suggest the appropriate action.

• If a player's infraction violated the rights or affected the lives of other players on the team, have the player participate in the resolution of the problem.

• If you want young athletes to love exercise and be proud of their fitness, don't use physical punishment *ever*.

• For those who can't follow the rules, withhold privileges such as playing in matches or making road trips.

MIXED MESSAGE

As a ninth grade varsity player on the Downingtown High School team, Brian Higgins felt pressure to perform because of his success as a younger player in the community. During an early preseason match Brian let out a vulgar outburst that couldn't be tolerated in a school setting. After a second warning, I defaulted Brian. I felt it was important to send a message early in his high school career so the problem would not escalate. After that, every time Brian used foul language he was defaulted. The default was meant to motivate Brian and help him control his temper. Instead, the discipline gave him a cop-out. When the going got tough, Brian used foul language so he would be defaulted and not have to face a loss. I had to find another way to help Brian control his temper.

What worked wonders was benching him for a match. And to this day, he has not blamed me for benching him. Instead he has thanked me for helping him learn to cope with adversity.

• Never withhold understanding and empathy for a youngster who makes a mistake. You've probably made a few errors in life, too.

• Keep internal team troubles within the group as much as possible. Public embarrassment and humiliation can devastate an adolescent athlete and likely drive him or her from the sport.

• Rewards are a powerful influence on behavior. Giving positive feedback when you see players doing something right is a good first step. Better yet, strive to say something positive to your players every day, and watch their eyes light up.

• If you've done a good job in setting individual and team goals, you have a built-in reward system. Recognition for players who achieve their goals is a key; reinforce their effort and discipline to accomplish the goal they set.

• Use your public relations skills to recognize player achievements, too. Is there anyone who doesn't like to hear her name on the school loudspeaker, see his name in the newspaper, or notice a picture on the bulletin board in the school capturing a memorable moment?

BORIS BECKER AWARD

One of our players, Brian Wills, would dive for every ball he could possibly reach. His skinned knees and hands and torn clothes and scuffed shoes were evidence of his determination. We created the Boris Becker award for Brian in recognition of his drive and style of play. Two-time Wimbledon champ Becker probably had softer landings on the grass courts than Brian did on our hard surface high school courts.

Brian's ultimate goal was to be an NCAA-ranked player and to play professionally. He earned a tennis scholarship to Drury College in Springfield, Missouri, where he played for 4 years, breaking the college's record for career wins. However, Brian's career took a detour, and his success in high school and college motivated him for the chain of events that he was to experience. This time the challenge he faced was far greater than any he had experienced on a tennis court: He had to beat a type of cancer that is usually fatal.

In the summer of 1988, I had the privilege of seeing him off to Europe, where he played the professional satellite circuit and earned a national ranking in France.

Brian's hard work and perseverance displayed in his comeback are unrivaled in my coaching career. Today he is teaching professionally near Richmond, Virginia, sharing his knowledge and motivating the stars of tomorrow.

Developing Mental Toughness

Players and coaches often cling to the theory that mental toughness is genetic, that a player either has it or doesn't have it. But, in fact, mental toughness is every bit as learned as the strokes in a player's repertoire. *Any* player can develop the skills necessary to handle match pressure.

Tennis is more mental than most sports. The benefits of mental training can result in reaching as high a level of performance as possible on any given day. This doesn't mean that a player will be at the top of his game every day. What it means is he has learned to maintain an inner calm no matter what is going on around him. With self-confidence, he is not trying to prove anything to anybody and can remain focused in the present. These skills, which maximize a player's performance potential, *can* be learned.

To improve mental toughness a player must honestly assess how well he handles match pressure. We all bring insecurities to competitive sport. Relationships with parents, friends, and teammates, as well as previous match results, mold each player's personal outlook and self-confidence under pressure. Help your players improve their match play coping skills with a plan that can measure their progress.

Our program includes seven components:

1. Self-confidence
2. Accepting the challenge
3. Sportsmanship
4. Relaxation-concentration
5. Self-talk
6. Visualization
7. Goal setting and measuring progress

These seven building blocks to on-court mental toughness allow a player to assess himself, develop a strategy for improvement, and measure progress.

Improving my players' mental side of the game is now an established part of our daily practice routine. Mental toughness is developed during our daily team talks by discussing each segment of our seven-step plan. I supplement these discussions with handouts illustrating important points that I've mentioned during team talks.

You too can use your practice court to implement mental toughness skills through talking with your team. We'll discuss each of the seven components of our program in the sections that follow.

Self-Confidence

This is the key to mental toughness. Without building personal self-esteem, no amount of positive thinking will work for the player under pressure.

As a coach you hold the key to building your players' self-confidence. They must know that you accept them for what they are, not what they think you want them to be. Let each of your players know that they are much more important to you than any win or loss. This total acceptance makes players feel secure, which raises their self-confidence.

Unfortunately, some players who lack self-confidence rely on putting others down or behave inappropriately in other ways, often to impress their peers. Players who become obnoxious during play or throw their racquets likely have low self-esteem. Such acts are unacceptable and should be dealt with immediately. When possible, take the player aside rather than embarrassing him in front of his peers. Praise his positive efforts, but above all explain to him that his behavior is only hurting his performance level.

Try to talk to all your players about dealing with their on-court insecurities. Gain your players' confidence by being fair to team members across the board. Once you and a player agree on what changes need to be made, immediate progress in the development of self-confidence has occurred. The player faces the personal problem and sets goals to conquer it.

As the coach, you can structure practice so that short-range success is within the grasp of every player on your team. If failure is all the player is experiencing during a skill-building drill, then exit the drill gracefully and go on to something the players can feel good about. Success breeds success, so don't let your players experience short-range failure at every turn under the guise that it will build character. Just the opposite is true—repeated failure destroys any semblance of self-confidence. As important as experiencing short-range success is to your players, they must understand that total long-range success is not always possible. Prepare your players to deal with failures they will inevitably encounter. Do this by turning failures into learning experiences that can be used to measure progress. A match may have been lost, but if performance goals were fulfilled that day, players come away with a victory. The goals they set for themselves are just that, goals, and they will not always be realized. The key is to continue to strive for realistic success by setting goals that are within reach.

Accepting the Challenge

Fear of losing is the single most counterproductive theme a player encounters when a match is on the line. The competition, not the victory, has to be what your players love.

When a player hits an inevitable slump and losses occur, he must have something to fall back on. The key to riding out these individual or team slumps is basing your postmatch self-evaluation on effort, not outcome.

Effort can be controlled. Seemingly lucky net cords, bad line calls, and inclement weather are not within your control. Only the effort exerted during a match can always be controlled by the player. Once you make your players realize that they hold the key to feeling good about themselves by giving a good effort every time out, then win or lose the match will be enjoyable and rewarding.

If a player develops the attitude that no matter what occurs around him during a match he will keep trying, uncontrollable situations will not faze him. His opponent may hit a winner or dribble the ball over the net on a very important point, but your player will recognize these situations as beyond his control. Be sure to praise your player if he gives an outstanding effort no matter what the score turns out to be.

Sportsmanship

A sad fact in today's sports world, even at the high school level, is that winning usually becomes the first priority of players and coaches. Fortunately, tennis doesn't come under the same public scrutiny, as, say, football, basketball, and baseball. As a result, very few tennis coaches feel the pressure, unless it is self-induced, of having to win to maintain job security. Thus, we can help each player in our programs learn the most important lesson we can teach them by making sportsmanship our first coaching priority.

Sportsmanship is a form of communication with your opponent during a competitive match. It's an aspect of mental toughness that must be applied in every competitive situation if a player is going to enjoy competition without looking for excuses. Teach your players to respect the effort of their opponents, as it is this effort that makes it possible for your players to test themselves during match play. Sportsmanship then becomes respect of your opponent while maintaining your personal dignity. Once the match is completed you can praise your player's effort regardless of the outcome. This all sounds so simple—what could possibly go wrong?

The "vibes" a player receives from his coach, parents, and teammates determines whether sportsmanship during match play will be possible. Unfortunately, what we say and what we communicate to the player with our body language and casual remarks is not always consistent. If you the coach place winning above any other individual goal, the pressure you transmit to your players will make sportsmanship impossible for them to achieve. Parents usually try to put winning in the proper perspective. However, if a child keeps hearing about how much money has been spent on lessons, with very little appreciable gain on the team ladder, then pressure to win will again erode sportsmanship. When you sense that parental pressure is a problem, take the parents aside and try to make them understand how they can best support their child's activity in tennis.

Peer approval is so important to today's teenagers. As coaches we sometimes overlook the fact that all players need to be accepted by their teammates. If the players on your team judge their teammates by wins and losses, then the pressure to win will again make sportsmanship impossible. Teach your players from day one to respect their teammates' efforts, as they would a doubles partner, because every member of the team is working toward the same goals. Positive support from teammates makes competing easier for everyone. I try to incorporate respect for teammates' effort into every facet of my tennis instruction. Have your team acknowledge effort by greeting a teammate at the end of a match and praising her whether she won or lost.

Once winning is put in its proper perspective, respect for opponents is possible. Your player does not use the opponent as a scapegoat. After a loss, he does not make excuses about an opponent cheating on line calls or using questionable gamesmanship. Instead, he accepts the loss and starts preparing for the next match.

 COACH'S LESSON

"Winning is important. That's why we keep score." This is a statement we have all heard as coaches. As a young and idealistic coach, I was

taught a valuable lesson early in my career. Looking back, I'm sure that I placed too much pressure on my players to win. I tried not to, but my body language and remarks often belied my true intent.

Once you have tasted success and coaching has "aged you," it's much easier to be gracious after a loss. In contrast, when you first begin a career in coaching, it's hard not to take losses as a personal sign of failure. My perspective was drastically changed by a young man on one of my first squads. His name was Paul Gregg, and he was diagnosed with leukemia during his junior year. I felt that his tennis career was over, but Paul would not accept that. Unfortunately, Paul's therapy was scheduled the day before most of our conference matches. The therapy left him nauseated and sleepless the night before competition. But this handicap did not phase Paul in the least. He was ready on game day, with a smile on his face, eager to compete as a member of our starting team.

Paul never made excuses. His love for competition made the effort to play much more important than the match outcome. Winning paled in comparison to the joy of competition that Paul exhibited with his positive attitude every time he took the court that year. I learned a valuable lesson from this courageous young man. Effort, not outcome, is the yardstick to evaluate all athletes by.

Relaxation-Concentration

Maintaining an inner calm when all around you is chaotic is easier said than done, especially with teenagers. But this inner calm is the emotional state all tennis players are trying to achieve during match play. When a player is in this frame of mind, her game flows effortlessly and free. Concentrating on stroke production and enjoying the competition become as simple as practice. Unfortunately, achieving this state during competition requires mental discipline and practice that most teenagers find much more difficult to master than hitting a forehand.

Tenseness and self-doubt are tough to overcome during a match that holds particular significance to a player. Excuses for poor play keep entering the player's mind and distract from the task at hand. When this happens, a player has to learn to blow the whistle on himself. Teach your players to dismiss this negative self-doubt by silently telling their mind to *stop* dwelling on the negative.

This technique of blowing the whistle on negative thought processes must be practiced continuously. Dwelling on the negative rather than the positive is a habit, and any habit takes time and discipline to change. A lot of young players will try it once, see no mental change for the better, and immediately say, "See, I told you it wouldn't work for me." Appeal to their competitive instincts to sell relaxation during play as a means of intensifying positive concentration. During your postmatch evaluation bring up the subject of relaxation as a technique to increase positive concentration. Keeping their self-talk positive, visualizing successful points, and walking away from errors help a player relax. Remind the player that mental training is similar to building great ground-strokes—perfecting a new technique takes practice and time.

Racing but Out of Control

During a match when a player feels as if she is in a movie being played at an accelerated speed over which she has no control, have her try one of the following techniques to regain control:

- Slow down preparation between points and deliberately take deep breaths. Take the racquet out of your dominant hand as you breath slowly and allow the muscles in your hand to relax.

- Focus on the strings of your racquet between points rather than on peripheral events occurring beyond your court.

- Visualize what you want to successfully accomplish during the next point before you continue play.

- Remind yourself that you alone control your effort and positive outlook.

Cement Feet and Elbows

Tension during match play takes many shapes, but one of the most common is when a player feels he can't react to the ball. This usually occurs during very important moments in a match. Have your players recognize the possibility of this happening to them, while arming them with solutions to overcome it.

- Remind yourself to be light on your feet. Visualize playing tension free in practice (light and quick).

- Between points bounce on the balls of your feet in the ready position as a reminder to react quickly.

- Concentrate on important points of focus during play. Key in on your opponent's stroke so that you can react to the direction of the shot as early as possible.

- Try to complete your stroke preparation before the ball bounces on your side of the court.

- Remind yourself to stay down on the point of contact as you hit your stroke.

These reminders to increase reaction time can be encapsulated in the following words: react . . . bounce . . . hit. Sometimes just repeating these three words will help a player increase reaction time and escape the tense feeling of slowness that has overcome her during play.

A Player for All Seasons

Distractions during play come in many forms. Some of your players probably have "rabbit ears." Whenever things are not going well on court, they find an off-court distraction to use as an excuse. I've even had a player who once used a chirping bird in a nearby tree as a handy distraction. Telling the bird to shut up was a way of showing everyone at the court that the chirping was causing her poor play!

Distractions to play can be dispelled for short times by following a positive method of visualization:

- Have each player coin a mantra. This is a personalized phrase that triggers the correct positive response during distractions in play. Most of my players have coined their own personalized phrase. One that worked for one player was, *hit the best shot possible.*

- When on-court distractions occur, repeat the mantra over and over again and visualize performing at an optimal level.

- Don't rely on your mantra all of the time. If it's used too much, it can become very tiring mentally. But it is the perfect solution to block out all distractions for short times during match play.

themselves down, it's like wearing a 30-pound anvil around their necks during play.

When a player starts beating himself up with negative self-talk on court, I try to give him some positives to combat this defeatist attitude:

• I tell the player to be good to himself. Be your own best friend rather than your worst enemy.

• Restrict your self-talk to things about yourself that you wouldn't be embarrassed for other players to hear. Some players will rip into themselves loud enough for others to hear, but most deprecating self-talk is inaudible. If it would embarrass you for others to hear how you were treating yourself, blow the whistle on yourself, and stop.

• Talk to yourself as if you were your own doubles partner. Just as you constantly try to pick up a doubles partner with positive remarks, be positive to yourself.

• Be able to laugh at yourself or the match situation. It is much easier to remain positive if you don't approach a match as a do-or-die ordeal.

• Don't feel sorry for yourself when everything is going against you. Accept the fact that your opponent is getting all the breaks today as part of the challenge of competitive sports.

• Dig in and accept the challenge presented by your opponent. Exhibit the "Challenge Response" to adversity.

Visualization

Many players can use visualization to picture themselves hitting their strokes correctly while maintaining a positive inner calm. A great way to use visualization is to have your players implement it in their prematch routine. Our players use the quiet time before matches to review their game plan for the upcoming match. Each player reads the index card that contains his game plan for the upcoming match and successfully plays the strategy out in his mind.

Many excellent books are available on visualization and how it relates to mental toughness in sports. Jim Loehr's book *Mental Toughness Training for Sports Achieving Athletic Excellence* (1986, Viking Penguin) as well as *Coaches Guide to Sport Psychology*

Self-Talk

It seems that talking to yourself during play is an occupational hazard of tennis players. Most players either talk to themselves audibly or mentally during a match. Usually the self-talk centers around personal cues to improve stroke production or deal with an opponent's tactics. As long as the self-talk is positive and motivational, the player can only benefit. Problems occur, however, when the talk becomes self-deprecating.

Tennis is difficult enough when your only obstacle is your opponent. When players become their own worst enemy by cutting by Rainer Martens (1987, Human Kinetics), and *Psyching for Sport* by Terry Orlick (1986, Human Kinetics) are excellent sources for further information on visualization.

These six steps can be used with your team each year to promote mental toughness on the court. The first three—Building Confidence, Accepting the Challenge, and Sportsmanship—are primarily conceptual, so you'll need to reinforce these three steps with your players at every opportunity. The next three steps—Relaxation-Concentration, Self-Talk, and Visualization—are mental skills your players can learn by themselves with your help. The seventh step, Goal Setting and Measurement (discussed earlier in this chapter) allows your players to swing into action using the first six steps and measure their success as it is occurring.

Summary

The following tips will help you motivate your players on and off the court:

- Motivation of adolescent athletes requires an understanding of their needs, including self-identity, peer approval, recognition, and perceived success.
- To be successful, you need to know how to make tennis fun, which, according to 10,000 high school athletes, is a lot more important than winning.
- Goal setting provides the roadmap for your players for the season. Goals should

  - be performance rather than outcome related,
  - include technique, fitness, and mental toughness,
  - progress from long-term to intermediate to short-term, and
  - include both individual and team goals.

- Punishment and rewards are effective tools for motivation if applied consistently with a cooperative coaching philosophy.
- Mental toughness is a learned skill.
- Mental training allows a player to reach a higher performance level on any given day.
- Develop a mental training plan that allows progress to be measured periodically.

Chapter 4

Building a
Tennis Program

Novice coaches often ask what the keys are to building a successful tennis program. It's a simple question, but there is no pat answer. Every program has its unique set of circumstances. What works so well at Astronaut High School will not necessarily work well in your school.

There are, however, some aspects of any successful program that you can look at and modify to your situation. Our tennis program has been formed piece by piece during the past 21 years. As I describe what has worked for us, see what you can use that fits the personality of your school, city, and you personally, and start putting together your dream.

Developing a System

A high school coach's task is to do the best job possible with the players available. Once the talent has been assessed, a coaching plan is formulated to enhance the current players' chances for success. Flexibility within this plan should be a coach's first priority. A willingness to adapt to the different players who come out for your team will enable you to maximize each player's skills. Your season will be compressed into 10 or 12 weeks of practice each year. During this time you will have to mesh players of various skill levels. There are generally three kinds of players you'll encounter:

1. Skilled tournament players who provide the playing core
2. Good athletes from other sports who bring athleticism and a team-first attitude
3. Program players (nonvarsity) who bring enthusiasm at practice and match support

As the coach, you blend these different groups of players into a cohesive unit in which each player contributes in his or her own way. How you involve each group in your program determines your chances for success.

If your team includes players with tournament experience, they will probably occupy the top slots in your lineup. Some high school coaches allow these tournament players to work exclusively with their teaching pros, interacting with the team only on the day of a match. This decision usually leads to poor team chemistry.

If the skill level of the tournament player is greater than your technical knowledge of the game, the best solution is to allow the player to work with her teaching pro during the week but also attend some high school practices. Players with tournament experience should work with other members of the squad during practice, sharing their experience and skills and thus giving something back to the program rather then just taking from it. Team unity will be enhanced and no members of the team will be perceived as receiving special treatment from the coach.

Team members who also play other sports usually form the backbone of your program. The team-first attitude of these players can be contagious to the more individual-minded tournament players. A good coach will use these players' team skills and enthusiasm during drills to strengthen the team's fiber.

The remainder of your squad will be composed of players who do not get to play regularly in matches. In some programs these players are ignored. I've discovered that if I give these players a meaningful role in achieving team goals, their contributions are immense. At Astronaut players chart matches, keep score in our umpires' chairs, and run the desk during tournaments.

Every coach has a favorite style of play. College tennis coaches often recruit players who can serve and volley and play an all-court game because they know this style of play can yield the greatest success in collegiate singles and doubles.

As a high school coach, if you have a player who is a baseliner and effective with long rallies, you probably won't want to redevelop him into a serve-and-volleyer. The style that best fits a player mechanically, physically, and psychologically is what you should enhance. You may feel that every player should charge the net at first opportunity, but if a player is not effective this way, you should help him develop a playing style that promotes his natural ability.

DOUBLES TROUBLES

In 1987 we were trying to win our fourth straight district title. Emblazoned on the front of our practice shirts was the slogan "4 in a row." The problem this particular year was that we had no offensive-minded doubles players. With the exception of our number one man, they all wanted to camp at the baseline. Seeing this, I made a mental note to stress approach shot and volley drills in practice. The serve-and-volley technique of this group had to be improved.

My zeal to implement this change in the players' game met with failure. After consecutive undefeated seasons, the 1987 team opened with two straight losses. Things got worse in our fourth match when we blew a commanding lead in singles by losing all the doubles.

Frustrated, we held a team meeting. The only senior on the team, Danny Brown, said, "Coach, we just don't feel comfortable at the net." Together the players and I devised a doubles strategy that enhanced their strengths. We had both players back at the baseline when returning the other team's serve. When we served, we used the I-formation that encouraged the net man to poach. This strategy, initiated by the players, turned our season around. Danny Brown and his partner Jon Sloan went on to win a district doubles title. And the team accomplished their goal of winning four in a row despite a dismal start.

As a coach you must remain flexible. If one style of play doesn't work, be willing to try another. Above all, don't force a style onto a player. If she is a baseliner with quickness and the mentality to grind out a match camped at the baseline, show her how to do this more successfully. If he is a big, strong, rangy player who likes to come to the net at the first opportunity, then help him develop this style of play. Take what each player does best and work with it. Your patience and willingness to adapt to different playing styles will pay dividends in the win column.

Components of a Successful Program

The players are the key ingredient to any good tennis program. But the talent on your squad will change from year to year, so you need some constants to make your program run smoothly. The components described below will help you achieve and maintain a solid program.

Team Rules

Don't make a rule that you can't or don't want to enforce. If your players have made a considerable investment in your program, they will take pride in what it stands for. Coaches who make a lot of nit-picking rules often find themselves bogged down trying to police them. Keep rules at a minimum but strictly enforce the ones you do set.

Our school has a standard set of rules to govern athletes in all sports (see Figure 4.1). I discuss these guidelines with our players at the beginning of the season.

We want all our athletes to realize that it's a privilege to represent the school. Not many athletes want to be deprived of that privilege. Over the years, I have applied the athletic department rules to only two members of my squads. In each instance the price paid by the guilty athlete deterred him from breaking the rules for the remainder of his career. On one occasion the guilty team member happened to be my son. When I announced the appropriate punishment at a team meeting, the team understood that no one was above the rules. We all had to abide by these rules to maintain team order and dignity.

Each year at our first official meeting our tennis team rules are debated democratically by the previous year's letter winners and me. At this meeting, which occurs a week before the first practice, possible changes in team policy are discussed.

Astronaut High School Athletic Department Policy

The athletic department strictly opposes the following actions by our athletes:

1. Possessing, distributing, or using illegal drugs or alcoholic beverages
2. Stealing

A player who violates these rules will be disciplined in the following manner:

First violation:

A. Player will be suspended for 20% of the team's regular schedule.
B. Player must attend at least one counseling session with the following groups of people in attendance:

1. Parents/guardians
2. Coach of the sport
3. Athletic Director
4. Principal

Second violation:

Player will be dismissed from all athletic teams for the remainder of that school year.

Parent signature

_____

Player signature

_____

Date _____

Figure 4.1

Common rules and their applications usually do not change from year to year. If a player is late to practice, he must perform the warm-up and conditioning work he missed before he can join the drill in progress. Absences from practice should be cleared through me in advance unless the player's name is on the school's absentee list. If an absentee list is not available, players must clear the absence with me before they can participate in the next practice they are able to attend. If as a result of a long absence from practice a player is not even close to his teammates' conditioning level, I will counsel the player and ask him to make a visible effort to improve. Until this occurs the player can practice but will not be used in a team match even if his position on the ladder would normally call for it.

Minor unsportsmanlike infractions during practice can best be handled by sending the player off court. Usually when players lose the privilege of practicing and interacting with teammates for a little while, they will not repeat their offense. Our players understand that their behavior will be scrutinized in the off-season at tournaments, on the public courts, or around the school building. As members of a high-profile program, they know that any individual misbehavior will be generalized to all of our players. There is thus a lot of pressure not to embarrass the program in any way.

I explain to my players that if they accept the positives that come with wearing our gear with the AHS tennis logo, a personal price is attached. They must exhibit the necessary personal discipline. We ask them to stop and think before getting into any situation that will dishonor all that has been built by those who preceded them. That tradition combined with the current players' personal investment is a powerful deterrent.

However, as coaches we all know that incidents will occur that require our attention. Whether the infraction is minor or major, I follow three simple rules in dealing with the player. I try to make the player understand that I care about him no matter what he did. The player must understand that he has to take responsibility for his bad decision. Last, and most important, the consequences each player must accept after making a bad decision are the same for every player on the ladder. Stars don't receive special treatment!

On- and Off-Court Behavior

The code of conduct I expect our players to live up to is detailed in the handout they receive when they sign up for tennis. The key word in our players' code is *respect*. Parents deserve respect for their commitment at home, which allows each player the opportunity to compete. At school the teachers who provide the students daily academic enrichment must be respected. And, last but not least, players must respect their opponents, who give them the chance to test their tennis skills. Adhering to these guidelines allows the on-court competitor the freedom to play hard, play fair, and enjoy the competition.

Captains

The word captain means leader. These are the keepers of our traditions, veterans who have been through a season or two. By providing leadership within the players' ranks, they are indispensable to team morale. A captain's duties include

- maintaining practice intensity and tempo when it is lagging,
- leading by example during conditioning work and drills,
- sharing their experience with underclassmen,
- helping the coach maintain team cohesiveness, and
- acknowledging good play or effort beyond expected levels at practice and during match play.

At the beginning of each season I used to traditionally name the team captains myself. I failed to realize that assigning a captain of my choice discouraged other potential leaders from emerging. If the captain I named failed as a leader, others with leadership potential didn't take up the slack.

I now let leaders emerge naturally as the season progresses. I talk to our players constantly about the need for team leadership from within. Veteran players who want a voice in the team's dynamics always emerge. It may be different players at different times in the season, but everyone who feels strongly about the program has a chance to lead by voice or example.

Our leaders are recognized at our annual team banquet. It might be only one player, or it could be as many as three or four. In front of their peers, parents, and friends, they are presented with captain's pins. After watching this presentation, many young players in the audience might want to gain similar recognition the next year. And that's great. You can never have too much leadership, so why limit yourself to one captain?

 PROVIDING A SPARK

Our team finished the 1985 season undefeated and we were very confident entering the district tournament. But, when on the first day our number three player was upset in the first round, tremors of doubt shook through the team. At the end of the first day's play we found ourselves 2 points behind the tournament's front-runner. At a team meeting in the hotel that evening a calming voice from the players' ranks emerged. Micah Medlock, a junior who was not a starter, stood to talk to the team. Micah was an average player who had earned the players' respect with his hustle at practice every day. When he stood at that meeting and reiterated all the key phrases I had used during the year, he had the attention of every player in the room. The next two days Micah moved from court to court exhorting his teammates to victory. On the last day we overtook the early team leader and realized our goal of winning a district championship.

At that year's team banquet, Micah was the proudest member of the team when he was honored with a captain's pin for his letterman's jacket. Although he had not scored a point for the team during district play, his enthusiasm and leadership were instrumental to our success.

Gaining Support

As one of many athletic teams on your school's campus and in your city, your tennis team has to establish its niche in the community. Gaining the support of the school's administration and staff is paramount to the success of your program. Support from the student body and the community at large goes a long way toward increasing participation and providing you with the little extras needed to run a successful program.

Administrative and Staff Support

At Astronaut High we're fortunate to have one of Florida's best principals. Mr. Fred Bynum fully supports athletics as an integral part of our students' education. I probably wouldn't have been at the school this long if it hadn't been for his tremendous support.

Communicate constantly with your administrators to let them know what you are trying to accomplish. As long as your program's goals fit into the philosophical and educational framework of your school, you will have their total support. Once you have gained administrative support, don't abuse it. If you ignore teaching duties during your tennis season, skip faculty meetings, or leave school early every day, you'll lose the respect of your fellow teachers and principal. Such behavior makes it impossible for the administration to side with you when you need them. Rather than putting yourself and your athletic program on a pedestal and expecting special treatment, strive to fit in with the flow of your school.

Student Support

Tennis is not usually viewed as a popular spectator sport in high school. However, as your program grows, students will express an interest if you make them aware of scheduling and results. If you are a nonteaching coach, your announcements can be delivered through a team captain. At our school we use the morning announcements and weekly bulletin to keep students abreast of tennis happenings. Individual accomplishments are underscored in the announcements by mentioning the athlete by name. Don't assume that no one is interested. It's up to you to promote your sport. As your success grows so will student support.

Community Support

At Astronaut, the community support generated for our tennis program has grown tremendously in the past few years. Signs at our city's entrance have been erected to recognize our three state championships. In 1990, local restaurants aided us in a fund-raiser to cover the expenses for a trip to the National High School Team Tournament at Duke University, where we finished as runners-up. Ball machine upgrades and other extras for our program have been donated by members of our business community.

If you're just beginning to develop a tennis program, start building a base of support in the community now. Go to your local tennis courts or country club and see who the business men and women are that play tennis. If you play, join the weekend round-robins and local tennis events. Our girls' tennis coach sponsors a Saturday morning men's and women's round-robin throughout the year. I often attend this activity to mingle with the adult tennis players in the community. Sometimes members of the boys' and girls' varsity participate, but this is just a voluntary activity by our players and doesn't break any eligibility rules set by our state. This event allows the men and women who play tennis in our town to meet and interact with our players and coaches. As they get to know us and what we are trying to accomplish, they want to lend financial support to our program. Businesses love to be associated with up-and-coming programs for the youth in their town.

If your school has a booster club, attend its meetings. If it's a general athletic support group, your presence will encourage their support of your program. If your school has specific booster groups for each sport, organize your players' parents and invite them to take on some of the fund-raising responsibilities.

In developing a successful tennis program, your responsibilities extend far beyond just coaching on the court. You must promote your program in the community. I begin by sending each parent and booster who has contributed to our program in the past a copy of our schedule and goals for the upcoming year. Communication is the key to community support. Tennis may not be a high profile sport at your school, but with promotional work on your part your program can get its fair share of interest and financial support.

WHERE IT BEGAN

When I think about how the Astronaut tennis tradition was built, what first comes to mind is our togetherness during the summer league tennis program. Although this was not directly related to the high school team, many of the high school players participated. Summer league embodied one of the most important building blocks of a tradition of cohesiveness and team play: an us-versus-everyone else attitude. Titusville was not a typical tennis town with country clubs. The kids who played tennis played because they loved sports, and summer tennis league provided another way to compete when traditional sports were not in season. Our team would go to those country clubs in the Orlando area, and in our recreation department T-shirts we'd beat the country club teams. Through this we built a cohesiveness that carried over for those who played on the Astronaut High boys' team. Astronaut was always the team to beat. Our reputation helped strengthen a team atmosphere—which isn't always there in a sport that is usually individually oriented.

These were the recollections of my son Tom's years in our summer program and high school team. A fierce competitor, he played in the middle of our lineup in the mid 1980s. For Tom, tennis was a second sport. He was an all-state offensive guard on our football team and went on to play football at Harvard. As the coach of this summer league team, Tom's us-versus-everyone else approach promoted a team-first attitude that became the cornerstone of our program.

Instituting the Program

To develop a tennis program from the ground level, start by developing a team-first, individual-second attitude. Not a single player on your squad can be more important than the team. Once you have fostered this team feeling, the ground floor of your program is in place.

Feeder System

Many school systems don't have junior high school tennis. Fortunately, the USTA schools program is addressing this lack of a feeder system in our elementary and junior high schools by training school personnel to begin tennis programs at every level below the high schools. If your state has such a program, give it your full support.

If you're interested in the USTA schools program, contact your sectional office of the USTA. After gathering some preliminary community profile information, a USTA representative will arrange to meet with you and other interested people in your town.

Depending on your school's needs, the USTA may offer to provide a motivational assembly for the students, in-service training for the physical education staff, a proven curriculum for instructional classes, and even some tennis racquets. All this is free to your school, provided you can ensure that kids will have some tennis program in your town to go to once they are hooked on the game.

The USTA will also help you start a short-court or mini tennis program in your feeder elementary schools. Get 3rd to 5th graders playing before school, at lunch time, or in after-school programs. You'll never run out of tennis players for your high school teams if you start them young and keep them excited about the game.

You can't expect your program to maintain any consistency if you don't have some type of feeder system. Because junior high sports don't exist in our school system, I try to maintain my own feeder system through the recreation department summer leagues and off-season clinics. I can't emphasize strongly enough how important this is to your continued success. As a USPTA certified teaching professional I'm directly involved in off-season tennis, running summer clinics and teaching private lessons to juniors in our city. You may not feel qualified to get out on the court and teach tennis, but you can still work on your coaching skills by volunteering to coach or manage summer junior teams. Your off-season involvement will pay handsome dividends when the high school season begins.

Establishing Your Team

How do you create a program at the high school level in which every player on the team has the opportunity to maximize her or his tennis potential? Every coach's goal should be to provide a quality experience for as many players as can be properly supervised on a squad. If you must cut players because of lack of court space or insufficient supervision, use preseason round-robin play to establish a squad.

Round-Robin Play

Developing a round-robin format of play rather than a single- or double-elimination tournament will give each new player an opportunity to play a set number of games against every other player trying out for your squad. A round-robin can be played as soon as your state allows practices to begin.

Hold your lettermen out of the round-robin. Once you have decided which new players have earned a spot on your squad, list them on the ladder in the order they finished the round-robin and below the previous year's letter winners. New players will then have an opportunity to improve their standing on the team by challenging up on the ladder against established letter winners.

At Astronaut High, the boys and girls tennis program tries to accommodate every player who comes out for the team. We do this by setting a fixed number of players that comprise the varsity squad. Varsity status is attained by winning matches on a challenge ladder. Once varsity status is attained, the player must defend his position on the ladder, which gives every player a chance to reach varsity status.

The varsity players, comprised of the top eight boys and top eight girls, are the only players who attend practice every day. Varsity matches in Florida are contested with five singles players and two doubles teams (which can include players who played singles). Nonvarsity players, under the supervision of an assistant coach who is aided by parents, practice and play ladder matches at a four-court alternate practice site. These nonvarsity practices are held 3 days a week, whereas the varsity practices daily. If a nonvarsity player is fortunate enough to beat a player in the varsity group in a challenge match, he or she takes that player's place at daily practice. However, once match season begins, challenge matches between members of the varsity eight and nonvarsity members must be cleared through me at practice. Once match season is in progress, challenge matches within the top eight are held to a minimum so that team cohesiveness can be maintained. This system allows any player the opportunity to move up the ladder during the season and become a playing member of the varsity or separate junior varsity squad.

To maintain order in this challenge process, ladder rules are implemented (see Figure 4.2). These rules allow challenges to occur throughout the period before dual match play begins. After match play begins, and the lineup is set, a player must beat a starting varsity member in two consecutive challenge matches to take her spot at varsity practice. This allows players to improve their status on the team during the entire season, while maintaining the integrity of the varsity in most cases. Very few changes occur once match play begins, but occasionally a player will knock the number seven or eight player into the nonvarsity group and take that player's place at daily practice.

Astronaut Ladder Rules

1. Letter winners are placed on the ladder in the order they finished the previous season.

2. New players are placed on the ladder in the order of round-robin finish below letter winners.

3. Before match season begins a player may challenge up to three positions higher on the ladder (e.g., player number 9 may challenge player 8, 7, or 6). All preseason challenge matches will be pro sets.

4. After match play begins a player may only challenge two positions up. These matches will be two out of three sets.

5. Once match season begins, challenge matches involving varsity members must be cleared through the coach and played at practice.

6. Players must accept a challenge from players below them on the ladder.

7. Players have 1 week to accept a challenge or forfeit their positions on the ladder. No excuses accepted except ill and out of school.

8. The top eight varsity players challenge once match season begins: Regular challenge of two out of three sets to take the place of numbers 6, 7, or 8 on the ladder. However, to take the place of one of the varsity singles players (top 5), challenger must win two consecutive matches against player.

9. New players coming from another sport whose season has just concluded or new students to the school have one free challenge and may play any player on the ladder. If they win, they take that player's position and everyone moves down one place. If they lose, they are put at the bottom of the ladder. This applies only until dual match season begins.

10. If player number 9 beats player number 6 on the ladder, 9 takes ladder position six, number 6 moves to ladder position seven, number 7 moves to ladder position eight, and 8 moves to ladder position nine. If player 9 loses to player 6, ladder remains the same.

11. If player number 9 challenges player number 6 but in the meantime player 6 beats player 4 and moves out of reach (more than 3 positions on the ladder), the match between 9 and 4 must still be played as it was scheduled in good faith.

12. Players not in the varsity eight must play a minimum of one challenge match per week to remain on the ladder in good standing.

Figure 4.2

Doubles Counts Too

In most states singles players are not allowed to play doubles. Thus, when you are choosing a squad, it becomes very important to look for players who have doubles skills. These players may not be as successful during the singles round-robin play but might fill the bill as a number two or three doubles-team player. Remember that the doubles-team points in a dual match are just as important as the singles points. Here are a few skills to look for when assessing a doubles player:

- Consistent deep serve with spin
- Good return of serve
- Likes net play
- Good communication skills (used when communicating with partner)

Maintaining Involvement

The end result of this type of system should be obvious. The sport of tennis is maintained at a varsity and junior varsity level, but no individuals are sacrificed. Each player can progress on the ladder as far as his talent and desire allow. Even if a player doesn't attain match-playing status, she will be active in the sport and be part of a team she can identify with throughout high school.

When you cut a player, his year—and maybe his tennis career—is over. But you never know if that gawky freshman will develop into a skilled player. This situation occurred in our program with a player named David Hennessee.

 PLEASANT SURPRISE

David was no factor on our team his first year. Then during the next summer he virtually lived at the courts, playing with anyone who would hit a few balls. He improved dramatically. I never thought David could rise above ladder status in our program. However, he had other ideas and diligently worked his way up to varsity status the next year, beating out a senior for the last singles position.

After a couple of early season dual match losses, he went undefeated into the district tournament. Painstakingly, he worked his way through the district tournament draw at number five singles. In the finals he faced a player who had dealt him one of his early season losses. Dave avenged that loss in a thrilling three-set match. With all his teammates cheer-

ing for him (including my son Dan, the senior Dave had beaten out for the last varsity position), Dave stood a radiant picture of success as a district champion.

If Astronaut had practiced the traditional cut policy, Dave would never have had the chance for success. As the coach I could see his lack of talent early in his career, but I couldn't look into his heart and see how brightly his competitive fire burnt.

The system of maintaining a squad with as many players as you can manage, supervise properly, and give a positive experience to has many benefits. A varsity team is established to compete. If your program allows, a separate junior varsity with an independent schedule can also be formed.

If you must cut players, use a system that gives you time to assess each individual's potential, not just her current playing status. Once you have decided which players must be let go, talk to each individually. Encourage them to continue playing tennis, support this year's team, and try out again next year.

Emphasis on Team

Creating a focal point for team pride, spirit, and loyalty is essential to building tradition. Our state championship, state runners-up, and district trophies are housed in a trophy case in the school for all to see. My guidance office houses our conference championship plaques, players' pictures, and countless other artifacts from teams of the past. This central display is tangible proof of what Astronaut High tennis is all about. Our players can touch it, gaze at it, and dream about their potential contribution to the team's history. Every player in our program looks at these exhibits with pride.

 THE WALL

For most players in the program, it's affectionately called "The Wall." At first it was just a concept, but now it's reality. On this particular wall in my guidance office at school are the pictures of 30 or so former players, all of whom have met the standard established by our program to receive such an honor. Any player who wins a singles or doubles district title, is a state champion or runner-up, or makes the

newspaper's all-star team is put on the wall. Crowded on makeshift shelves are numerous trophies. Match memorabilia, such as balls from important team victories, and other mementos fill almost every available inch of space. Your eyes, however, are inevitably drawn away from the individual players' pictures to the large plaque in the center of the wall on which is a picture of the 1990 state championship team and their coach minutes after victory. The gold inscription is simple but dramatic: "The Dream Comes Alive." This dramatic effect accentuates the single most important concept: Team successes *always* take precedence over individual achievements.

You, the coach, are the only constant in your program from year to year. Team pride must be instilled in every player each year. Make sure your players know what the program stands for.

One of the easiest ways to begin developing pride and confidence in your team is by having team uniforms. There are few things more intimidating to your opposition than arriving for a match with each team member dressed in identical shirts, shorts, and sweatshirts. You might also include your team slogan on the shirts. The mental advantage uniforms provide your team will be apparent immediately. Too many high school teams allow their players to wear whatever they want to school matches. If complete uniforms are too expensive, at least have each player purchase T-shirts monogrammed with your school's logo.

Constantly nurture team spirit, a common bond determined by the goals you set each year. The veterans on your team can help you instill this spirit in new members.

Most tennis players are used to playing for themselves in tournaments. The spirit that builds through working within the team concept makes playing matches easier. Each player picks up his teammates with positive encouragement during a match. Such team spirit can pick up the confidence level of players who are struggling or in very tight matches.

Players will be loyal to the program when they feel like important cogs in your machine. Treat each player with respect and provide generous praise—especially for outstanding effort and proper conduct. Treating your players this way will win and maintain their loyalty to your program.

Summary

The keys to building and maintaining a successful program include the following:

- Develop a system of play flexible enough to accommodate the different styles of play you'll encounter from year to year.
- Promote proper conduct on and off the court using athletic department policy and specific tennis team rules.
- Allow leadership to surface by acknowledging positive contributions by any team member.
- Nurture administrative, faculty, student, and community support.
- Implement a feeder system through summer play.
- Stress the team-first, individual-second mentality.
- Use round-robin play and a ladder system to establish your team.
- Look for doubles specialists as well as singles players.
- Instill pride and loyalty to your program in every member of your team.

Part II
Coaching Plans

Chapter 5

Planning for the Season

The joy of coaching comes from watching your players execute the skills they have been taught. The mundane tasks such as collecting player/parent forms will never compare favorably with on-court teaching. However, every successful coach realizes that many important responsibilities must be addressed before match play begins each season. These early season tasks include

- medical screening, insurance, and eligibility,
- scheduling matches,
- providing proper equipment,
- formulating a master plan,
- conditioning your athletes,

- providing medical care,
- scouting opponents,
- traveling to matches, and
- helping players with their college plans.

Medical Screening, Insurance, and Eligibility

No athlete should be allowed to attend the first practice until she has provided you with medical clearance. At Astronaut, local medical clinics provide our athletes with a reasonably priced alternative to a private physician's physical. Once an athlete has secured a physician's signature on our athletic department's health form, she is allowed to attend practice.

A related task is the securing of proof of insurance. Our county school system does not provide insurance coverage for any students. Thus it is the parents' responsibility to show the school system that their daughter has insurance coverage.

Certification of health and insurance coverage are combined in one school form called The Player/Parent Agreement Form, which also grants the school permission from the parents to transport the athlete and seek medical care in an emergency (see Figure 5.1). In addition to the medical and insurance form on file at school, each coach carries on his person a notarized list of each player on his squad. This list grants any medical facility the right to treat an injured athlete.

Determining athletic eligibility is the last piece of the puzzle a coach must understand when screening athletes. States, and even individual school districts, have different standards. Most standards are based on grade point average minimums and in-district residency requirements for the parents or guardians of the athlete. Your source of school-based eligibility standards is your athletic director.

Scheduling Matches

Scheduling team matches can be very easy if your school belongs to a conference or quite difficult if your school is independent. Even with conference affiliations, you'll be responsible for scheduling some nonconference opponents. Work closely with your athletic director to develop a match schedule that will help your team develop as the season progresses.

My scheduling philosophy depends on the relative maturity of our current team. If I have a young team, I want to schedule a few matches at home early in the season with teams that we have a chance of competing with successfully. Veteran teams need to be tested early and on the road against the best competition available.

Balance your schedule with teams weaker and stronger than your squad. Road matches develop mental toughness that will pay dividends during your conference or district championship play. Remember that your scheduling strategy should be aimed at peaking your team for championship play at the end of the year.

BEEFING UP THE SCHEDULE

Before the 1990 year began, and coming off a second-place finish at the state tournament the year before, our team realized that this year we had a chance to win it all. However, if we were to get the chance to compete for a state title, we would have to get past a great team in our own district. With this in mind we added to our schedule two teams that would likely provide us with tough competition during the dual match season—the type of competition our schedule lacked in 1989.

The first of these teams was a Florida school scheduled for early in the season. The players on this team were drawn from a tennis academy of international repute. Our players were pushed to the limit during this match, but we finally won in doubles. The second team we added to our schedule was the McCallie School from Tennessee. As a private school they paid their own way during spring break to come to Florida and play some of our high school tennis teams. Their players from throughout the southeast proved too tough for us on that day. The loss was the only blemish on our dual match record that year.

Our 1990 team went on to win our district and thus secure a spot in the state tournament, where we captured the school's first state team title. To this day, I'm convinced that making our dual match schedule tougher that year was instrumental in the team's late-season success. Don't be afraid to schedule teams that may beat you during the year if it increases your team's chances for success in championship play.

Providing Proper Equipment

Tennis is expensive. Players are responsible for providing their own racquets, shoes, and practice clothing. The school provides three practice shirts each to the top eight players. Match shirts and shorts are purchased by

Parent and Player Agreement

School Board of Brevard County
Titusville, Florida 32796

Sport _____ Grade level_____ School year_____

Name of student (please print)

_____

Address

_____

Home phone_____ Date of birth_____

Place of birth_____

Parent's work phone_____ Other emergency phone_____

This application to compete in interscholastic athletics in the Brevard County Schools is entirely voluntary on our part and is made with the understanding that we have not violated any of the eligibility rules and regulations of the State Association or the Brevard County Junior High/ Middle School Activities Association. It is also agreed that we will abide by all the rules set down by the School Board of Brevard County, the State Association and the school.

The School Board of Brevard County and its school principals and coaches desire that athletes and parents or guardians of athletes have a thorough understanding of the implications involved in a student participating In a voluntary extracurricular activity. For this reason, it is required that each student athlete in the Brevard County Schools, and his/her parent, parents, or guardian, read, understand, and sign this agreement prior to the athlete being allowed to participate in any form of athletic practice or contests.

1. I/We, the undersigned, as parent, parents, or guardians give my/our consent for the athlete identified herein to engage in athletics as a representative of his/her school.

2. I/We will not hold the School Board of Brevard County, anyone acting in its behalf, or the Florida High School Activities Association responsible or liable for any injury occurring to the named student in the course of such athletic activities or such travel.

3. I/We understand that no portion of the insurance premium for the player identified herein is to be paid from school funds.

4. I/We understand that school officials will complete required accident insurance forms after which all claims under insurance policy, or policies, for injuries received while participating in school athletics shall be processed by the player, and his/her parents, or guardian through the company agent handling the player's insurance policy, and not through the school officials.

5. I/We hereby accept financial responsibility for athletic equipment lost by the athlete identified herein.

6. I/We authorize the school to transport the student to obtain, through a physician of its choice, any emergency medical care that may become reasonably necessary for the student in the course of such athletic activities or such travel. I/We also agree that the expenses for such transportation and treatment shall not be borne by the school district or its employees.

(continued)

Figure 5.1

7. I/We accept full responsibility and hereby grant permission for my son/daughter to travel on any school-related trip by bus or car. This statement remains in effect until the end of this school year unless canceled by me in writing to the school.

8. I/We know the athlete identified herein is in good health and physically able to compete in interscholastic athletics and has had no past illness or injuries that would prevent him/her from participating in said activities.

9. All parties should understand that in all athletic competitions there is the possibility of serious injury or even death to a participant. Consequently, all athletes must have insurance.

10. I/We undersigned, as parent, parents, or guardian hereby agree to provide insurance coverage for the athlete shown above as indicated below:

(Check one or more, as appropriate)

❑ a. Basic 24-hour student insurance available through the local school for the current year.

❑ b. Supplemental senior high football insurance available through the local school for the current school year. (This covers other athletic activity. Student will also need basic coverage under a above.)

❑ c. Insurance coverage by insurance policy #_____ written on the _____ company. We do not desire additional coverage and will assume all liability and responsibility for injuries received by said player in athletic participation not covered by the above identified insurance policy.

_____
Student's signature

_____
Mother/guardian's signature

_____
Date

_____
Father/guardian's signature

Figure 5.1   *(continued)*

players at a reasonable price from local merchants who work with me annually to keep the cost of clothing as low as possible. These match shirts and shorts are then the personal property of the players and can be used in the off-season.

I try to update my knowledge of trends in the tennis industry so that I can advise parents and players about suitable equipment that fits their needs at a reasonable price. Tournament and match play demand two identical racquets in case a player breaks a string during play. Be prepared to tell your players where they can get racquet advice and purchase equipment.

If your school is just beginning a tennis program, you may be able to get equipment donated. Call your local tennis teaching professional and find out if a schools program is available in your region. The USTA schools program collects used racquets for school use and may even have a source for obtaining practice balls. As your program develops,

better players may become eligible for preferred-player discounts from the tennis racquet manufacturers.

Racquet strings break often, and restringing can be very costly for the average high school player. Consider buying a team racquet stringer through a fund-raising project. You may even be able to raise enough money to buy string for your players. Learning to string their own racquets not only saves money but also teaches players responsibility.

Our racquet stringing machine is at my home, and every player on the squad uses it. I have found that this builds camaraderie among players of different grade levels. It also gives me an opportunity to interact with my players away from the courts.

Maintaining Your Courts

If your practice and match site is a public tennis facility, ensuring that the courts are safe for play should be handled by the managing agency's maintenance department. However, take it upon yourself as the tennis coach to actively discuss the facility's safety factors with the public agency's director. If your courts are on campus, take pride in their appearance. Keeping the courts clear of debris, the nets mended, and the windscreens properly attached to the fences can be easily handled by you and your squad. Painting court lines and helping with resurfacing can save the school thousands of dollars if that's the only way the job can be accomplished. Volunteering your help in the never-ending battle to maintain a safe and pleasant playing site goes a long way toward showing your school's administration that money spent on your facility is worth the investment.

Essential Equipment

The addition of a ball machine to your facility is essential. This piece of equipment enables your players to do repetitive drills to master stroke production. A ball machine is almost as important as nets to your tennis facility. Also consider purchasing targets and barriers for drills. Many teaching aids are available on the market. You can keep such purchases within your budget by buying locally. For barriers, use small red cones that can be found in most sporting goods stores. Use colored ropes and hula hoops as targets for drills. Ask your industrial arts department to help you construct singles sticks for your nets. Singles sticks are placed on the net in the middle of the alley to prop up the net height at the singles sidelines to the required 3 feet, 6 inches. Because many courts are set for doubles play, the net height at the singles sidelines will be too low unless you use singles sticks. Resourcefulness on your part will allow you to acquire the necessary equipment so that your program can be first class.

Formulating a Master Plan

Formulating a course of direction for the upcoming spring tennis season begins for me during the summer. I don't have the luxury of assistant coaches helping me develop a master plan. I need time to weigh decisions that will have an impact on team progress. Once you have a master plan, any changes you need to make during the season are easy to accomplish.

Developing a master plan becomes much easier for a new coach if all the general topics that need to be addressed during a season are spelled out. From informing each player in a preseason handout of the important dates for your tennis team to summarizing the just completed season, everything that you will encounter during your season must be addressed and planned for. Make your list as inclusive as possible, but expect to add to it after each season. Here are some of the items that will likely appear on a list for formulating a master plan:

- Preseason handout
- Stroke production (incorporated in master practice plan)
- Conditioning
- Singles match strategy
- Doubles pairings
- Doubles strategy
- Mental toughness
- Coaching advice during crossover games
- Prematch and postmatch procedures
- Letter to players and parents summarizing the season

The result of this well thought-out planning is a blueprint for structure within each practice session. Write daily practice plans that cover the broad topics you want to introduce to your team. At the end of each week, review your daily practice plans to see if you have adequately covered the topics you wanted to cover. Paper clip each week's practice plans together and at the end of the month conduct another review about how cohesive the month's practices flowed. At the end of each season a final review allows you the luxury of overseeing the entire season so that you can plan for the next year. After a few seasons, you'll be able to use your past daily, weekly, and monthly practice plans to prepare for the upcoming season.

CHANGING GEARS

In the early 1980s our team had emerged as the premier tennis program in our county. But after graduating most of our 1981 team, the talent level decreased in 1982, and the team was struggling. The previous 3 years' practice plans were useless because the 1982 squad required basic skill-building drills rather than the advanced drills of the previous teams. Looking back at monthly and daily practice plans from the mid 1970s allowed me to gear practice plans to the level of players currently on the squad. Two years of using practice plans from the past to help the 1982 team progress eventually led to a veteran 1984 team that went undefeated.

You can digress from a planned structure if special situations needing your coaching attention arise during a practice. However, without daily, weekly, and monthly plans to comprise your master plan, practices will quickly become chaotic. Use your periodic written plans to structure practices, allowing leeway to change as necessary as special situations present themselves.

Preparation separates championship programs from unsuccessful programs. On our practice shirts for the 1993 season was inscribed the motto "The Will to Prepare."

 **INCENTIVE TO PRACTICE**

By adopting the motto "The Will to Prepare," we position ourselves to take advantage of whatever opportunities present themselves. Many athletes are eager to play in the "big match" on game day. However, few are willing to take the steps every day that put them in a position physically and mentally to seize the opportunity for success on game day. That's what separates the champion from all the rest: The Will to Prepare.

Conditioning Your Athletes

Tennis requires athletes to be in top condition. During the high school season, conditioning should be part of the daily practice schedule. You will need to develop a conditioning and nutritional plan to prepare your players for the dual match season and peak them physically at the end of the season for conference or district tournaments.

Physical Conditioning

At the beginning of the season, before dual matches have begun, I stress aerobic development by having my teams run long sprints

Player's name: Murphy Payne		
	Test	*Circuit*
Step-ups (45 seconds)	53	27
Push-ups (20 seconds)	29	15
Sit-ups (30 seconds)	39	20
Lunges (30 seconds)	19	10
Line jumps (60 seconds)	95	43
Knee-chest jumps (30 seconds)	52	26
Line run twice across lines of 1 court (no test time)		

(front of card)

Dates and times Murphy completed the seven-exercise circuit twice:

3/26	6:55
3/30	6:46
4/2	6:49
4/7	6:19
4/10	6:22
4/20	6:19
4/27	5:39

(reverse side of card)

Figure 5.2   Sample circuit.

and do distance running. Once players have achieved cardiovascular fitness, maintenance of this conditioning level is the goal. Thus, during the middle of the season sprints are shortened and distance running reduced.

I have found that circuit training is a perfect way to maintain proper conditioning. During match season, my teams circuit train at least twice a week. Players use circuit index cards to maximize their individual conditioning potential.

Each player uses an index card with seven exercises listed on it (see Figure 5.2). At the beginning of the season, we have a test day when each player goes through the circuit and performs as many repetitions of each exercise as he can in the time limit (for example, as many step-ups or push-ups as possible in 45 and 20 seconds, respectively). The test day results establish a player's baseline for each exercise. During the season, the circuit amount for each exercise is half what the athlete scored on test day. As Figure 5.2 shows, Murphy Payne's circuit will be comprised of 27 sit-ups, 15 push-ups, 20 sit-ups, 10 lunges, 43 line jumps, 26 knee chests (half of the amounts he performed, respectively, on test day), and a line run.

On the days players circuit train, they begin at assigned stations on the court for each exercise on their index card (see Figure 5.3). The goal is to complete each exercise's circuit amount on the index card in the shortest time possible. Each player goes through the seven exercises twice to complete a circuit. When a player finishes his seven-exercise circuit twice, he hollers "time." I will give the time in minutes and seconds, which the player will record, along with the date, on the back of the index card (see Figure 5.2). Each player tries to better his circuit time as the season progresses.

The player's conditioning has been maintained at a proper level for dual matches with

Position 1: On-court lunges. Player stands upright, bends, and places both hands on the court as the legs are thrust out behind. Player then returns to the upright position.
Position 2: Push-ups.
Position 3: Line jumps. Player jumps across any line in the designated area of the court.
Position 4: Sit-ups.
Position 5: Player executes the line run by following every line on half a court. The player should sprint forward when moving from the baseline to the net and backpedal when moving from the net to the baseline.
Position 6: Knee-chest jumps. Player stands upright and jumps by lifting knees as high as possible toward the chest.
Position 7: Step-ups. Using the lowest bleacher seat or a box, the player lifts one leg at at time onto a bleacher seat or box as quickly as possible and then reverses steps to return to the court surface.

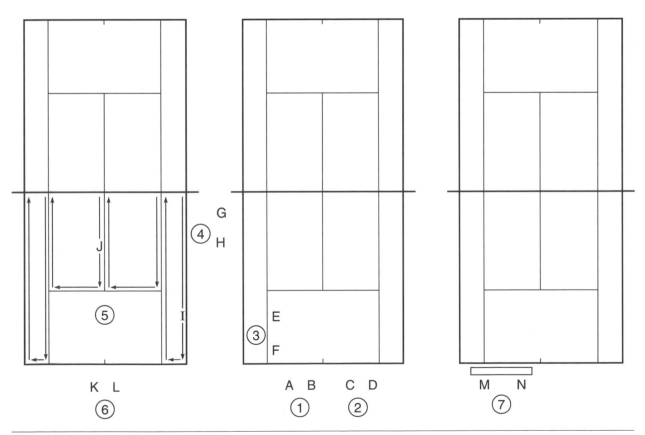

Figure 5.3 Court diagram for circuit work. Two players start at each station.

circuit training, intermediate distance sprints, and in-season strength training (see page 180). The intermediate distance sprints typically include five 3-court sprints and three or four 440-yard sprints. The sprints are run at the beginning of practice and the more demanding 440s at the end of practice. As the championship part of our season approaches (2 weeks before tournament play), we fine-tune the player's conditioning by shortening the sprint distance and stopping the strength training with weights. Shorter sprints include one-court dashes and net-to-fence sprints.

Proper Nutrition

Now that the player's conditioning is maximized for tournament play, the remaining ingredient needed for achieving success is proper nutrition. Addressing a player's nutritional needs increases her chances for success. Eating and drinking the right foods will decrease fatigue and cramps brought on by heat exhaustion. Hydrating by drinking plenty of water is essential. Remember that once a player is thirsty during play, it is too late. Begin hydrating with six to eight 8-ounce glasses per day for the 48 hours leading up to the moment of competition.

Your athletes will need guidance from you about proper nutrition—it's as important as talks about stroke production. Many high school athletes don't realize just how much nutrition can affect their ability to function properly during the strenuous practice and match season. Nutrient-rich food will help your players maintain good health and top performance. Players should try to get 60% of their calories from carbohydrates such as breads, grains, fruits, and vegetables. Protein, essential for building and repairing muscles, should comprise 15% of your players' diet. Protein-rich foods include chicken, fish, and beans. Your athletes should limit their fat intake to 25% of their daily total calories. Vegetable fat is less harmful than animal fat. A good nutrition game plan also provides your players with the vitamins and minerals their bodies need. An excellent resource is Nancy Clark's *Sports Nutrition Guidebook: Eating to Fuel Your Active Lifestyle* (Human Kinetics, 1990).

Pre-event nourishment is a matter of personal preference. What works for one athlete might not for another. The key is to eat foods that will prevent low blood sugar, help settle the stomach, and fuel the muscles far enough in advance to be stored as glycogen. Help your players discover which pre-match foods serve them best. A daily diet of high-carbohydrate, low-fat meals will keep players' muscles fueled for action all the time, and they may not need to do anything special before a match. The day of a dual match or tournament play, an athlete should consume small amounts of food rather than big meals. This will provide the player with enough calories to supplement the reserves built up without making her feel bogged down while playing.

Some athletes nearly starve themselves to maintain what they feel is the proper weight. Alarmingly, eating disorders among sports-active people continue to rise. If you suspect that one of your athletes has an eating disorder, don't ignore this threat to the player's health and well-being. Notify the athlete's parents or guardians and work with them to get the athlete professional help. Be supportive and patient, for the healing process may be long and arduous. Another resource to add to your coaching library is *Helping Athletes with Eating Disorders* by Ron Thompson and Roberta Trattner Sherman (Human Kinetics, 1993).

FITNESS INCREASES SUCCESS

During the 1994 state high school tournament, one of my volunteer assistant coaches pointed out that our players had been involved in four three-set matches during the tournament and won all of them. When I questioned the players,

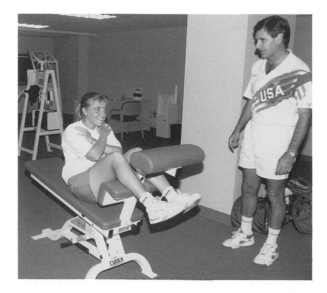

their response left little doubt about the importance of conditioning and proper nutrition. "Coach, when we got into a third set, we knew we were in better shape than our opponent." This physical and mental edge helped the 1994 team achieve a state championship.

Off-Season Conditioning Work

The high school season is completed in 3 months. Strength training should be accelerated in the off-season. Some of your athletes will ask your advice on how to prepare for tournaments during the off-season. *Periodization,* which simply means cycles of activity leading up to tournament play after taking some time off, has become a buzz word in tennis circles. The cycle of periodization leading up to important tournament play in Appendix A is what I give my players to follow in the off-season.

Strength Training

One of the little extras that separate our tennis program from others is the in- and out-of-season strength training our athletes do. The era of the underdeveloped tennis player is over. Tennis doesn't require a bodybuilder's physique, so our strength program stresses muscular endurance, not building muscle mass. Appendix B illustrates our 3-day per week out-of-season and our 2-day in-season strength training program.

Progress in strength training is made in the off-season. When an athlete can perform two to three sets of 12 to 15 repetitions per exercise, it's time to increase the weight by 5 to 10 pounds. By contrast, in-season weight training is a maintenance program. We ask our players *not* to increase the weight they are lifting for each exercise. If 12 to 15 repetitions start to get too easy, the player will do as many reps as possible on the second or third set.

Proper strength training that accentuates muscle groups used in tennis provides our players with strength and power. There are three major muscle groups frequently used in tennis. When it comes to strength training, tennis players should be built from the ground up. Begin with the lower body. Push-off by the legs of a tennis player is accomplished primarily by these muscle groups:

soleus, gastrocnemius, quadriceps, hamstrings, and gluteals. A second group of muscles provides trunk rotation for groundstrokes and the serve and overhead. The muscle groups that accomplish these tasks for a player are the obliques and spinal erectors. The upper body muscle groups that help a player execute a stroke vary with the stroke, but the tennis player should be sure to train the pectorals, upper latissimus, rhomboids, middle trapezius, deltoids, triceps, biceps, shoulder external and internal rotators, and the wrist flexors. Strength and endurance combined with speed and flexibility, gained from plyometric exercises and sprints, develop a properly conditioned tennis player. A complete guide to strength training for tennis can be found in the USTA publication *Strength Training For Tennis.* Contact the USTA Publications Department at (914) 696-7000 for more information.

Providing Medical Care

Few tennis players incur serious injury on the court. An emergency plan for proper and immediate care of an injured athlete should be discussed with the athletic director to make sure it meets the standards. As a coach, preparing for emergencies can save your athlete valuable practice time and might even keep you from being liable if litigation should occur.

At Astronaut, every coach is responsible for a written emergency plan that adheres to the guidelines set by our athletic director. This plan states what will happen in the event of serious injury. The coach goes over the plan with his team at the beginning of every season. Who will stay with the injured athlete, who will go to the nearest phone, and what the other athletes on the team will do are the major considerations of the plan. It's a good idea to do a dress rehearsal of the emergency plan with your team.

Most tennis programs will not have an athletic trainer present at practice. Thus, you will have to take care of minor injuries. Assemble a first-aid kit for use at practice and during matches. Your first-aid kit should contain the items listed in the sample first-aid kit shown on page 58.

✚ Sample First-Aid Kit ✚

- A list of emergency phone numbers
- Bandage scissors
- Plastic bags for crushed ice
- 4-inch and 6-inch elastic wraps
- Triangular bandages
- Sterile gauze pads—3-inch and 4-inch squares
- Saline solution for eyes
- Contact lens case
- Mirror
- Penlight
- Tongue depressors
- Cotton swabs
- Butterfly strips

- Bandage strips—assorted sizes
- Alcohol
- Benodine
- Antibacterial soap
- First-aid cream
- Tape adherent
- Tape remover
- 1-1/2–inch white athletic tape
- Prewrap
- Sterile gauze rolls
- Insect sting kit
- Safety pins and elastic bands
- Disposable rubber gloves
- Mouth shield (for CPR)

In the case of a sprained ankle, which occurs quite frequently on the court, the availability of ice is critical. Know where you can get ice so that it can be applied immediately, as ice, elevation, and compression of the injured limb is critical to suppress swelling. The quicker you treat these minor sprains, the sooner your athlete will be ready to return to the court.

Your school likely has a team doctor. If not, find a physician who has children at the school or an interest in athletics. The team doctor can get your athlete in for an office visit at a moment's notice. The strained back, pulled muscle, or torn ligament can be examined and diagnosed before it becomes chronic. Fortunately, at Astronaut we have such a man, Dr. Ben Storey, and heaven knows how many wins are directly attributable to his timely care.

Scouting Opponents

Before a match I believe a player should concentrate on what she or he does best rather than on the opponent. However, knowing beforehand what your opponent's strengths and weaknesses are is an advantage worth pursuing.

New players or those who have just moved in from another section of the country can appear invincible until a "book" is compiled on them. This book is no more than the advice of someone who has played this new player, or a coach's observations after watching the player in action.

🎾 LOOKING FOR AN EDGE

As our program began to take off in 1975, it was clear to me that to become the dominant team in our conference we would have to overtake Coach Norm Holmes' program. Coach Holmes was my tennis mentor, and his teams had crushed mine the previous 3 years. As a young, zealous coach, I wanted any advantage possible in our upcoming match with his team. A week before we were to meet, I drove the 40-minute drive to their courts to scout his team. Not wanting him to know I was there, I hid behind the tennis hut, out of sight. To my chagrin, as I was furiously scribbling notes about his players' strokes, he appeared behind me. Like a child caught with his hand in the cookie jar, I awaited his admonishment. He looked down at me, smiled, and said, "I can't believe you drove down here to scout my team. I guess I better take you seriously."

He took me seriously by beating Astronaut teams again for the next 3 years. It was 6 years into our program before I finally achieved success against one of Norm Holmes' teams.

A player's prematch itinerary should focus on personal strengths and how they can be used against his next opponent. Knowing what to expect from the opponent gives my player the opportunity to formulate a game plan. Being armed with scouting information about how to disrupt an opponent's game with your strengths is a distinct advantage that I try to provide my players.

I watch players at tournaments, especially if they will be future opponents during the high school tennis season, and take notes. I keep the information in a notebook to be used at the appropriate time. Such information about future opponents is quite specific, and my scouting notes can be divided into three categories:

- Opponent's stroke production (topspin, flat, slice)
- Opponent's style of play (baseliner or attacker)
- Opponent's match stability (maintains focus or easily distracted)

Scouting is an important component of prematch preparation that should be incorporated into your coaching. Once you have compiled a scouting report, share it with your player before she encounters her next opponent. Tell her how she can use her strengths to exploit the opponent's weaknesses. See chapter 10 for more information on scouting.

Traveling to Matches

Our team usually travels in parents' cars. During our parents' meeting, before the season starts, I ask for volunteer drivers. Each parent who volunteers to drive fills out a liability form provided by the school that verifies insurance coverage as well as assuming liability for the players they drive to a match. Parents of players have granted permission for their athlete to be transported by bus or car in statement seven of the parent and player agreement form. This is the transportation system we use at Astronaut, but don't assume it is the best plan for your program. I have been fortunate that parents have made themselves available to transport players to away matches. As an alternative, many school districts provide team transportation. If yours can't, consult your school's risk-management advisor to learn the best option for transporting your players to away matches.

Our team travels together to numerous amateur tournaments in the off-season. During the high school season, I plan at least one away match that will require an overnight stay. These weekend tournaments and in-season trips are a valuable experience to adolescents. Bonds that are impossible to develop at home are formed between players living together over the weekend.

Seniors and experienced lettermen are given the responsibility of schooling the younger players in proper travel etiquette. Players are reminded to be courteous in restaurants and hotels. Removing hats in a restaurant and not becoming too boisterous are part of the image we try to groom in our young players. I remind all my players that they are representing their school and team. With few exceptions their behavior is exemplary.

Helping Players With Their College Plans

As they mature during their tennis careers, players are asked to make better decisions on and off the court. One of the most important decisions players will make while under your tutelage is choosing a college. This

choice should always be made by the player and his family. I try to remain neutral during the selection process. My input is never meant to sway the player in one direction or another.

The USTA publishes a *College Guide* for tennis players that lists alphabetically by state schools that offer tennis for men and women. The guide includes every school that offers tennis, from the largest to the smallest.

Any player interested in playing college tennis is counseled into making a list of suitable choices from the *College Guide* in the spring of her junior year. The player and I scan the list after it has been approved by her parents. The athlete then writes a letter to the coach of each college on the list, which I supplement with a letter of my own about the player.

At some levels of collegiate play over the past few years tennis scholarships have been reduced. However, with the possibility of supplements for scholastic achievement, a player's scholarship can be handsomely rewarding for excelling on the court and in the classroom during his high school career. New NCAA standards require each player to register with an athletic clearinghouse. Check with your high school guidance counselor for applications to the clearinghouse.

Summary

These are the items that need to be handled or considered before the season begins:

- All players must have complete medical screening and insurance coverage.
- Understand player eligibility standards at your school.
- Schedule team matches that will help your squad mature and peak at the right time.
- Know where your players can purchase tennis equipment at a reasonable price and get advise on racquet technology.
- Provide your squad with a safe facility and equipment including a ball machine and targets that will enhance the learning environment.
- Maintain order and structure during the season by developing a master plan.
- Structure in-season practices to provide the necessary conditioning and nutritional information.
- Provide your players with workout plans for the off-season. Maintaining a proper conditioning level for tennis is a year-round process.
- Institute an in- and out-of-season strength program that benefits the muscle groups used in tennis. Emphasize strength rather than building bulk.
- Establish a relationship with a doctor who can treat your athletes when necessary.
- Develop a system for scouting that will provide your players with information about upcoming opponents.
- Thoroughly plan away match and tournament travel so the players will have an opportunity to develop bonds with teammates.
- Assist your players in every way possible with college plans while keeping in mind that the final choice must be made by the family.

Chapter 6

Planning Practices

Preparation for the season must begin long before the first day of practice. Managing practice time efficiently and effectively will help your players improve their tennis and fulfill their potential. You should work from a Master Practice Plan that varies little from year to year, add more detail and specifics in a Weekly Plan, and finally flesh out the schedule each day in the Daily Practice Schedule.

Most high school tennis seasons vary in length between 12 to 16 weeks. It's probably helpful for you to divide the season into three distinct units: the preseason, regular season, and championship season. The activities and priorities within each of these periods can change significantly, and separating them will help you focus practice sessions on specific instructional objectives.

The preseason is the time to focus on player fitness, including strength, power, flexibility, and endurance. Tennis technique should be heavily emphasized, although major changes in style should be done in the off-season, not now. Principles of percentage tennis need to be stressed in classroom sessions, drill situations, and simulated match play. This is the time for your players to understand and apply the basic strategic concepts of both singles and doubles.

During the regular season you need to develop a maintenance program for physical training (see chapter 5). Running should be for short distances, with emphasis on footwork, balance, and explosiveness. Emergency first aid should be applied to tennis shots or strokes that cause problems in competitive matches. A major emphasis during this time is to help players deal with the pressure of competition, winning and losing, concentration on performance goals rather than outcome of matches, and improving their skill in planning and executing a specific game plan.

During the championship season, shorten the length of practices, allow more time for rest, and train physically by eating correctly, stretching often, and tapering the training load. This is not the time to improve or add strokes or skills; instead players need to maximize what they can accomplish with the skills they already possess. Mental training skills and match play competitive skills should be emphasized to help players cope with the excitement and pressure of important matches.

An overview of a comprehensive fitness plan is shown in Figure 6.1. As you move through the year, different aspects of physical training should receive emphasis to allow players to peak physically during the weeks of championship play.

Special Circumstances

Planning for the tennis season is influenced by the time of year the matches are played. The time demands on your players may vary, too, depending on whether the school year is just beginning or ending. Another major factor for you to consider is the effect of cold, windy weather on preseason practice and early spring matches.

Tennis in the Fall

When there are only enough courts to accommodate either the boys' or girls' team, typically the girls' season is in the fall and the boys' in the spring. A fall season may require a preseason practice schedule in mid-August before school starts (similar to that of the football, soccer, or cross-country teams). Two-a-day practices can be exceedingly effective if handled correctly, and the opportunity for your players to concentrate on tennis before school starts can produce terrific improvement.

The two-a-day practice pattern usually includes skill work and conditioning in the morning session, when temperatures are

	Energy fitness[1]	Weeks	Muscular fitness[2]
Offseason			
Beginning	Aerobic training	•	
Middle		•	Strength
Preseason (4-6 weeks)	Anaerobic threshold	1	
		2	
		3	Endurance
		4	
		5	
		6	
Competitive (1st 4 weeks)	Anaerobic training	1	
		2	
		3	Power
		4	
Competitive (2nd 4 weeks)	Speed training	1	
		2	
		3	Speed
		4	
Championship (2-3 weeks)	Tapering	1	
		2	Tapering
		3	

[1]Energy fitness is the ability to store and use fuels to power muscular contractions. It includes both aerobic and anaerobic energy systems along with the respiratory, cardiovascular, and endocrine (hormonal) systems.

[2]Muscular fitness includes flexibility, strength, endurance, power, and speed. It also involves the nervous system that controls muscular contractions.

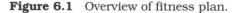

Figure 6.1 Overview of fitness plan.

cooler. Game situations or challenge match play is best in the heat of the afternoon or maybe early evening.

Tennis in Cold Weather

Unfortunately, all tennis teams don't have the luxury of warm, pleasant weather in which to practice or compete. The typical northern climate team that plays in the spring will find the weather just turning nice at season's end. How then can you get a team ready to play good tennis?

First, you have to be creative in seeking indoor court time, even if the hours are a bit unusual. Many club owners are glad to help school teams if you'll agree to practice times like 10 PM to midnight, 6 AM to 8 AM, or on a weekend night. Modest court charges can be paid by your players (maybe $2 to $5 each), a booster club, one generous donor, or through fund-raising events.

Second, if your school has a gymnasium, use it for conditioning, footwork and movement drills, practice against the wall, and volley and overhead practice. If the gym has a weight room, you can also teach your players the basics of strength training for tennis. One thing you should not do on a wooden gym floor is have players return serve or practice groundstrokes. Balls come off a wooden floor so fast that playing them off a bounce is frustrating and will likely produce poor stroking habits.

Third, use a classroom to teach the fundamental strategies and tactics of percentage tennis and mental training skills. Show videos and films of great matches (including high school matches depicting past players) and spend time on team and individual goal setting.

Fourth, any day when the temperature is 32 °F or above, take the team out to the courts. Plan your practice activities to be vigorous and continuous and insist on layered clothing for players and Arctic wear for the coaches. Shorten the length of practice and end with some significant physical training before you head for the showers.

If you blend indoor court time, gymnasium workouts, classroom sessions, and outdoor practices as weather permits, the preseason can be a very productive time. Make the best of your conditions and resources and help your players enjoy the experience.

The Master Plan

The Master Practice Plan sample in Figure 6.2 provides a blueprint for your tennis season and ensures consistency from year to year. You'll need to adjust your master plan a little each year to meet the needs of your players, but the plan should help you make sure nothing is left out when preparing for a season.

The natural flow from the master plan is a weekly plan that can be adjusted depending on the progress of your team, results of competitive play, the weather, and other school events or community happenings. See the sample weekly plan in Figure 6.3.

Daily practice plans (see the sample in Figure 6.4 on page 66) give you the opportunity to adjust each day and set aside the time you need for each component of practice. Be sure to include variety from day to day, frequently change practice partners and opponents, and allow time for some fun every practice. How much time you spend with a given player will depend somewhat on the impact of the outcomes of recent matches and how successful she has been in working toward the performance goals you agreed on.

Sample Master Practice Plan

Preseason

	Technique	Physical training	Mental training
Week 1	Control of ball Percentage tennis Baseline play Ladder play	Aerobic Endurance Flexibility Strength	Intrinsic motivation Managing mistakes
Week 2	Midcourt play Net play Defensive play Ladder play	Endurance Flexibility Strength Footwork skills	Goal setting Performance versus outcome goals
Week 3	Consistency and accuracy Offensive play Develop weapon Ladder play	Endurance Strength 440s Movement skills	Breathing techniques Watching the ball Review goals
Week 4	Review fundamentals Practice style of play Doubles principles Doubles positions	Endurance Strength 220s Movement skills	Develop game plan Handling line calls Sportsmanship

Competitive first half

	Technique	Physical training	Mental training
Week 5	Serve and return Serve and volley Doubles receiving Stroke first aid	Strength Movement skills Nutrition basics	Match play behavior Relaxation techniques Pace of play Doubles teamwork
Week 6	Doubles serving Poaching and signals Net play review Modified set play	Strength Agility drills Hydration	Between-point behavior Coping statements Concentration skills Doubles teamwork

(continued)

Figure 6.2

	Technique	Physical training	Mental training
Week 7	Holding serve Breaking serve Work on strengths	Circuit training Agility drills Sprints	Percentage play Tiebreaker strategy Postmatch emphasis
Week 8	Patterns of play Style of play Work on weaknesses	Circuit training Movement skills Sprints	Review performance goals Coping with winning or losing

Competitive second half

Week 9	Review baseline skills Consistency Doubles skills	Power Speed	Relaxation training Pressure drills
Week 10	Review defensive play Serve and return skills Work on strengths	Power Speed	Concentration skills Pressure drills
Week 11	Review midcourt play Practice weapon Play singles sets	Begin tapering Movement drills	Between-point behavior Review performance goals
Week 12	Review net play Serve and volley skills Doubles skills Play doubles sets	Rest and diet Movement drills	Emphasize positive attitude Build confidence

Championship season

Week 13	Review style of play Review percentage tennis Practice strengths	Continue tapering Rest and diet Shorten practices	Review game plan Review relaxation skills Deal with pressure
Week 14	Review doubles principles Stroke first aid	Movement drills Take time off	Have fun Emphasize teamwork
Week 15	Emphasize consistency Practice strengths	Rest and diet Quickness drills	Have fun Emphasize teamwork

Figure 6.2   *(continued)*

Sample Weekly Plan

Week 5 out of 14

Day	Technique	Physical training	Mental training
Monday	Serve and return First serve percent	Sprints	Emphasize pace of play
Tuesday	Patience at baseline Doubles receiving team	Competitive sprints	Emphasize posture and coping statements
Wednesday	Match day		
Thursday	Stroke first aid	Fun ball skills	Discuss match results
Friday	Play points Tiebreaker matches	Light running and stretching	Relaxation concentration and pressure drills
Saturday	Match day		

Figure 6.3

Sample Daily Practice Plan

Week 2, day 2   *Equipment—Balls and targets*

Time	Activity	Key points	Drills
10 minutes	General warm-up Jog and stretch	Seniors lead	Basic 10 stretches Jog around 3 courts (3 times)
10 minutes	On-court warm-up	Use *one* ball	Hit all shots, especially serves
20 minutes	Review groundstrokes	Emphasize consistency Height and depth	F to F, B to B Figure 8
30 minutes	Teach and practice Approach shots	Use targets Underspin, down-the-line Do forehand and backhand Emphasize *depth*	Start with feed Add volley after approach off short ball
30 minutes	Competitive practice Modified game situation	Serve underhand Receiver must approach and follow to net	Weak serve
15 minutes	Conditioning	Record scores and times	Push-ups, sit-ups, and mile run
5 minutes	Cool-down	Announcements	

Note. Remind new players to turn in copy of birth certificates to AD by tomorrow . . . or else no practice!

Figure 6.4

Setting the Practice Schedule

Short practices of high intensity and focus are far superior to long practices that drag on endlessly. Generally, you should plan for 2-hour practices, perhaps a bit longer early in the season and certainly shorter near the end of the year. Gradually decreasing the length of practice helps keep players fresh and eager throughout the season. Your goal is to have your players at their peak for the end-of-season championship play.

Conducting Practice

Once you have established a seasonal, weekly, and daily practice plan, the key to success is making every practice fun. To do this, listen to and observe your players. Keep your drills and instruction moving and, above all, interesting. After a long day at school your players' attention span will be limited, even for an enjoyable extracurricular activity. One foolproof way to stimulate interest is to add a competitive element to each drill. You can cater to your players' competitive spirit by constantly inventing new individual and team competitions to practice skills necessary for match success. Also, don't neglect to use some competition against their own previous best scores, records, or times rather than just against the other players. When a practice appears to be dragging, don't hesitate to move on to another drill, even when the current skill is being badly practiced. Just plan to come back to that skill another time or day.

IF A DRILL WORKS, STOP IT

I remember returning from a coaching conference with new drill ideas to try with my team. We got so engrossed in trying to perfect them that we spent too long a time on the same drill. After that if I even mentioned "continuous figure 8" or "2-up—3-back" my players groaned.

I've since learned that when drills or modified play is going well, stop it then and return to it another day to work on the perfection of execution—don't risk overkill. Players will be eager to report to an activity they remember as fun and avoid those they associate with boredom or fatigue.

Player Preparation

On normal school days, practices should start 30 minutes to 1 hour after classes are dismissed. This gives players time to see a teacher for extra help, get a homework assignment they missed, or change clothing and have a snack before practice begins.

Begin practice with several slow laps around the courts to raise the body temperature and begin the warm-up. Then have every player join in stretching major muscle groups, which can be done in a circle formation. After you have taught the team the proper procedures, you can appoint different exercise leaders for each week or for each day's warm-up and stretch.

At a minimum, have your players do the Basic 10 Flexibility Exercises recommended by the USTA. You might want to order enough of these cards for each of your players to keep in his racquet cover. You can order the Basic 10 Flexibility Exercises from the USTA Publications Department at (914) 696-7000. The cost of ordering one to forty-nine cards is 50 cents/card. Further price discounts are also available.

Whether they are practicing, playing a competitive match, or playing for fun on the weekend, help your players get in the habit of warming up and stretching anytime they step onto the tennis court. You may prevent an unnecessary injury, especially in cold climates.

 TAKE THE TIME

Late one fall afternoon, as the sun was setting, the JV players were patiently waiting to play once courts became available after the varsity match. Finally, it was Kathleen Gillooly's turn. She rushed onto the court, hit a few groundstrokes, and began her match without any stretching. Within 10 minutes we had to stop the match and take her to a doctor for treatment. The result was a torn muscle—and a cast from hip to ankle for 6 weeks!

At the beginning of practice let players visit with each other and talk about events at school that day. If you want practice to be fun and players to feel a sense of camaraderie, you've got to give them time to chat, mingle, and enjoy being part of the team. Once the stretching is over, though, it's down to business.

Time to Get Serious

After the stretching period it's time to set the tone for the day's practice. Begin by outlining

the skills and activities for the day and how you expect the team to work on them. Demonstrate what you expect rather than just describing it, and encourage any questions. If players truly listened, once the drills begin you shouldn't have to repeat directions. If necessary, a few times sitting in the bleachers watching will help them pay closer attention in the future.

Next, players pair off and warm up on the court. This time is frequently misused. How often have you watched players try to impress a teammate by how hard they can smack each shot? During warm-up shots should be kept under control as rhythm and timing are established. Wild, aimless hitting results only in wasting time chasing balls. It can help to give each pair only one ball and to limit the total warm-up time to 5 to 10 minutes. Encourage them to hit all the shots at about half speed right back to their partners. The object should be to maximize the number of hits made in the 5 minutes.

Experienced players are accustomed to the following warm-up sequence:

- Both players rally groundstrokes from baseline.
- One plays at net (volleys and overheads) and the other at baseline (passing shots and lobs). After a few minutes, they switch positions.
- Players alternate serving and returning.

Skill-Building Time

This is the most critical time of the practice and your chance to be a master teacher. The first part of building skills is to review the skills or shot combinations learned previously. Set the habits by repetition, and as players demonstrate competence, step up the challenge a bit. For example, if you've worked on keeping groundstrokes deep in the court, make a rule that all shots must land beyond the service line or the hitter loses the point.

The next part of practice is spent introducing and practicing new skills or concepts. The topics are easy to choose because they naturally flow from your master plan and weekly plan. Usually you will want to limit

this time to 20 to 30 minutes of intense work on just one new skill. That is enough challenge for one day and short, intensive work periods produce more efficient learning.

After a while, you may want to add the element of competition into drills to stimulate interest. Here are some ways to do this:

- Divide the squad you're working with into two teams by having different players each day choose sides. This is a perfect time to work on positive encouragement between pickup team members as they compete. Highlight any skill you want, such as the split-step and volley. After the player split steps, feed her a volley. If the volley lands crosscourt behind the service line, she has scored a point for her team. Play two out of three games to 10 points. You are the scorekeeper and award points. Don't hesitate to stop the drill and point out deficiencies in technique as the drill progresses. Many variations of games can be devised, and you can structure the games for any skill level.

- Individual competitive situations for drills can be used very successfully as well. Combine the split-step and volley sequence with an approach shot. Ask the player to hit an approach shot from midcourt down the line with cones or a rope as a visual target. After the player has hit the approach shot successfully, feed him a volley that must be hit crosscourt. The two-ball sequence of approach shot and volley earns the player 1 point. When one player earns 10 points, he moves on to the next court and a new activity. Often players stay at the task until they achieve success. If you are feeding during the drill, adjust the difficulty of the feed to the player so that weaker players aren't stuck in one place all day.

- A third scenario would involve timing the drill. Using the approach shot, split-step, volley sequence again as an example, divide your players into two groups on opposite sides of the net. Feed a midcourt ball from the side of the court to player A, who must come in and hit an approach shot. Player B on the opposite side of the net tries to pass. The ball is played out until an error occurs. If player B passes player A cleanly, both players switch sides of the net. Using a 10-minute time limit, all players caught on the side of the net where passing shots were attempted suffer a penalty decided on before the drill begins. The level of intensity will increase dramatically as you inform the group that only 1 minute remains in the drill!

The final skill-building session in daily practice should be spent perfecting prescribed patterns of play, on modified play situations, or by simply playing normal sets with specific objectives agreed on for each player. Your players will look forward to this part of practice because it's fun to play games, but watch out for the frustration that comes from their inability to transfer to game situations the new skills and strategies they've learned in drills.

At the early part of the season expect players to focus on sound technique and strategy during play and encourage them to try new ideas or modify ineffective playing styles. As you move into match play during the season, it's better to emphasize match play skills and tactics and reduce the emphasis on technique unless there is an obvious problem, such as late preparation. Keep in mind that too many objectives will simply confuse any competitor, so try to focus match play practice on the one or two factors that will produce quick improvement and success in competition.

If you have players who compete in only singles or doubles, practice plans and modified game situations should be specific to the skills they need. On the other hand, if your team members play both singles and doubles during the season, be sure to devote adequate time to the skills of each game.

Some examples of modified game situations or match play follow:

• Players are allowed only one serve—exposes lack of a dependable second serve.

• Players must attack the net anytime opponent hits a short ball or they lose the point—encourages getting to the net.

• Points count only after 3 shots are hit: serve, return, and first groundstroke. Helps players get into points without foolish errors too early in the point.

• Award 2 points anytime the winning shot is hit from the net—to encourage attacking play.

• On all second serves, the receiver must chip and charge to put pressure on the server.

• Players lose the point if they try to change direction of the ball when standing behind the baseline. Instead they should aim high and deep and send the ball back in the direction from which it came.

• Encourage players to open up the court by hitting wide to one side with a short angle and following with a deep shot to the opposite side.

• Ask players to imitate a particular style of play—perhaps that of a famous player—and force the opponent to counter that style.

• Be sure to add pressure to some practice play so that players get accustomed to handling their nervousness in real matches. Some ideas:

1. Play best of 3 tiebreakers.

2. Use audience pressure by gathering teammates to watch the final game of a set.

3. Have teammates divide into two teams and cheer their assigned player on.

4. Offer a tangible reward for winning the set such as the chance to practice the next day with your team's top two players.

5. Have one player serve the entire set and expect him to win.

6. Ask one player to serve underhand and expect the opponent to win.

7. Start every game with the server behind 15-30.

8. Play no-add scoring. (When game is tied at 3-3, or the first deuce, the receiver chooses the side of court to receive and the next point wins the game.)

9. Play handicapped scoring so that the player who trails in the set score is awarded a point in the succeeding game—one for every point behind. Example: Player A leads player B in games 2-0. In the third game player B starts the game with a 30-love lead. Even with unequal abilities, set scores will stay close.

10. Invite a team alumnus, local college player, or good adult player to practice. Let your young players cope with wily veterans in practice so they will be ready for anything.

Physical Conditioning

Every practice should include some time for physical training near the end. You need to improve strength, speed, power, flexibility, and endurance but vary the length of time and stress levels depending on the time of the year and schedule for matches.

Scheduling conditioning at the end of practice makes sense because you usually will want to stress the athletes and, after a sufficient cool-down period, send them on their way. If you demand heavy physical work before skill work, players will become too fatigued to concentrate and muscles won't respond.

Once in a while you might want to tire your players (perhaps with a long run before playing a set) to give them the challenge and experience of competing when physically fatigued. This is a great mental toughness test and might simulate what your players will face at year's end in district or state championship play.

Footwork and Movement

Footwork and movement drills are extremely important for tennis because they help players learn efficient movements at the same time they help anaerobic training. Because short, powerful bursts of speed are the most typical moves in tennis, during the season you should be specific in types of sprints and agility runs you ask players to perform.

The USTA has two outstanding videos on movement skills—*Movement Training for Tennis* and *Advanced Footskills for Tennis*—that show how to make these drills fun, creative, and competitive. Borrowing from basketball, football, and baseball, tennis coaches can take basic movement ideas and make them specific for tennis. The variety shown on these videos will let you try a new movement drill every day so your players will never be bored and dread the prospect of wind sprints. You can order these videos through Human Kinetics at (800) 747-4457.

If you follow a few key points, most high school players, both male and female, will enjoy fitness activities and take pride in their physical abilities.

• Keep training fun, emphasize the benefits, be enthusiastic, and expect a positive attitude.

• Never use physical training as punishment—you'll produce a mindset that physical activity is to be avoided. That's just the opposite of your goal.

• Be creative and use great variety in physical training. New ways of accomplishing the same workouts will keep motivation high.

• Test your players periodically (every 4 to 6 weeks) on a few simple fitness tests and show them the improvement. They'll love getting stronger and faster!

• Be sure every player has personal fitness goals that are specific and realistic. Reminders and sharing goals with teammates can be powerful incentives to train harder.

• Use team competition and peer pressure to urge the less enthusiastic players to train harder.

EAT TO WIN

One of the favorite activities of adolescent boys is eating. One year our team captains came up with this incentive to get the guys to train harder. We divided the team into two equal groups based on the preseason fitness test results. Then we gave each group 8 weeks to train and improve their scores. The team that showed the most improvement would be the guests of the losers at a favorite local all-you-could-eat restaurant. I can tell you, that competition was a great motivator combining peer pressure and a tangible reward. It became a team tradition that lasted 6 years before a new group came up with a better (or at least different) idea.

Tips for Effective Practices

- Take time to prepare for each practice with a practice plan.
- Keep each drill segment short and quickly moving. Concentration lags when drills drag for too long.
- Remain positive and be constructive with your criticism. If a player is having a hard time, praise a strength before picking on a weakness.

- Get into the moment yourself by having fun with your players and devising situations that allow them to practice a stroke in a match-like situation.
- Use the pickup team method to get all the members of your squad involved in drills, with an equal chance at success.

Summary

Here are the key planning points outlined in this chapter:

- Have a plan in mind for each practice. Start with an overview for the season, then break your planning down into weekly and daily plans.
- Vary the emphasis during the preseason, competitive season, and championship season. Players need change depending on the challenges they face in competition.
- Remain flexible by using your daily practice plan to address needs that you couldn't foresee when you wrote a weekly plan.
- Keep your practices upbeat and competitive.
- Keep practices fun.

Part III

Coaching Tennis Skills and Strategy

Chapter 7

Stroke Production

The level of tennis coaching experience at the interscholastic level varies a great deal from school to school. Many of you have been recruited into coaching by your athletic director despite having little or no tennis teaching experience. But no matter what your playing or teaching level, you can help your players improve on court. Make a commitment to increase your tennis teaching knowledge, and don't be afraid to try something new.

As coaches, one of our primary goals is to provide each of our players with a biomechanically sound basis for each stroke; the stroke should be comfortable and not lead to overuse injuries. Let your players maintain some individual style to their strokes. As you know from watching professionals, many different styles of play can be successful. Don't try to make every member of your squad's strokes exactly the same.

The style you and the player choose should suit your player's physical and mental abilities on court. Maintain an open dialogue with your players as their strokes are taking shape, and listen to their feedback so that a cooperative exchange occurs, which makes learning much easier.

Use this chapter as a reference point for stroke production. Add your coaching flair and the player's individual style, and the result will be sound strokes that each player can rely on during match play.

Coaching to Learn Versus Coaching to Perform

Every coach is faced with the problem of analyzing why a player didn't succeed during match play. Was it poorly learned racquet skills, or was it just nerves? The easy way out for a coach is to blame the failure on the player's lack of effort or poor shot selection during a match. Assessing the failure as stroke related reflects badly on a coach's ability to teach.

To coach successfully we must be able to assess the player's on-court problems correctly. If further basic training on stroke production is necessary, then we must "coach to learn," which is done by repeating the proper technique for the stroke that broke down during play. If nerves or poor shot selection were the reason for failure, then we must "coach to perform," which can be accomplished by talking to the player about shot selection and handling match pressure better so strokes remain fluid and confident.

Mental Stage of Learning

When a player first learns new tennis skills a lot of thinking is required. The player must slowly process each step of a particular stroke as a new sequence of movements is ingrained. Be careful not to overload a player's mental circuits during this phase. Follow this sequence for success:

- Simplify the basics of each stroke. The player can digest only so much at once.
- Correct one flaw in the stroke at a time. Overlook the minor details and concentrate on teaching the major biomechanical movements involved in the stroke.
- Give your player positive constructive feedback as often as possible.

Practice Stage of Learning

After learning the basic sequence of a stroke's mechanics, a player needs to spend quality practice time refining the skill. At this point less conscious thought is necessary to execute the stroke, which allows the player to concentrate on coordinating and refining the individual segments of the stroke until it is smooth and flowing.

Once the fundamental movements of a stroke become familiar to the player, errors decrease and performance becomes more consistent. You the coach are still coaching to learn, but now coaching feedback and dialogue with the player changes. Rather than your having to point out errors in the stroke's execution, the player can begin to detect these flaws himself. Dialogue about error detection is no longer one-sided from the coach—the player can tell you what he should do to solve the error. Work closely with your student during this phase. Continue to use the player's feedback and opinions rather than asserting your view about what went wrong with a faulty swing. Doing this will allow your player to develop independent thinking so that he can correct a flawed stroke himself during play. To plan quality practice time for your player during this stage of development, consider these factors:

- The player's capacity to learn. Everyone learns at a different rate. Allow the player time to absorb each phase of the stroke.
- The player's motivation to change or learn a new stroke. The desire for change must come from the player himself—not solely from you.
- Fatigue during practice. No one can learn a new skill on court if practice time lasts too long and causes fatigue. Players trying to master new skills need to be mentally and physically fresh.

Automatic Stage of Learning

After much repetition and correction the player will reach a point where he knows how to perform the stroke. As errors occur, he is capable of adjusting automatically. In fact, player overanalysis in this phase usually interferes with stroke production. You can now coach the player to perform. Tell him to relax and let his stroke flow without dwelling on each movement required to execute it. Breakdowns in the stroke are now usually mental.

- If match pressure is causing stroke breakdown, inform your player that the stroke is not at fault. Once she can admit to being bothered by match pressure, you can help her adjust to overcome the problem (see pages 154-155).

- Shot selection from different areas of the court could be the problem. Watch the player during match play and suggest changes that will make each stroke more effective from different areas of the court.
- Offer suggestions about when your player should use a particular stroke to attack or defend his position on court.

With practice, you'll become better at analyzing on-court problems correctly, which will allow you to decide whether to coach for learning or performance. As player confidence in you increases, don't be afraid to say, "I don't know." Then you and your player can solve the problem together.

If a player has entered the automatic stage of learning using incorrect technique, "relearning the stroke" can become very difficult. Self-taught strokes with faulty mechanics must be taken back to the mental stage of learning to relearn proper stroke production. Provide the player with simple cues to make the mental stage of learning flow more easily. Vidcotapc is an excellent venue to point out improper technique to a struggling student trying to relearn a stroke.

Grips

Much has been written about grips. Many coaches use terminology created to describe where the dominant hand is placed on the racquet. Others use numbering systems, labeling the panels of a racquet handle where the pad of the index finger and the heel of the hand should be placed. I have found that tennis students really don't care about artificial methods of proper grip description—they just want a grip that works for them without their having to think about it every time they prepare to hit a shot.

The best way to make this happen for your students is to give them simple parameters as a guide to a functional grip. (By now you may have recognized that the central theme running through all of my teaching is to keep instruction as simple as possible.) If a stroke requires a complex sequence of movements, it is like a machine with too many moving parts—it will break down under pressure.

Most players await their opponent's shot in the ready position with a forehand grip. I want my players to experiment with whichever forehand grip feels comfortable. I ask them to do two things before experimenting: keep the racquet face perpendicular to the ground and keep a firm wrist. Doing so allows better contact with the ball through the hitting area. Achieving this racquet position requires the dominant hand to be placed along the backside of the racquet's handle, which results in an eastern or semiwestern forehand grip. Once a base forehand has been established, grip variations can be added to handle different situations.

Advances in racquet technology and different playing surfaces force most players to use more than one grip during a match. Height of the ball's bounce and speed and trajectory of the shot must be considered in selection of a functional grip. The area of the court at which the shot is executed (baseline, midcourt, or net) will also determine what grip to use.

Because he will use more than one grip in a match, a player needs to be comfortable with how he is going to change grips quickly during a point. Grip changes should be accomplished by using the nondominant hand. Cradle the racquet at a point between the throat and top of the grip, with the nondominant hand. As the shoulders are turning into the shot, use the nondominant hand to turn the racquet to the proper grip required. The nondominant hand also aids in balancing the racquet between points and allowing the dominant hand some rest (see Figure 7.1).

Anatomical differences in hand sizes and different racquet handle shapes make it very difficult to standardize grips. With your assistance, each player should experiment to find what grip is most comfortable for each situation that develops during a point. For reference while discussing grips, refer to the following review of general grip terminology.

- Eastern forehand—the "shake hands" grip. To get this grip, place your palm flat against the strings and slide down the shaft to the handle (see Figure 7.2a and b).

Figure 7.1   Using the nondominant hand makes grip change easier.

- Eastern backhand—from the eastern forehand grip for a right-hander, turn the racquet 90 degrees to the right. Left-handers turn to the left. (See Figure 7.2c.)
- Semiwestern forehand—the "frying pan" grip. Put the racquet flat on the ground and pick it up. Your palm will be further under the racquet handle than in an eastern forehand grip (see Figure 7.2d).
- Continental forehand—the "hammer" grip. The palm is on top of the racquet handle, similar to holding a hammer before pounding a nail (see Figure 7.2e).

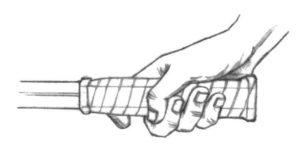

a

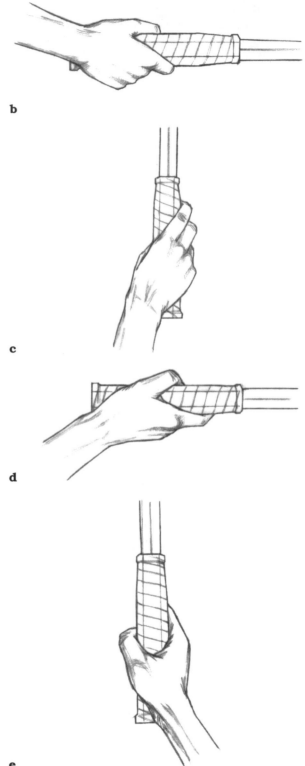

b

c

d

e

Figure 7.2   (a) Front view of eastern forehand (the "shake hands" grip); (b) Rear view of eastern forehand grip; (c) Eastern backhand grip (leverage for your backhand); (d) Semiwestern forehand (the "frying pan" grip); (e) Continental grip (the "hammer" grip).

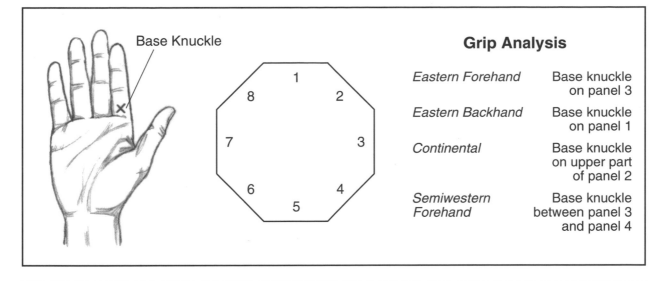

Figure 7.3 A way of analyzing grips is determined by the alignment of the base knuckle on the panels of the racquet.

Another way of analyzing grips is shown in Figure 7.3. Hand position for the eastern forehand, eastern backhand, continental forehand, and continental backhand is determined by the alignment of the base knuckle on the panels of the racket.

Grips' Application to Strokes

Each stroke requires a decision as to what grip will work best. Factors such as ball speed, height of bounce, and spin have to be instantly analyzed as the ball approaches. Occasionally these quick decisions will catch a player in the wrong grip. However, if a player knows which grip is best suited for her game in each circumstance, chances are she will be in the right grip most of the time before striking the ball. The following outlines what to consider before choosing a grip for each stroke.

Forehand Grip

Hard-court play, which usually produces a consistent high bounce, has seen the forehand evolve into a powerful stroke. On hard surfaces, I recommend having your players consider a forehand grip somewhere between an eastern and semiwestern. Due to grip changes, I have found the eastern forehand is usually picked by players with one-

handed backhands, whereas two-handed backhand players are more likely to choose a semiwestern forehand. The eastern forehand grip requires less rotation of the hand to achieve a one-handed eastern backhand grip. A semiwestern forehand grip requires a severe grip change to achieve a proper one-handed eastern backhand grip. However, the two-handed backhand requires less adjustment by the dominant hand to achieve a proper two-handed backhand grip. The palm of the hand should be lined up with the racquet face. Have players prepare for a forehand, freeze in the ready position, and tell you without looking how their racquet face is angled. If the palm of the hand is lined up with the racquet face, the racquet will be perpendicular to the ground. Presenting the racquet face to the ball in this position creates a powerful and consistent shot. The grip allows the elbows to remain closer to the body and the wrist in a firm and comfortable position, which results in maximum power.

One-Handed Backhand Grip

This grip allows more flexibility when reaching wide for a backhand. Midcourt backhand slices are usually achieved easier from this base backhand grip than from a two-hander's grip. At the net your players will already have the second hand off the racquet, unlike a two-hander, so teaching the volley is usually easier because the best grip at net is the continental, which is easier to achieve with one hand on the racquet.

The grip change from the forehand required to hit a one-handed backhand allows the player to present the racquet face flat to the ball and keep a firm wrist. If the player doesn't change grips, then her wrist will be contorted. Keeping a firm wrist without a grip change will cause the racquet face to be too open when presented to the ball. Thus a grip change is imperative.

For a right-handed player, the degree the racquet should be turned to the right to comfortably achieve an eastern backhand grip depends on the strength of the player. However, as a reference point, the inside pad of the thumb on the dominant hand should be in line with the racquet face (see Figure 7.4).

Two-Handed Backhand Grip

This is the most popular backhand grip for most junior players. The knock on this stroke is that it restricts reach on the backhand side. However, the control and power most young players develop with two hands on the grip usually outweigh the lack-of-reach factor. Baseline players, especially girls, find this grip advantageous because the factor of wrist strength is negated with two hands on the racquet.

The two-handed backhand grip is sometimes used by players with a semiwestern forehand without much noticeable change in the dominant hand's position on the handle between forehand and backhand. However, to present the racquet face to the ball in a perpendicular fashion, the dominant hand should rotate to the top of the grip, resembling a continental forehand, and the nondominant hand should resemble an eastern forehand grip (see Figure 7.5).

Slice Backhand Grip

When college coaches ask me about one of my players they may be recruiting, one of their first questions is, "Can he come under the ball at midcourt or is he just another baseliner?" These coaches know that opening the racquet face up to slice an approach shot is crucial to a complete game. To have a chance at the net, a player must be able to hit a sliced approach shot on a low bouncing ball

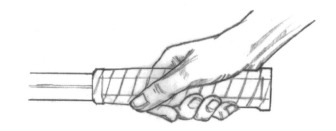

Figure 7.4 You line up your thumb pad to execute a one-handed eastern backhand.

Figure 7.5 Align your wrists on a two-handed backhand.

at midcourt. Once our players are past the beginner stage, countless drills are used to hammer home this important lesson in midcourt play.

For the slice, your grip will resemble a continental or eastern backhand grip. Think of delivering a karate chop with the base of your dominant hand. If your player has a two-handed backhand, I recommend that you try to convince her to take the nondominant hand off the racquet to effectively hit the slice backhand (see Figure 7.6). Doing so aligns the shoulders with the target as the racquet moves from high to low to create underspin on the ball. This is achieved by pushing the dominant hand forward while the nondominant hand moves away from the point of contact.

Slice Forehand Grip

The forehand slice requires an open racquet face and an eastern forehand grip. Many

Figure 7.6 Use a karate chop for a better backhand slice.

players who use a western grip find this shot difficult if they are unwilling to change grips as they come in from the baseline. The western grip makes it difficult to open the racquet face and slice the ball. This problem usually keeps players at the baseline rather than trying to approach the net on a low-bouncing ball at midcourt.

Service Grip

Besides groundstrokes, which include the return of serve, the most often hit shot is the serve. It's hard to convince a beginner that she should not use her forehand grip to serve. After all, she may be competing against other beginners, who will not pressure her serve, so a flat serve is usually sufficient. But as players gain experience, they will need to add some spin to their serves for better control. To convince an advanced beginner to change her service grip to one resembling a continental have her serve to a better player. Once she sees a few of her soft second serves blow back by her, it will be much easier to persuade her to try another service

grip. A flat serve simply lacks the control of a spin serve. Once a player has adjusted to a proper service grip, first-service power can be tempered by the spin imparted.

The spin required for a reliable second serve also demands a continental grip. It may be difficult for an inexperienced player to grasp initially, but once he gains confidence in this service grip, he'll notice how much his control improves.

Volley Grip

Quick exchanges at the net make grip changes for a volley impractical. Most beginners will attempt to hit volleys with their forehand grip, which usually means the player will have a very weak backhand volley. Convince your players that a continental grip should be used at net as soon as their wrist strength allows. The grip will resemble a continental with the heel of the hand rotated toward an eastern grip. This rotation is particularly evident on a high volley. If you have players who use both hands on the backhand side to volley, convince them to take their nondominant hand off the racquet as soon as possible. This will allow them to keep the lead shoulder lined up properly and punch through the volley.

The test of a good grip for any stroke is getting to the ready position and knowing how the face of the racquet is slanted. Have your players prepare and take a swing at an imaginary ball. Can they bring the face of the racquet to the imaginary ball and hit it nice and solid? Ask them if they can feel that this is going to happen. A good grip makes the execution of a stroke easy. A bad grip makes proper stroke production nearly impossible. Impress on your players that failure to have a functional grip for all the strokes they must manage during play will cause glaring weaknesses in their game. Focus your players on proper grips as soon as you begin practice for the year. Without proper grip technique, all other stroke production work will be wasted.

Swing Patterns

Stroke production is a matter of individual style. Style, however, must be secondary to function if you hope to be successful in the game of tennis. How many players have you coached who wanted to look good on court at all costs? They take an exaggerated backswing and huge follow-through, resulting in either a winner or, more likely, an erratic unforced error. Style over substance is unfortunately a pitfall young players get caught up in all too often.

🎾 PLAYING THE PERCENTAGES

In 1988 I began working with a young player who also happened to be an excellent baseball pitcher. His stocky build, even at a young age, made him look like anything but a tennis player. His service motion was excellent due to the similar wrist pronation used in delivering a pitch in baseball. However, his lack of foot speed made him hit many forehands off balance. He would snap his wrist through the shot and try to hit every forehand as hard as he could. Occasionally he would hit a screaming winner, but more often his forehand went awry. He would always remember the winners but quickly forget all the unforced errors.

My solution to this problem was to chart his matches until he conceded that the unforced forehand errors he made by hitting the ball too hard was the reason he lost matches. I worked with him on getting to the ball earlier so that he would be balanced when he swung. However, the most important change we made in his stroke was to shorten the backswing and firm up his wrist before contacting the ball. These changes along with a conscious effort on his part to keep the ball in play longer improved his winning percentage markedly.

The solution is focusing on contact area first and backswing later when beginners are learning a swing pattern. The most important part of any tennis stroke is when and where the ball meets the strings. I feel that instruction should emphasize a short backswing for beginners. When the racquet, in the preparatory position, disappears behind the hitter, the backswing is excessive. Fast courts, windy conditions, or playing an opponent with powerful strokes would usually favor shortening of the backswing. Slow courts or playing an opponent who hits softly (pushes) might favor lengthening the backswing to build more racquet head speed before contacting the ball.

Loop or Straight-Back Preparation?

There are two basic ways to prepare your racquet on the backswing. In the loop, the racquet is brought back at about shoulder height and dropped below the waist during its forward motion to create a semicircular pattern. Picture the letter C to execute the loop backswing (see Figure 7.7). Straight-back preparation is just that—the racquet and arm are brought straight back below the level of the ball's bounce, then driven up and through the incoming ball.

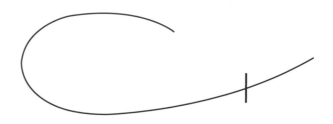

Figure 7.7   Picture the letter C to execute loop backswing.

As each type of preparation has its advantages and disadvantages, I feel a player should be able to use both types depending on the situation. For instance, on a fast-playing court surface where a short backswing is advantageous a straight-back swing might be advisable. But on slow-playing court surfaces where more power needs to be generated, a loop backswing will usually work best. However, I find that most players develop a favorite backswing on their groundstrokes and stick to that method rather than trying to match their backswing to the circumstances.

Swing patterns that develop from a straight-back preparation are usually easier for a beginner to grasp. The wrist is under control in most cases, and it's easier to handle pace. With this swing pattern, low to high groundstrokes allow a beginner to achieve a better margin of error when the ball crosses the net. For the advanced player who uses this basic swing pattern, hitting the ball on the rise is easier to accomplish. The racquet is close to the ground during the preparation phase, where the ball must be contacted in order to "live off their opponent's pace."

Disadvantages associated with the straight-back swing pattern involve spin and pace. The path of the racquet makes it more difficult to impart topspin on the ball. Racquet head speed is cut down because of the shortness of the backswing. If your player allows the ball to reach the top of the bounce before swinging, pace can be difficult to achieve.

The loop (or elliptical) backswing is currently very popular. Many of the big hitters in today's game generate tremendous pace with this swing pattern. The freedom allowed the wrist maximizes racquet head speed. Control is accomplished through spin. The loop should be smaller if the playing surface is fast or if your opponent is a big hitter. On a slower surface, such as clay, you will have more time for preparation. The loop backswing is perfect to generate more power while maintaining control with topspin.

The disadvantages of the loop backswing are quite obvious. A young player can become power crazed and lose all semblance of control. The freedom afforded the wrist coupled with a late contact point may further compound the problem of control for beginners.

If your player naturally hits topspin and contacts the ball at the top of its bounce, then a loop backswing might be appropriate. However, if the player is well coordinated and strong enough to take the ball on the rise, a straight-back swing pattern might be more efficient.

Regardless of which swing pattern is used, the key is to avoid excessive backswing. The problem of too much backswing usually occurs on the forehand side. (Excessive backswings are less likely on the backhand side because the player prepares by reaching across her body.) If the racquet disappears behind the player during preparation, the contact point may be late, making control and pace more difficult to achieve.

Preparation to swing must be early enough so that the contact point is out in front of the player. For some players this means using a short, compact swing. This means that when teaching swing pattern, moving from minimum swings to maximum is best. With a short, compact swing pattern, whether it's a loop or straight-back, your player is more likely to contact the ball out in front.

Once the player becomes comfortable with the swing pattern he is using, rhythm and flow can be introduced. The timing involved in hitting balls coming at different speeds and various spins requires hours and hours of practice. Basic groundstroke drills are the ticket to developing a consistent stroke. I use the one-, two-, three-, or four-ball drills outlined in my monthly plan to build this important skill. These drills should be varied often to prevent boredom. Used correctly, the drills help develop the most important basic skill of stroke production, the player's swing pattern.

Footwork and Movement Training

Tennis is a movement game. An excellent swing pattern will be of little use if a player's legs can't get her to the ball. In most sports, the arms are pumped to gain momentum

while running. Tennis is different. Running to the contact point, a player's upper body must remain still as the legs work to get into position to hit the shot. An advanced player might pump his arms to gain momentum, but as he approaches the ball and initiates stroke preparation his upper body is still. However, beginners are better equipped to execute a stroke if racquet preparation is initiated as they run toward the ball and keep the upper body as "quiet as possible" until they execute the stroke.

Anticipation and Preparation

Footwork is actually the art of remaining balanced as a player anticipates an opponent's shot, runs to the ball, and sets up to hit a shot. In the ready position, a player will feel balanced when her feet are shoulder width apart and her knees slightly bent. The player should be on the balls of her feet, ready to move in whatever direction the ball is hit. Bending her knees slightly as she awaits the next shot will lower her center of gravity and prepare her to react (see Figure 7.8). The best way to react to an opponent's shot and gain momentum quickly is by using a hop step, which is usually associated with approach shot–volley technique. However, we practice this technique before ground-

Figure 7.8 The ready position, with the shoulders squared-up to net.

strokes as a means of developing explosive speed to the ball. Have your player take a quick little jump step onto the balls of both feet as her opponent takes the raquet back in preparation for the next stroke. This action squares the shoulders, lowers the center of gravity, and allows the player to react quickly to an opponent's shot.

Balance and Recovery

As an opponent hits a shot, a player must maintain proper balance while reacting to the ball. Long strides are effective until the player gets close to the point of contact, when steps must be shortened. Shortening the steps as the shoulders rotate allows the player to lean into the contact point with a prepared racquet, which makes recovery easier once the shot is hit. Recovery is the number of steps a player has to take to stop forward momentum past the point of contact after the ball is hit.

Many beginners make the mistake of bending at the waist to reach the ball at the point of contact. This throws the center of gravity out over the legs, which is the base of balance. The resulting stroke is all arms and does not use the body as a linked system. No help is received from the legs, hips, or shoulders.

To use the body as a linked system, the player must step into the ball, which allows the power generated by the legs to transfer to the hips and finally through to the shoulders as the player rotates into the shot. This power can then be used by the player's arms and hands to execute a stroke.

After completing a stroke, many players make the mistake of stopping flatfooted to see what happens to the ball they just hit. This loss of momentum makes working their way back to their opponent's possible center of returns more difficult. Teach your players to work just as hard between shots as during their execution. If they bounce on the balls of their feet between shots, the time they'll need to prepare for the next shot will decrease considerably.

Take a Chance

Unfortunately, every shot hit does not land as deep as your player intended. If they hit a short ball—which their opponent can often stroke for a winner—teach them to gamble. While bouncing on the balls of their feet, they should guess where their opponent may hit the ball and sprint to that side for a possible play on the ball.

Footwork Tips

- Maintain balance with a proper ready stance. Player should be on the balls of her feet, with knees slightly bent.
- Use a hop step to react quicker to an opponent's shot.
- Steps should be shortened as the player gets close to the ball.
- Use the body as a linked system. Power is generated first in a player's legs. Step into each shot so that this power transfers to the upper torso.
- Minimize recovery steps.
- Continue to work between shots. Don't stand flatfooted.
- When hopelessly out of position gamble. Sprint to the side you think your opponent will most likcly try to hit your short ball.

Enhancing Footwork Drill

Purpose. To develop better footwork and balance.

Procedure. Set up pairs of red cones on opposite sides of the singles sidelines. Three players with their racquets are stationed in the middle of the court between the pairs of cones. On your command, players take a hop step and move toward a cone. Executing proper racquet preparation and footwork as he approaches the cone, the player executes a shadow swing, recovers, returns to the middle of the court, and does another hop step before moving to the cone on the opposite side.

Coaching points. Properly executed, simulated shadow drills develop excellent footwork much quicker than when players must be concerned about hitting a ball after a feed. Try this drill to develop balance and footwork.

Three Stances

There are three stances a player can use to set up to hit a shot.

Square Stance

This stance is the simplest way to teach young players good balance and weight transfer into their shots. The back foot lands first and the front foot steps forward toward the net just before contact with the ball. The front foot is directly in line with the back foot. This classic style assures good weight transfer and keeps the body sideways to the net at contact (see Figure 7.9a).

Open Stance

This stance makes it more difficult for players to establish good balance and weight transfer, although many top players use this technique successfully. The back foot lands last and is closer than the front foot to the contact point. The back foot will generally be directly to the side or slightly behind the point of contact (see Figure 7.9b). This stance is typically used by players who use a western or semiwestern grip.

Closed Stance

This stance is sometimes used by players with two-handed backhands. The back foot lands first and the front foot steps across the body and beyond the point where the back foot landed (see Figure 7.9c). This stance is seldom seen for a forehand except when a player is running all out for a wide ball, and is forced to flick the ball back with their arm. The closed stance makes adequate hip rotation virtually impossible.

The square or open stance is acceptable for groundstrokes. I will leave a player's open stance alone if he uses a western grip and can maintain balance and stability during the shot. However, for most high school players, I believe that the square stance allows a player to put his weight into each groundstroke, which transfers power from the legs into the upper torso. By stepping into the shot with this stance, the knees can bend during preparation and the player can stay down on each groundstroke. This total package of balance and weight transfer makes groundstrokes easier to control and much more powerful.

Figure 7.9 Stances. (a) Square stance for proper weight transfer; (b) Open stance for a quicker recovery; (c) Closed stance.

Control of the Ball

Tennis is a game of restrictions. Specifically, the barriers are the lines and the net. If your players cannot control the ball when executing a stroke, no amount of power will do them any good.

Once a player has arrived at the hitting area and is properly prepared to hit a ball, the moment of truth has arrived. She must be able to control the ball as she hits it. From this point in a stroke, ball control is a five-step process:

- Mastering swing speed
- Managing the contact point
- Applying spin for control
- Equating ball direction to angle of racquet face
- Following through to the target

Mastering Swing Speed

Control begins when a player determines how he will use the potential racquet head acceleration provided by his legs and hips as they uncoil into the ball. At this point the player should line up the ball at a distance far enough away from his body to allow the shoulder and arm to move comfortably through the hitting area. A "slow arm" at this point in the swing will do wonders for control. No matter what the playing surface, if racquet preparation is completed early enough, moving through the contact point with the arm under control will enhance the chances for success. Control implies guidance, which gives a player the image of taking care of the ball as he begins the swing. Players must understand that power comes from timing and rhythm, not necessarily arm speed. Managing racquet head acceleration will determine the stroke's chances for success.

Managing the Contact Point

Each player must learn where the perfect contact point is for each stroke. Widening the base created by spreading the feet apart in a square stance as the player strides into the shot creates a potentially longer contact area.

On the forehand side have the player envision pushing the palm forward into the ball. Each player can determine her perfect forehand contact point by initiating an imaginary swing. The player should stand sideways to the net and stop her swing with her weight on the front foot and the racquet face pointed directly forward toward the center of the court. This is the recommended contact point for a forehand that is just in front of the lead foot (see Figure 7.10).

Figure 7.10   Forehand contact point.

For a one-handed backhand have the player repeat the imaginary swing. Standing sideways, prepared to hit the ball, he should stop the swing when the racquet head is slightly ahead of the front foot. The racquet face again should be pointed directly forward toward the center of the court. This is the perfect contact point for a one-handed backhand (see Figure 7.11a). For a two-handed backhand the contact point should be virtually the same as for the forehand drive (see Figure 7.11b).

- Ball and racquet face should meet at the contact point while the player is balanced.
- Grip variations will vary contact point for each player.

Applying Spin for Control

Putting spin on the ball is like applying the brakes to speed. Spin creates friction on the ball as it travels through the air. To impart spin, you need a firm but flexible wrist, which can be achieved by tightening the last three fingers of the hand around the racquet handle before a stroke.

Three types of spin can be imparted on a ball. To accomplish these three spins the racquet head must accelerate through the hit, as follows:

- Brush the back of the ball upward for *topspin*.
- Brush the back of the ball downward for *underspin*.
- Brush across the ball sideways for *sidespin*.

Figure 7.11   Backhand contact points. (a) One-handed backhand; (b) Two-handed backhand.

There are many reasons to use spin when executing a stroke. By imparting spin players can vary the depth, angle, height, speed, and bounce of a shot. If a player always hits the ball flat, she will be unable to hit some of the target spots, which makes it difficult to use the entire court. The six areas available to a player as target zones are the two baseline Ts, the two service line Ts, and the two drop shot Ts at the net (see Figure 7.12).

Topspin

When topspin is put on a ball, the top of the ball spins in the direction of travel. The looping trajectory caused by topspin allows the ball to clear the net with a greater margin of error. This loop is effective in producing either a deep groundstroke or a sharply angled crosscourt shot.

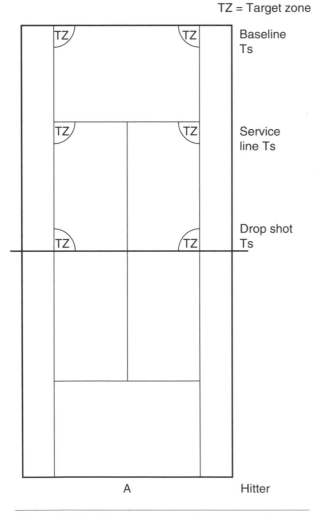

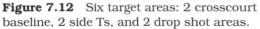

Figure 7.12 Six target areas: 2 crosscourt baseline, 2 side Ts, and 2 drop shot areas.

- To hit topspin, swing the racquet from low to high. The top edge of the racquet's strings should contact the ball first. The faster the racquet head accelerates through the shot, the more topspin produced.

Underspin

When underspin is hit, the top of the ball spins away from the direction of travel. Because there is less air pressure under the ball, an underspin shot tends to stay in the air longer. An underspin shot that strikes the court at an angle greater than 45 degrees tends to "sit up" as in a drop shot. If an underspin shot strikes the court at an angle of less than 45 degrees, it tends to skid and stay low as in an approach shot. Underspin can also be used to control volley placement.

- To hit underspin, swing the racquet in a somewhat downward direction. The bottom edge of the racquet's strings should hit the ball first. The swing pattern should begin slightly higher than where impact will occur.

Sidespin

When sidespin is hit, the side of the ball spins in the direction of travel. This is often referred to as *sliding* the ball. Sidespin is used to hit the ball at an angle off the court as in an approach or midcourt putaway. It can be used while serving to hit the ball wide and pull an opponent off the court. It is also helpful when attempting to change the direction of the incoming ball.

- To hit sidespin, swing the racquet head across the back of the ball. Contact the ball close to the throat of the racquet and drag the ball across the strings to the racquet tip.

Equating Ball Direction to Angle of Racquet Face

Elongating the contact point provides a player the time to tell the ball which direction he wants it to go. Ball direction is controlled by the angle of the racquet face at impact. Once a player learns the contact point for the center of the court for each stroke, she can adjust slightly to hit the corners of the court.

- Right-handed players standing at the center of the court hitting a forehand drive should picture hitting the ball at 6 o'clock for the center target, 5 o'clock for a crosscourt shot to the left corner, and 7 o'clock for a shot to the right corner.

Players need to realize that disguise is important in controlling the direction of the ball. To disguise direction as long as possible from their opponent, preparation should look the same. Subtle variations of contact point and angle of the racquet will vary the direction of the ball.

Clearance height over the net on groundstrokes can be controlled by opening the racquet face slightly or by imparting topspin. This will also cause the shot to land deep in the court. On a fast-playing court, the ball should travel over the net at about 3 to 4 feet. On a slow-playing court the height over the net should be 6 to 7 feet. If the choice of shot requires the player to hit a shorter ball into the opponent's court, closing the racquet face slightly will help the ball travel in that direction.

Following Through to the Target

It is very important to push the racquet through the entire contact area, with head still and eyes on the ball. The follow-through should extend toward the target.

- Players should have a target for a variety of situations. If an opponent stays back after serving, for example, the return should be deep in the court. If an opponent serves and volleys, the return should be low to the feet of the opponent.

Your players should practice a progression of stroke production every day. If they follow a plan for each stroke, they'll quickly progress. The first priority should be getting the ball in play at all cost. Second, control needs to be gained over each stroke's direction, crosscourt or down the line. Third, have your players learn to control the depth of each shot. Of course baseline groundstrokes are usually hit deep to the opponent's baseline. However, players should be able to hit short balls as well. Fourth, work on a player's ability to put the correct spin on each shot. Spin

allows a ball to be hit with more power and still remain in court. Fifth, the players should learn to control ball speed, varying the pace of the ball during each point played.

Key Coaching Concepts on Technique

Along with the principles of grips, swings, footwork, and factors that control a tennis ball are key coaching concepts for each stroke. Most coaches develop their own favorite concepts based on their experience and the skill level of players on each year's team.

Working on player technique often requires individual attention from a coach to evaluate the player's current stroke and suggest improvement. However, it is most efficient for a coach trying to help an entire group of players to present some general concepts for each type of shot and then organize a series of drills for practice of that stroke.

While players drill, the coach can troubleshoot by reinforcing proper technique and make brief suggestions for improvement that do not interrupt the flow of the drill. Players really struggling will need some individual attention, but I suggest that you schedule special help before or after a regular practice. Keep in mind that your role as coach during team practice is to coach all the players for the entire time.

Hints for Using Drills

Helping players learn rapidly requires drills that isolate attention on and repeat a particular shot. The drills shown in this chapter and chapter 8 are examples that you can modify or adjust to fit the needs of your team.

Over your years of coaching you'll develop a repertoire of favorite drills that become the backbone of your practices. However, you should continually search for new ideas, adjustments to old drills, or invent new drills to fit particular situations.

The following hints may help you use drills more effectively in your practices:

✔ Determine the purpose of a drill and make it clear to your players before they begin.

✔ Demonstrate each drill along with your verbal explanation. Point out the key points for players to focus on.

✔ When designing or choosing drills, it's helpful to think of the sequence in the development of a shot, as shown in the pyramid in Figure 7.13.

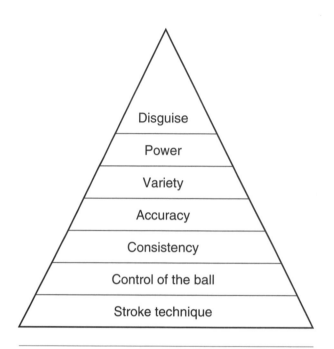

Figure 7.13 Consider this sequence of the development of a shot when designing or choosing drills.

✔ Early in the learning of any shot, emphasize technique and control of the ball (e.g., height, direction, depth, and spin). As players' skills progress, drills should provide practice on consistency and accuracy.

✔ Whenever possible, simulate game situations and natural shot sequences so that your players begin to use patterns of play that transfer to playing points.

✔ As often as possible use live ball rather than dead ball drills so that players learn to adjust to a ball in play. The coach should feed dead balls (i.e., a ball not in play) to players who are just learning a shot or a sequence of shots so that they can experience early success.

✔ Simulate the typical length of a point in drills so that players get used to playing out 3 to 6 shots in succession.

✔ Use targets on the court when drilling for accuracy or consider targets above the net when emphasizing control of direction and height.

✔ Use a variety of drills each practice and change drills before players become tired and bored of the repetition.

✔ Vary the challenge to your players by adjusting the purpose of a drill. For example, you may perform a drill for a certain amount of time, a certain number of trials, until there is a winner, until players master the skill, or until the coach blows the whistle. Each of these criteria has its place and by varying the instructions and purpose, the same drill can present a new and different challenge to players.

✔ Maximize court space by using some drills that can accommodate 6 to 8 players on one court, thereby freeing other courts for singles drills or game situations.

✔ Adjust drills to the ability level of players on each court. Although all players may be performing the same task, challenge your better players by adding the challenge of depth, accuracy, or increased penalty for errors.

✔ Integrate enough frequent rotations and movement within each day's drills so that your players are getting a good physical workout without even noticing it. Make sure players do not have to stand in line for a turn more than 30 seconds—nothing is more boring.

✔ Look for opportunities for positive reinforcement while players are drilling. Try to catch them doing something right. If you need to correct their technique or performance, do it clearly, concisely, and without emotion.

✔ Remember to make drills fun. Players like challenges. They like competition and love to beat the coach. Plan some time each day for fun—especially after periods of intense concentration and hard work.

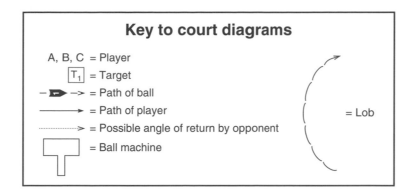

Key to court diagrams

A, B, C = Player

T_1 = Target

- ▣ -> = Path of ball

⟶ = Path of player

·············> = Possible angle of return by opponent

⊥ = Ball machine

= Lob

The following coaching concepts for the serve, return of serve, groundstrokes, midcourt shots, net play, and passing shots and lobs are generally accepted as important to high school players. You may find it helpful to extract some of the suggestions that follow and develop a team handout or workbook so that each player has a personal copy of key concepts on technique. I've found it useful to require team members to review these written concepts before and after practice time spent on specific shots.

Serving

Teach your players the wisdom of adopting the following priorities when serving:

❶ Get the serve in the court—consistently, even under pressure.

❷ Vary the placement to the opponent's backhand, forehand, or at the body.

❸ Adjust the amount of spin—if serves are long, add more spin; if serves fall short, use less spin and aim higher.

❹ After you control the skills above, add speed and power to force a weak return.

Before each serve, urge players to take some time to perform a ritual before beginning the motion. The ritual should include a deep breath or two to relax, a few bounces of the ball, and a decision on the placement and type of serve to be delivered. One of the telltale signs of nervousness and choking is rushing between first and second serves. The pre-serve ritual should help to relax and focus the server by slowing the process.

The aim on the service toss should be in line with the tossing shoulder and out in front of the body. The distance in front will vary depending on the service motion of each player and the type of serve hit. For example, a flat serve will be hit further in front than a kick serve.

Power on the serve is generated from the ground by bending the knees and then straightening them during the reach to contact the ball. A 20% turn of the shoulders

away from the starting position provides good body rotation and, when combined with a continuous swing of the racquet arm, allows for maximum velocity.

Second serves should be hit with exactly the same motion and speed as first serves but the margin of safety increased by adding quite a bit more spin to bring the ball down into the court. Help your players resist the temptation to push the second serve, as this will risk an attacking shot from the receiver, especially if the serve lacks depth.

Serving Drills

Pressure Serving

Purpose. To test serves in a pressure situation.

Procedure. Create the following scenario: "Imagine it's the third set of a tough match and you're up 6-5. Odds are if you hit four first serves in you'll win the match." Have each player attempt these four serves in succession (see Figure 7.14):

1. Serve to the outside half of the deuce court.
2. Serve to the inside half of the deuce court.
3. Serve to the outside half of the ad court.
4. Serve to the inside half of the ad court.

If all four serves land in, you've got a winner. If a player misses on the first serve, she must go and hit 40 practice serves before trying again. For a miss on the second serve, the penalty is 30 practice serves, and so on.

Coaching points. Remind each player to take time for his serving ritual and focus on the task at hand. If your players try to ensure success by hitting serves too softly, simply add the rule that the ball must pass the baseline on the second bounce. You can increase the pressure on the server by gathering an audience of cheering players, which often happens at the end of a crucial match. An excellent variation of this drill that promotes cooperative teamwork is to assign a receiver to work with each server. They work together to accomplish four serves and four returns successfully with the returns required to land crosscourt beyond the service line.

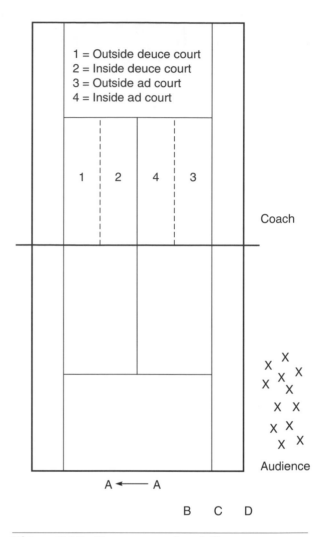

Figure 7.14 Pressure serving drill.

Serving Power

Purpose. To measure the depth and power of the first and second serves.

Procedure. Players serve 10 serves from the serving position. A partner marks the spot of the second bounce of all serves that land in the service box with enough power that the ball's second bounce lands behind the power line 8 feet beyond the baseline (see Figure 7.15).

Coaching points. Players who have difficulty with this drill should be open to additional practice on their serve and probably welcome suggestions from you to improve technique. To maximize the use of space, have players serving from both the left and the right sides of the court at once. After serving 10 serves, they should switch roles with their partners

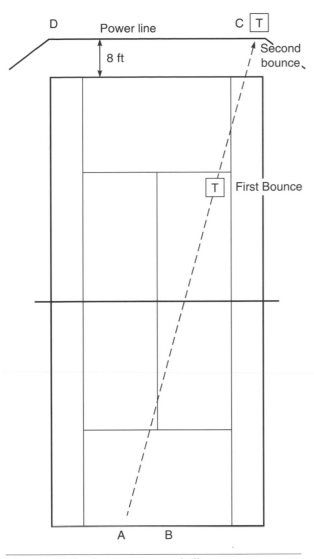

Figure 7.15 Serving power drill.

across the net. After both players have hit 10 serves from one side, repeat the procedure from the other side.

Serve and First Volley

Purpose. To practice the serve, split-step, and first volley.

Procedure. Servers line up at the baseline and one at a time try one serve to the service box straight ahead, split-step as the receiver begins the forward swing, and then volley the ball beyond the service line. The purpose of serving straight is to maximize space as the identical drill can proceed simultaneously on the other half of the court. This will free other courts for singles drills or play.

Coaching points. Emphasize getting the serve in (faults cause a loss of turn), perfecting the

technique and timing of the split-step, and hitting the first volley deep. After players achieve repeated success, let them play the point out using the center line and doubles sideline for boundaries. Because the playing area is limited, the ball tends to stay in play longer and the serve-and-volleyer will gain confidence to move in for volleys or retreat to hit an overhead smash.

Returning Serve

Although every point requires a return of serve, this is probably the least practiced shot in tennis. Emphasizing the following points with your players will help them improve their service returns.

1 Adjust your position on the court based on the speed and depth of the opponent's serve. Move inside the baseline to attack a weak second serve. Move behind the baseline to counter a hard first serve.

2 Watch the ball as the server tosses it, split-step just before she contacts the serve, and begin your return with a quick shoulder turn. If the serve hits the net, check to see if your shoulders are turned.

3 As there is usually less time for the swing on a service return, shorten the length of your backswing from your normal groundstrokes.

4 Hit most of your returns crosscourt or deep down the middle to increase the margin for safety. If the serve is weak, attack it by going to your opponent's weakness.

The receiver's position should bisect the angle of possible serves from her opponent. If the server varies her serving position, the receiver should adjust to the left or right accordingly.

For most players, I suggest waiting with the forehand grip if that is their preferred shot as they'll have to make only one grip change to the backhand. Waiting with a grip between forehand and backhand is inefficient because there are then two possible changes to make. If the server is hitting a high percentage of serves to the backhand, it may be wise to adjust by starting out with the backhand grip.

The key to an early reaction to the location and type of serve is for the receiver to watch the ball closely during the service toss, then look and listen to pick up the spin and direction of the ball just after the server contacts it. Some servers provide clues unknowingly by varying their stance or service toss for different types of serve. Watch closely for clues as the server begins her serve.

If the server hits a spin or kick serve that bounces high and kicks up to shoulder height, you may be forced to play a return out of your preferred hitting zone. The most common counterstrategy is to move forward and take the serve on the rise before the spin takes full effect. Many players find it easier to chip or slice a serve with a lot of spin. Whether driving or slicing, however, the key to success is to move forward to attack the ball and close the racquet face a bit or to cover the ball to control the upward movement that results from the heavy spin.

The safest return with the best margin for error is returned at the same angle it was hit from. On serves that are less difficult to handle, you may wish to change the angle of return and hit to the opponent's weakness.

Practicing service returns should start with a series of drills that emphasize consistency. A modified game that focuses on the serve and return can be structured by limiting each point to those two shots. Keep score the same way as a normal set but end each point after the service return. Increase the difficulty of the task by limiting the placement of serves and/or returns. If the players in the drill are of uneven ability, you can increase competitiveness by limiting the choices for one player and not the other.

Because many points are ended during the first couple of shots, emphasize the importance of consistency early in the point by requiring a serve, return, and one groundstroke before the point begins. This will help your players grow accustomed to playing their way into each point.

Return of Serve Drills

Service Return to Targets

Purpose. To promote consistency, depth, and accuracy on returns.

Procedure. Players return serves to a predetermined target area of the court. Targets 1, 2, and 3 emphasize depth of the return against a baseline player, whereas Targets 4, 5, and 6 are valuable to practice returns against a serve-and-volleyer (see Figure 7.16). Balls returned to Targets 4 and 6 will also force a defensive baseliner to move forward and sideways away from her more comfortable home position behind the baseline.

Coaching points. After players gain consistency in placing the return, add the element of competition by using conventional scoring or some adaptation. Another twist is for the coach to assign the target area for each return.

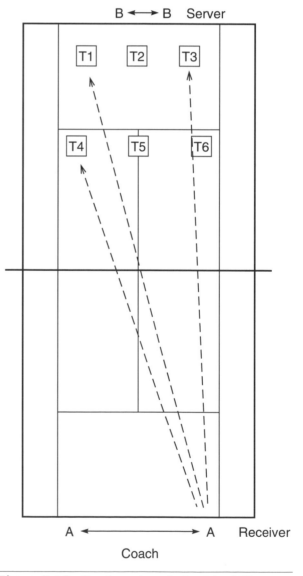

Figure 7.16 Service return to targets drill.

Punish the Server

Purpose. To develop an offensive, punishing return of serve.

Procedure. The receiver assumes his normal position for returning serve. As the server begins his service toss, the receiver quickly runs around his weaker stroke to hit the return with his favorite shot (typically a forehand drive). The objective is to hit an aggressive return out of the server's reach (see Figure 7.17). Normally this strategy is useful against second serves, so you should limit the server to hitting second serves.

Coaching points. Be sure your receivers practice this shot from both the deuce and the ad courts. You can add a competitive element by scoring 2 points for an outright winning return, 1 point for eliciting an error from the server on the first groundstroke, and 2 points to the receiver if he can hit the return deep to the server.

Cutting Off the Angle

Purpose. To practice moving forward on the diagonal to defend against wide serves.

Procedure. The server is limited to serving to the wide angle on the outside of the service boxes. The receiver must cut off the angle by moving forward at 45 degrees to intercept wide serves. The return should normally be played crosscourt to prevent the server from hitting the next shot to a wide open court (see Figure 7.18).

Coaching points. Insist that the receiver think forward first and sideways second to cut off the angle. The most common errors with this return result from a lateral movement that requires more steps and then a crossover step with the inside leg that blocks the hip rotation during the hit. This shot is usually critical against a left-handed slice serve in the ad court or a right-handed slice serve in the deuce court. It is often a particularly

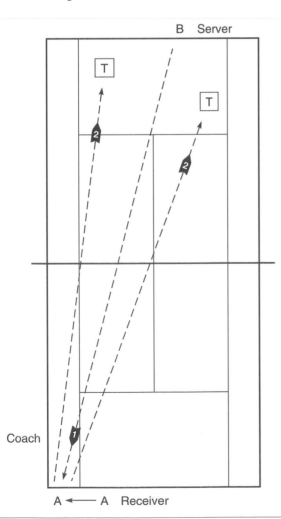

Figure 7.17 Punish the server drill.

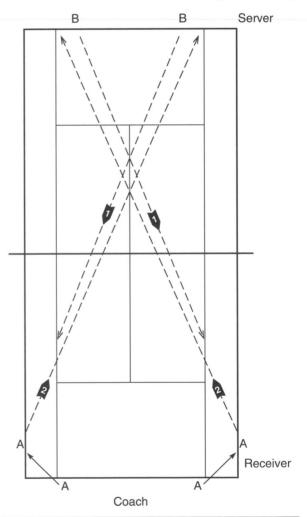

Figure 7.18 Cutting off the angle drill.

troublesome return for two-handed players due to their problems in reaching for wide balls. Vary the drill by letting the server serve to either the inside or outside corners of the service boxes. This will keep the receiver from cheating to the outside in anticipation of a wide-angle serve.

Groundstrokes

After the serve and return, most points begin with an exchange of groundstrokes. Keep the following concepts in mind as you work with your players on groundstrokes.

1 Aim for steadiness on groundstrokes. Generally hit crosscourt and deep to prevent your opponent from taking the offensive.

2 Hit more aggressively when you move inside your baseline to play a shot.

3 Vary the height, spin, and pace of your strokes to keep your opponent a bit off balance—just like a baseball pitcher changes speeds and types of pitches.

4 Aim for target areas well inside the lines to give you a good margin for error. Establish your target at the intersection 6 feet in from both the baseline and the sideline.

A key to consistent and accurate groundstrokes is keeping good balance while moving to the ball and during the stroke. Explosive longer strides are necessary for covering long distances to reach the ball, but short adjustment steps are required as players position for the shot. The footwork options—square, closed, or open—were discussed earlier in this chapter (page 85), and choices should also be based on the grips, swings, and technique of each player's shots. Urge players to get to the ball early so they have time to set up properly for their next shots rather than having to hit on the run.

Early preparation of the racquet is important to produce smooth, relaxed ground-strokes. As players begin the small adjustment steps before the stroke, they should turn their shoulder to prepare the racquet for the shot. Encourage players to begin preparing their racquet about the time the ball crosses the net. If they wait until the ball bounces to begin their swing you can be sure they will be too late.

Once your players have improved their consistency and accuracy from the baseline, have them experiment with playing the ball on the rise after the bounce. This will reduce the time the opponent has to prepare between shots and is the foundation shot for an aggressive baseliner. Because the ball is moving upward after the bounce, a slight closing of the racquet face at contact is required to cover the ball and counteract the upward flight.

Groundstroke Drills

Alley Rally

Purpose. To promote steadiness and accuracy on groundstrokes.

Procedure. With two players to a side, one puts the ball in play by a self-drop and hit and players begin a rally. All shots must land in the alley to be considered good. After an error, the same player begins the next point until she has begun play five times. The other player then initiates the next 5 points and the game continues until one player reaches 21 points.

Coaching points. Players are positioned toward the center of the court and players A and C are allowed to hit only forehands, whereas players B and D may hit only backhands. This drill is fairly difficult because the alley is only 4-1/2 feet wide. Tell players to keep their strings to the target (alley) as long as possible. Doing so will lengthen the stroke. At the end of the game, players switch to the other side of the net for a new game.

Wipers

Purpose. To practice moving along the baseline and hitting groundstrokes deep in the court.

Procedure. Feed 6 balls to each player, alternating forehands and backhands. Players move to the ball and drive it crosscourt and deep. After six hits, the player runs around the net to retrieve the six balls and then rejoins the line to wait for her next turn.

Coaching points. Stress the importance of aiming the ball high enough over the net to achieve good depth.

Two on One

Purpose. To develop good court coverage and consistency.

Procedure. Two players at the net volley balls to the baseline player. Any player can begin the point, but have the volleyers hit every ball crosscourt and the baseline player hit down the line (see Figure 7.19).

Coaching points. After 3 minutes of nonstop action, players rotate positions. After all three players have had a turn as the baseline player, repeat the sequence but have volleyers hit down the line and the baseline player hit crosscourt.

Figure 8

Purpose. To work on directional control of groundstrokes.

Procedure. Player A begins the rally by hitting crosscourt to the forehand of Player B. Player B returns the ball down the line to the backhand of Player A, who again plays the ball crosscourt to the backhand of Player B (see Figure 7.20). The sequence continues with the ball in play until an error occurs and a new point begins. Player A may hit only crosscourt while Player B hits down the line.

Coaching points. After a few minutes of play, switch the players' roles. You'll notice that the player assigned to hitting down the line does the most running, which reinforces the value of a crosscourt shot. A good variation when court space is limited is to have partners for each player who take over the play after every six hits.

Moving Your Opponent

Purpose. To learn to vary the spins, speed, and trajectory of groundstrokes.

Procedure. Player A begins the play from his forehand side of the court and varies his

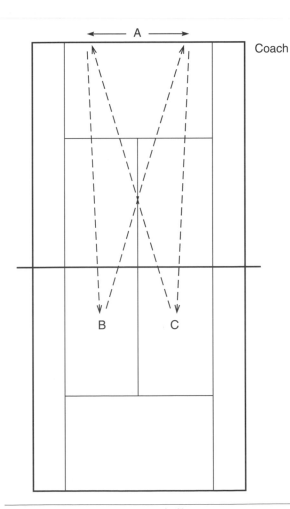

Figure 7.19 Two-on-one drill.

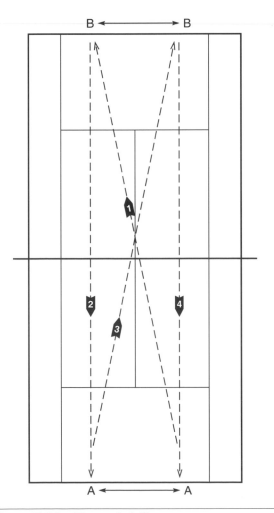

Figure 7.20 Figure 8 drill.

shots to player B by moving him around the backcourt. Player B must return every ball to the forehand quadrant of A (see Figure 7.21). When B makes an error, C takes his place.

Coaching points. Encourage players to change the speed, spins, and trajectory of every shot. This drill practices topspin drives, slices, moonballs, and angles. As this is a groundstroke drill, neither player is allowed to approach the net.

Scramble

Purpose. To promote court coverage and fitness.

Procedure. A coach stands at the T and feeds balls in rapid succession to various points of the baseline. The baseline player must get to each ball, prepare, and return the shot into the court. Each player hits 10 shots, but if he misses a ball, 3 more shots are added.

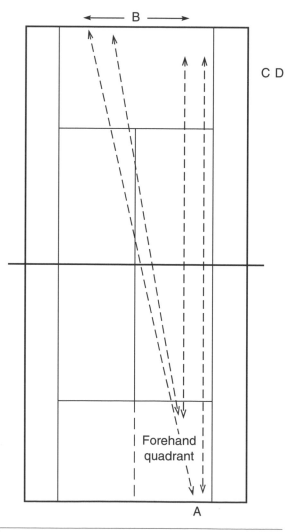

Figure 7.21   Moving your opponent drill.

Coaching points. Adjust the level of difficulty to the skill of your players by asking them to hit to target areas or changing the interval between feeds. Your intention is to tire players enough to reveal stroke breakdowns and encourage them to be mentally tough even when fatigued.

Midcourt Shots

Midcourt shots require major changes in stroke technique. The most important decision a player has to make at the midcourt is whether to play a safe shot and move in to volley or to go for an outright winner. Keep these concepts in mind as you work with your players on midcourt play.

1 Go for a winning drive from the midcourt when

    a. you can contact the ball above the height of the net,

    b. your opponent is out of position, or

    c. you are balanced and prepared to hit the shot.

2 Most of the time, hit an approach shot down the line to reduce the angle of your opponent's passing shot. Aim the ball deep and low by keeping the trajectory flat and adding a little backspin for control.

3 Use an occasional drop shot to confuse your opponent, who may be looking for a deep attacking shot.

4 To disguise your intention, prepare exactly the same for a winning drive, approach shot, or drop shot. However, as you move closer to the net you may want to shorten the length of your backswing a bit.

Because of the range of options available to players in the midcourt, it's helpful to establish some rules for choosing which shot to play. The most important rule and first lesson to be learned is that balls that bounce even with or lower than the net should be sliced as an approach shot and followed to the net.

A second rule of play is for balls that can be taken above the height of the net. In this case, consider the capabilities of each of your players and choose the shot with the best

percentage for success for that individual. For some it will be a winning forehand or backhand drive; for others it may be a sliced approach. Consider, too, that the same player may be better off driving the forehand but slicing the backhand. The key point is to choose the option that makes sense and then practice it so that it becomes automatic during match play.

A third rule is to decide how often to use drop shots. For many players, the drop shot is too delicate a touch shot to hit on hard courts or in pressure situations. Drop shots with the wind at your back are also risky. I'd suggest a very limited use of drop shots for the majority of high school players.

Body balance and movement is vital to successful midcourt play. Teach your players to move forward at a controlled speed, keep good balance during the shot, and move through the shot upon contact. Unlike baseline shots in which you want players to plant their feet firmly before the shot, approach shots should be played while moving to the net.

The length of the backswing on most shots from midcourt should be reduced from the normal size on baseline groundstrokes. Because you are closer to the net and moving forward, the ball will tend to carry deep into the court even with a shorter swing. Tell your players that midcourt shots should have a backswing longer than volleys but shorter than baseline groundstrokes.

One vital shot to learn in the midcourt is a half-volley, especially for serve-and-volley players. Teach your players to avoid this shot if possible, but when they have no choice but to play a ball at their feet, they should use a shortened backswing with a long follow-through to guide the ball deep into the opponent's court.

Midcourt Drills

Approach to Targets

Purpose. To practice the technique of the sliced approach shot.

Procedure. Players form two lines on either side of the court with the first player in each line in 3/4-court. The coach feeds a short ball alternately to the lines on the left and right. The first player hits a sliced approach shot down the line to the target and rotates to the opposite line (see Figure 7.22).

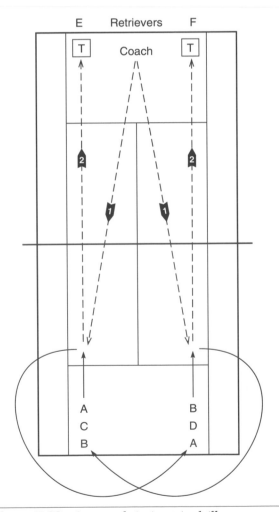

Figure 7.22 Approach to targets drill.

Coaching points. The main point of this drill is to allow for multiple repetitions of approach shots on both sides of the court. Players hit forehand approach shots from the right side of the court and backhands from the left. Coaches should feed balls rapidly to keep the drill moving or designate two players as feeders to free themselves to coach on the same side of the net as the hitters.

Continuous Approach

Purpose. To develop control and rhythm of baseline rally followed by an approach and volley.

Procedure. Two players form a team on each side of the net at the baseline. Player A begins the drill with a crosscourt forehand to C, who returns short to the forehand of A. Player A hits an approach shot to C's backhand, and C hits a passing shot down the line. Player A volleys the ball crosscourt to D, who repeats the sequence with B as his partner (see Figure 7.23).

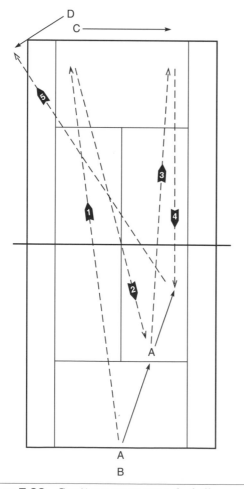

Figure 7.23 Continuous approach drill.

Coaching points. This drill promotes consistency and control of midcourt shots to simulate a typical game situation. Players should be encouraged to keep the ball under control and in play by hitting at about 3/4 speed in the beginning. Each player should have an extra tennis ball in his pocket so that if he misses a shot he can quickly put another ball in play at the same spot and continue the drill. After a set amount of time, repeat the drill using backhand shots.

Winner or Approach

Purpose. To practice choosing whether to hit a winner or an approach shot based on the height of the ball.

Procedure. Players line up to take turns from the baseline and play a groundstroke on the first ball, which a coach has put in play. On the second ball from the coach, coach varies feeds above the net and below the net. Players must choose the correct shot, winners off high bouncing balls and approach shots off low bouncing balls (see Figure 7.24).

Coaching points. Mix up shots to the forehand and backhand sides. Reinforce players who choose the right shot even if they miss.

Approach From the Air

Purpose. To practice approach shots taken in the air.

Procedure. Player A is fed a groundstroke that must be hit deep in the opponent's court. The opponent answers with a moonball, which normally gives him time to recover. Player A steps in to midcourt to play an approach shot out of the air, takes the net, and plays the point out.

Coaching points. This is an essential drill to learn to pressure defensive baseliners. The technique for the approach shot is the same as is used on a bouncing ball, but it may be a bit more difficult to time the hit correctly.

Half-Volley Deep

Purpose. To practice hitting half-volleys deep down the line.

Procedure. Player A feeds a ball to player B who is just behind the service line. Player B half-volleys the ball down the line, aiming for depth and closing in to the net. Player A may try a passing shot or a lob and the point is played out. The next player, C, repeats the sequence, followed by D, and so on.

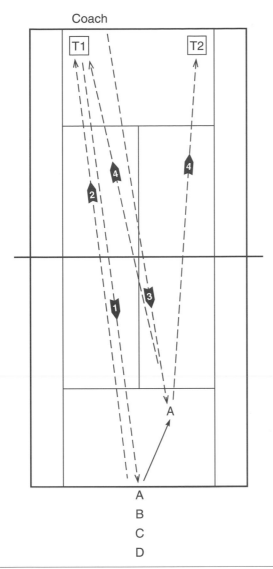

Figure 7.24   Winner or approach drill.

Coaching points. Be sure that players work on both sides of the court so that they can practice half-volleys using the forehand or backhand. Emphasize a short backswing and long controlled follow-through to produce depth on the half-volley.

Net Play

Play at the net requires quick response and decisive movements to end the point in your favor. Here are the key concepts for net play.

1 All volleys involve a short, compact movement with a follow-through toward the target. Prepare for the shot with a quick turn of the upper body and align the racquet face behind the flight of the oncoming ball.

2 Balls that you can hit above the net should be angled off to the open court (offensive volley). Balls below the net should be played safely deep down the line and wait for the next shot (defensive volley).

3 As your opponent strikes the ball, close in quickly to volley or retreat to hit the overhead smash. Closing in makes passing shots difficult and opens up more angles for winning volleys.

4 Keep your shoulders and back relatively straight and bend from the knees for low balls. On wide balls, move diagonally toward the net to intercept the shot.

Volley technique must be efficient because there is less time to react to the oncoming ball. The racquet head should be above waist level and out in front of the body. A continental grip is preferred by advanced players because it requires no grip change from forehand to backhand. If your players must change grips, be sure they do so by using the

nonracquet hand at the throat of the racquet to change the angle of the racquet face and grip.

Two-handers should usually be encouraged to convert to a one-handed volley to extend their reach and defend against balls at the body. This is probably a change to make in the off-season as it will take time.

Good balance is essential at the net to allow quick recovery for the next shot. Players should maintain a relatively straight upper body and bend from the knees for lower shots. When possible, the volleyer should transfer weight forward by moving diagonally toward the net and step into the shot with a crossover forward step.

The primary objective at the net is to end the point, and normally the flight of the ball is down into the opponent's court. Most winning shots are achieved by angling the ball away from the opponent, which is done by setting the wrist angle and maintaining a tight grip and firm wrist upon ball contact.

Balls directed at the body are best covered by the backhand from waist to face. Encourage your players to hold their ground or step forward on every volley rather than stepping back. A good way for you to prevent the backward step is to stand directly behind a player as she prepares to volley.

The overhead smash is a spectacular shot hit with a grip and swing similar to the serve. The first move should be to turn sideways and retreat to a position just behind the expected contact point. Both arms should be raised together to maintain balance and, after the racquet arm bends, reach up to meet the ball. The contact point is about a foot in front of the body so that the ball will be directed downward into the court. The head and chin should stay up throughout the hit to avoid pulling the ball downward into the net.

On very high defensive lobs or on windy days, urge your players to let the ball bounce before they try an overhead smash. Because the ball picks up speed as it falls, very high lobs are difficult to time correctly.

Net Play Drills

Volley to Targets

Purpose. To develop accuracy on eight possible volleys.

Procedure. Use a ball machine or feeder to give each volleyer eight shots in a row. Begin with forehand volleys deep crosscourt and down the line (Targets 1 and 2 in Figure 7.25). Follow with short angled volleys to the short crosscourt angle and finally down the line (Targets 3 and 4 in Figure 7.25). Repeat the sequence using the backhand volley.

Coaching points. Tell players to move forward on the diagonal to cut off the ball. If you notice that a player has difficulty with one of the eight shots, allow some time for individual help and practice as soon as possible. Be sure that every player uses some underspin on each volley to control the depth of the shot. Short volleys may prove especially troublesome for players who take too big a backswing. Teach them to "soften" their hands and simply deflect the ball to accomplish the short angles.

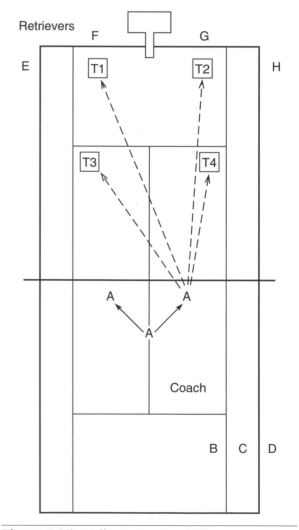

Figure 7.25 Volley to targets drill.

Two-On-One Volleys

Purpose. To work on consistency and directional control of the volley.

Procedure. Two players at the baseline feed groundstrokes to the volleyer. Any player can begin the point, but have the baseline players hit every ball crosscourt and the volleyer down the line (see Figure 7.26).

Coaching points. After 3 minutes of nonstop action, players rotate positions. After all three players have had a turn as the volleyer, repeat the sequence but have volleyers hit crosscourt and baseliners down the line. A good variation is to ask baseliners to mix in lobs occasionally to prevent the volleyer from crowding the net.

Kamikaze Volleys

Purpose. To practice closing into the net and reacting quickly to the speed of the oncoming ball.

Procedure. Have two players on each half of the court begin the play from 3/4-court. Either player puts the ball in play and both players must volley the ball out of the air back to their partner straight ahead and take one step toward the net and then split-step to prepare for the next volley. The object is for both players to close in to the net while the ball is in play.

Coaching points. Encourage players to keep the ball under control and reduce the size of their backswing as they move closer to the net and have less time to react.

Overhead Countdown

Purpose. To promote teamwork and add pressure during practice of overhead smashes.

Procedure. Begin the drill by assigning four to eight players to a team. Multiply the number of players by 10 to arrive at the number of successful smashes to be hit. For example, six players × 10 = 60 smashes.

The first player in line begins to smash lobs from the coach while the group chants backward from 60 with each successful smash. If the first player misses after 7 successful smashes, the next player in line replaces him and the group takes up the count at 53. Once the second player misses, the third player replaces him. Continue until all six players have had a turn.

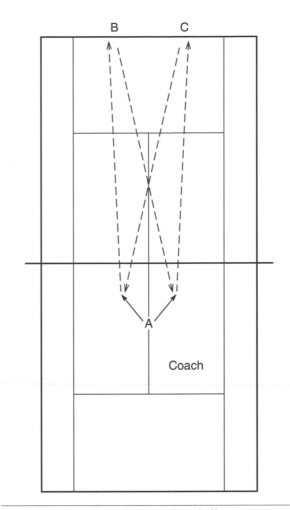

Figure 7.26   Two-on-one volley drill.

Of course you hope to reach 0 smashes before you run out of players. If not, assign every player in the group to hit the remaining number of smashes left before they leave practice that day. For example, if the countdown ended at 17, each player must perform 17 successful smashes at the end of practice.

Coaching points. Because you are feeding the lobs you can vary the difficulty according to the ability of the group and particular players. Challenge the best players with difficult lobs and boost the confidence of less skilled players with easy chances.

Passing Shots and Lobs

Defensive play against a net player involves hitting the ball past her to the left or right or lobbing a shot over her head. Emphasize these key concepts with your players:

1 Think of passing as a two-shot sequence. First, get your opponent in trouble and after a weak volley pass her on the second shot.

2 Use heavy topspin on passing shots to keep the ball low and topspin or backspin on lobs to control their depth in the court.

3 Choose a lob when
  a. your opponent is close to the net,
  b. your opponent has an undependable overhead smash,
  c. the sun is in his eyes or wind in your face, or
  d. you are deep in the court behind your baseline.

4 Choose a passing shot
  a. when your opponent does not close in to the net,
  b. your opponent has an undependable volley,
  c. the wind is at your back, or
  d. you are inside your baseline.

Because the objective is to prevent the net player from hitting a winning volley, passing shots should be hit lower to the net than normal groundstrokes. Ask players to aim 1 to 3 feet over the net and apply plenty of topspin to the ball so that it dips downward after crossing the net. The extra topspin can be achieved by emphasizing the upward path of the racquet from low to high and accelerating the racquet head through the hitting area.

The most important concept to stress with your players is to keep the ball low so that the net person must play a defensive shot. Although most young players tend to slug away when the opponent reaches the net, speed and power alone will not produce successful passing shots. Of course the key to defensive play is learning to disguise and integrate lobs along with passing shots.

Lobbing is the only answer to counter the attack of the volleyer who closes in very tight to the net. Many players are vulnerable to a lob over their backhand side, so urge your players to aim that way most of the time.

To disguise the lob, its technique should look identical to that for groundstrokes. The loft of the ball can be achieved by opening the racquet face just enough through the hitting area. Using backspin on lobs to control the depth of the shot is the first order of business for your players. Topspin lobs are more offensive and may require more touch and practice to gain good control. However, some players who use semiwestern or western grips and apply heavy topspin to their groundstrokes may find topspin lobs to be an easy addition to their repertoire.

Defensive lobs are hit high in the air to allow recovery for the next shot. Because the ball will fall rapidly from greater height, your opponent will be faced with a more difficult shot if the lob is hit at least "three stories high." Tell players to aim high defensive lobs to land just behind the T at the service line to allow plenty of room for error.

Passing Shot and Lob Drills

Perfect 10

Purpose. To learn to adjust the height and depth of groundstrokes for effective passing shots.

Procedure. Players are fed four balls in succession, which they try to hit in sequence to the following locations: deep crosscourt, short crosscourt, deep down the line, and short down the line (see Figure 7.27). Each successful shot earns the point value shown in Figure 7.27, and all four shots hit correctly earns a perfect 10. After their turn, players retrieve the four balls they hit and replace them in the feeder's basket.

Coaching points. This is a basic drill to help your players learn to adapt their normal groundstrokes to passing shots. Emphasize two changes that must be made to hit the shorter balls: apply more topspin to the ball and aim lower over the net. You might try stretching a rope 3 feet above the net and asking players to aim over it for deep shots and under it for short ones.

Passing Shots

Purpose. To develop the feel of crosscourt angled passing shots.

Procedure. Players A and B put the ball in play from the service line and stay right there for the returning shot. Players C and D try to hit a topspin passing shot aimed at the short crosscourt angle low to the net, and the point is played out (see Figure 7.28). Players A and

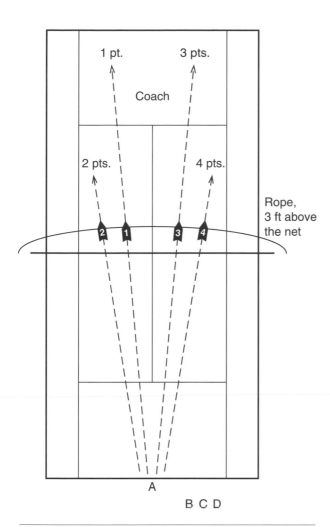

Figure 7.27   Perfect 10 drill.

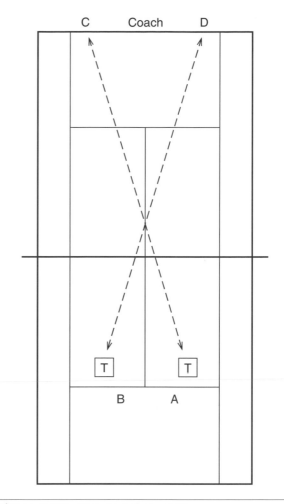

Figure 7.28   Passing shots drill.

C work together at the same time that B and D are performing the drill on the other side of the court. Perform this drill on the forehand side first, then switch to the backhand side.

Coaching points. Although Players C and D are forced into the unnatural position of remaining at the service line instead of closing in, they will get good practice at digging out low volleys and half-volleys. After about 3 minutes of work, players should rotate clockwise to the next position until they have practiced from each of the four spots.

Two Balls Across, One Wide

Purpose. To develop better groundstrokes and defensive lobs.

Procedure. Players line up on one side of the court and move across the baseline as you feed two balls in succession across the baseline. You then feed a third ball to the opposite side of the court so that the player

has to sprint back and throw up the defensive lob (see Figure 7.29).

Coaching points. This drill allows groundstroke work as well as practicing the art of hitting a high defensive lob that allows the player hitting the lob time enough to get back into the center of possible returns.

Lobs and Smashes

Purpose. To develop the touch and technique of defending against the smash with high defensive lobs.

Procedure. Player A tries to put away overhead smashes anywhere within the doubles court. Players B, C, and D defend by lofting defensive lobs and trying to return every smash (see Figure 7.30). Players rotate clockwise after 2 minutes in each position.

Coaching points. Add the element of competition by scoring a point for each successful smash.

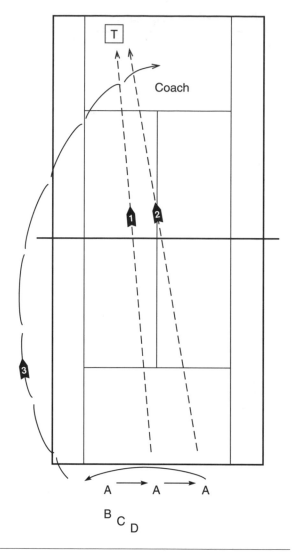

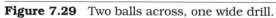

Figure 7.29   Two balls across, one wide drill.

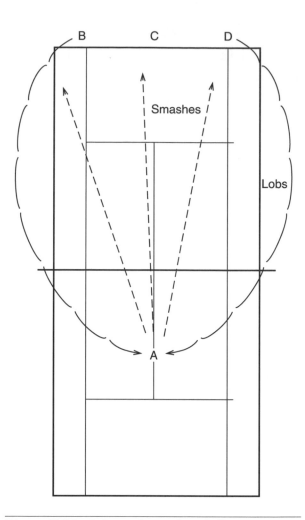

Figure 7.30   Lobs and smashes drill.

Summary

Use the following points to help your players develop sound stroke mechanics:

- Carefully analyze match play performance to determine whether poor play is the result of pressure and nerves or simply poorly learned fundamental skills. Structure practice time to address the cause of the problem.
- Help your players understand the importance of grips—how they affect the stroke and the limitations of each one. Assist them in choosing grips that fit their style of play and competitive objectives.
- Emphasize the technique and skills of footwork, movement skills, and body balance for every shot. Court coverage, power, and consistency are all directly affected by player skill in these areas.
- Help your players solve the mysteries of controlling the tennis ball so that they can self-correct during play. Be sure every player knows how to adjust the height, side-to-side direction, depth, spin, and speed of the ball.
- Establish several key concepts for each tennis shot that every player should understand and consistently reinforce proper application of these coaching tips during practice.
- Be creative in planning and developing drills to practice specific shots or sequences of shots. The purpose of each drill should be clear to players so that they can transfer their knowledge and skill to game situations.

Chapter 8

Singles Strategy

While your players are working on their tennis skills, they also need to be learning the key concepts of strategy for singles and doubles. By learning skills and strategies together, they will see the need for stroke changes and improvements to accomplish certain styles of play. Chapters 8 and 9 present the key concepts and drills for singles and doubles strategy.

Although the information is separated by chapters, you'll likely want to use the material and drills in chapters 7, 8, and 9 in an integrated way. These three chapters will become your primary resource and guide during the tennis season.

Singles Strategy

At the most fundamental level, singles strat-

egy is simply hitting the ball over the net and into the court once more per point than your opponent. After just a few sets, most players realize that it is also a good idea to aim the ball out of the opponent's reach or hit to an obvious weakness such as a suspect backhand. At the same time you want your players to hit their favorite and most dependable shot as much as possible while covering up their weaknesses.

A good framework for teaching singles strategy is to help your players understand it as a combination of these basic features:

• The principles of percentage tennis
• Your players' strengths and weaknesses
• The opponents' strengths and weaknesses

Your first task as a coach is to teach your players the principles and applications of percentage tennis while they are developing their skills. This approach will help them understand the reasons to learn certain shots or the necessity for changing an inadequate stroke.

Eventually, your second task is to help each player analyze her personal strengths and weaknesses. Once the two of you agree on the analysis you can begin to fashion an individual style of play that makes sense to both of you and which the player enjoys. Tips on building a style of play are covered in the next section of this chapter.

The final task for you and your team is to learn to analyze the opponent's game and tailor a game plan for each match. Sometimes it's possible to collect such information by scouting opponents before a match. But if that's not possible your players will need to perform a quick study during the warm-up period and during the first few games of the match. It's up to you to help them learn to take a quick inventory of each opponent's strengths and weaknesses and then factor this information into their game plan for the match. Scouting is discussed further in chapter 10.

Percentage Tennis

The height of the net, dimensions of the court, and the rules of the game provide consistent parameters for all players. To those limitations you must add the collective wisdom of the coaches and players of the game accumulated over more than 100 years. Once your players have a good grasp of these principles of percentage play they will be launched on a steady path of improvement throughout their high school career, collegiate tennis, and even during adult and senior tennis years.

Use all the teaching aids and methods at your disposal to help your players learn the principles quickly and retain the knowledge for years. Classroom talks, reading assignments, videotapes of the great players, and periodic written examinations are all appropriate tools.

Over my years of coaching I have collected and constructed test questions on the principles of percentage play. After a few weeks of preseason practices, each of my players is given a series of questions to answer in writing during a classroom session. I vary the difficulty of the test from year to year and among team members depending on what they could be expected to know at that point in their career. A passing grade of 80% is required, or I ask them to repeat the test each day until they earn a passing grade. My players know I take their learning of percentage play seriously. Maybe the best part of the experience is watching them help each other study for the test.

On the tennis court you should use carefully planned demonstrations by skilled players to support your points. Follow each demonstration with a series of drills that progress from simple to more advanced concepts and focus specifically on the concept you just demonstrated.

Check each drill you plan to use in practice to be sure it replicates the correct shot or series of shots strategically. If your drills mirror a game situation and provide plenty of repetition of the right shot at the right time, your players will quickly improve in match play. Along with the drills presented in this chapter, review the drills in chapter 7 as well as the hints for using drills effectively, beginning on page 89.

Finally, during "set play" practice, stop play to reinforce good use of percentage play and choice of shots. On the other hand, if players make poor choices, resist the temptation to dwell on the mistakes they make. For example, if you notice two players sparring from the baseline with shots landing near the optimal aim points well inside the lines, stop play and call attention in front of the entire team to their good percentage play. It's so natural for onlookers to notice and be impressed by shots that land on a line, but you have to emphasize that line shots are poor risks and not deserving of applause.

In my experience players make a poor play for one of these reasons:

- They don't understand the correct shot.
- They understand what to do but use poor technique.
- They are affected by the pressures of match play, a loss of concentration, or fatigue.

Take the time to determine which of these reasons produced the poor play and help your players find an alternative. A few gentle but direct questions will produce better results than orders, sarcasm, or negative criticism. Your job is to help your kids become their own coach on the court and learn from each mistake. Your conversation might go something like this:

Coach: I wonder if that was the best choice of shots, Jim?

Player: I dunno coach. I thought I had him dead at the net.

Coach: Did you notice where he was in the court?

Player: I'm not sure . . . I guess he was kind of close to the net.

Coach: Ummm . . . what might have worked better?

Player: I should have tried a topspin lob like we practiced yesterday.

Coach: Good idea. Next time he comes in, try the lob and see what happens.

Tennis Is a Game of Errors, Not Winners

At almost every level of play, 85% of tennis points are lost as a result of an error. It follows that 15% of points are earned by a winning shot. Understanding that statistic will help your players realize that smart strategy is to get opponents in trouble and force them to take a risky shot. A well-coached team will practice using a singles strategy that will be obvious even to the casual spectator. From every position on the court your players should automatically choose the shot that will put them in the best position to stay in the point or result in an error from the opponent.

Of course many errors in high-level tennis are forced by the placement or power of the shot. Errors that are not forced are the result of poor choice of shots or faulty technique. Naturally the player who can force errors from her opponent while limiting her own unforced errors has a great chance for success. The few winners she collects will be icing on the cake, but they really don't win matches because they are so rare.

Keys to avoiding errors involve playing each shot with a low risk for error. Here are some specific suggestions:

• The first objective on every shot is to clear the net. When both players are at the baseline, groundstrokes should be aimed about 3 to 5 feet over the net. This will not only ensure clearance but will tend to keep your shots deep in the opponent's court.

• The second objective is to direct the ball inside the lines. Smart players aim well inside the baseline and sidelines for a comfortable margin of safety. Measure 6 feet in from the sideline and 6 feet in from the baseline and use that intersection as the target for most groundstrokes (see Figure 8.1).

• Anytime your players are in trouble or forced to play the ball from behind their

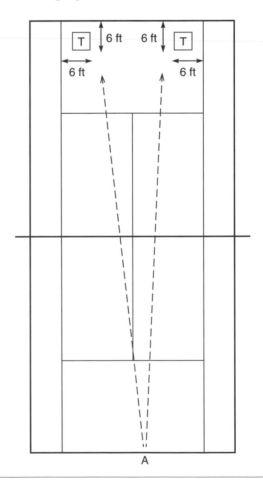

Figure 8.1 Six feet in from the sidelines and six feet in front of the baselines are the aim points for the majority of groundstrokes.

baseline, outside the sideline, or on the run, have them hit the ball high and deep to allow themselves time to recover for the next shot.

• When in doubt, a shot hit deep and down the middle of the court reduces the chances for making an error and keeps the opponent from attacking.

• It is generally safer to play a ball back to the same direction it came from rather than trying to change its direction. For example, a crosscourt forehand is easier to return crosscourt. If you try to change the angle of the racquet face at contact, even just a few degrees, the timing is delicate and risky.

• Early preparation for each shot is the key to consistency. Urge your players to get in position early, set up for the shot, and aim to hit every ball in their strike zone (about waist high) with good balance.

• Most errors occur early in a point, especially in returning serve. Develop a mind-set to begin each point from a neutral position and "work" the point before attacking, particularly on slower courts.

Areas of the Court

Strategy is influenced significantly by the area of the court where a player is positioned. Most tennis coaches divide the singles court into four general areas:

1. Baseline
2. 3/4-court
3. Midcourt
4. Net

The closer players get toward the net to play a ball, the more angles they have available to hit a winning shot. Figure 8.2 shows how the angles increase closer to the net.

Tips for Baseline Play

The objective of players at the baseline is steadiness, and the flight of the ball should be upward from the racquet to achieve net clearance and depth.

❶ A crosscourt shot is safer than a shot down the line because the net is lower in the middle (3 feet) than at the sidelines (3 feet, 6 inches) and the diagonal shot from corner to

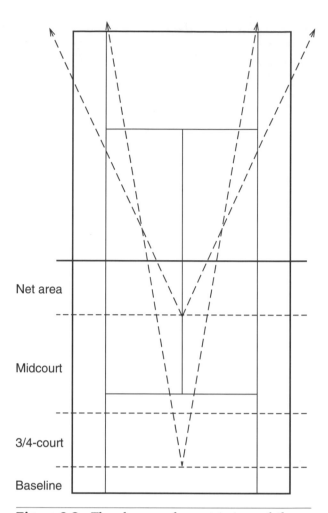

Figure 8.2   The closer a player gets toward the net, the more angles she has to hit a winning shot.

corner adds about 4 feet to the length of the court.

❷ Players must learn to bisect the angle of possible returns. This doesn't mean the player returns to the center of the court each time but that he stays diagonally opposite the ball. Figure 8.3 shows the proper baseline positioning for court coverage based on the possible angles of return by the opponent.

❸ Stress to your players that a position on or behind the baseline is a defensive one. Their objective should be to remain steady, stay in the point, vary the shots by changing the spin, speed, and trajectory, and wait for a short ball from the opponent.

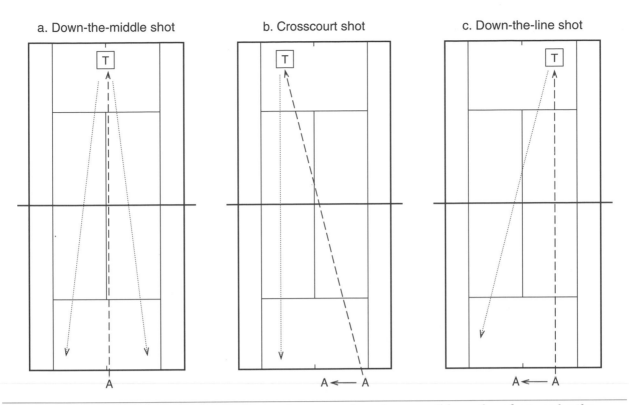

Figure 8.3 Proper baseline positioning for court coverage, based on possible angles of return by the opponent. (a) Down the middle; (b) Crosscourt; (c) Down the line.

Notice in Figure 8.3a the player is positioned in the middle of the court when his shot is hit down the middle. In Figure 8.3b the shot is crosscourt, so the returner's position is just to the right of center, diagonally opposite the ball. If the shot is hit down the line as in 8.3c, the player should move to the left side of center to bisect the angle of possible returns.

Bisecting the Angle Drill

Purpose. To practice bisecting the angle of returns.

Procedure. Feed three balls to a player who hits the first ball down the middle and recovers to the middle (see Figure 8.4a). Hit the second ball crosscourt, and make the recovery to the right of center (see Figure 8.4b). The third ball is hit down the line, and recovery is to the left of the center mark (see Figure 8.4c).

Coaching points. After players are recovering correctly each time, add a second shot. For example, the player hits the ball crosscourt and recovers; you then hit a second ball angled sharply back crosscourt. If the player has moved too far to the center he will not be able to reach the second shot.

Tips for 3/4-Court Play

The objective from 3/4-court is to force an error from the opponent. This is the time to hit your favorite shot, such as the inside-out forehand.

1 Playing a ball from 3/4-court opens up better angles to move your opponent. A good combination of shots is to hit sharply crosscourt to one side and then follow up with a deep shot to the opposite side. Your opponent will have to cover a lot of ground to catch up with both shots.

2 As the skill level of your team improves, have your players take a ball early off the bounce (as it is rising) to reduce the time the opponent has to recover position.

3 On shots of medium difficulty, a good play from 3/4-court is to run around a weakness and hit your favorite shot. For most players this means a forehand.

4 If the opponent is quick to cover the open court area, direct the ball back where she came from and force her to change directions.

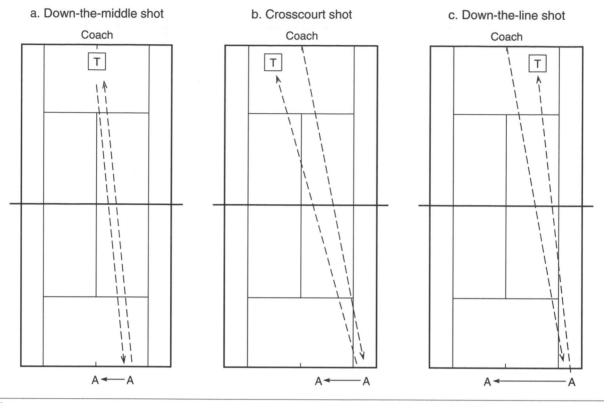

Figure 8.4   Bisecting the angle drill.

Inside-Out Forehand Drill

Purpose. To develop an attacking inside-out forehand.

Procedure. Players line up at the baseline on the backhand side. Feed the ball from behind the service line, short and high toward center of 3/4-court. Players move up in turn and hit aggressively with a forehand drive to T_1. This shot should be hit firmly, and the path of the ball should exit the court across the singles sideline, not the baseline (see Figure 8.5).

Coaching points. For variation, have the player add a fore-hand down the line by hitting the outside of the ball and hooking it down the sideline. The ball should land deep in the corner to your left (T_2). After a number of trials, let players choose their best shot.

Tips for Midcourt Play

Balls that land in the midcourt are an invitation for you to hit a forcing shot or an approach to the net. The flight of the ball should be straight, and you should aim for good depth.

1 A ball in this area of the court can be hit for an outright winner if you can play it above net height. Play it flat with just a little spin for control, using either topspin or backspin, whichever works best for you.

2 On balls below or even with the net, slice an approach shot down the line and follow the path of the ball toward the net. This allows you to bisect the angle again by keeping you on the same side of the court as the ball.

A crosscourt shot forces you to move across the center line as well as forward to bisect the angle. It's a risky play unless your opponent has a significantly weaker shot on one side, in which case you simply approach to his weakness.

3 To keep your opponent guessing after a series of approach shots down the line, hit a deep shot to the other side. If you disguise the shot well, you'll catch your opponent deep in the opposite corner.

Three-Ball Drill

Purpose. To develop the habit of approaching the net on a short ball.

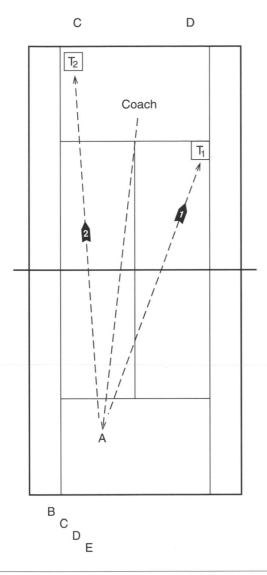

Figure 8.5 Inside-out forehand drill.

Procedure. Feed a deep ball to first player, who drives it deep crosscourt. The second feed should land short and the player should hit an approach shot down the line and move through the shot to the net position. The final shot is a volley angled crosscourt (see Figure 8.6). The next player performs the same sequence.

Coaching points. After players achieve some success, add a fourth ball that should be fed as a lob. The player should hit an overhead smash to the backhand side of the court.

Tips for Net Play

Once you've reached the net position, end the point by hitting the ball down into the court, using the angles to put it out of reach of the opponent.

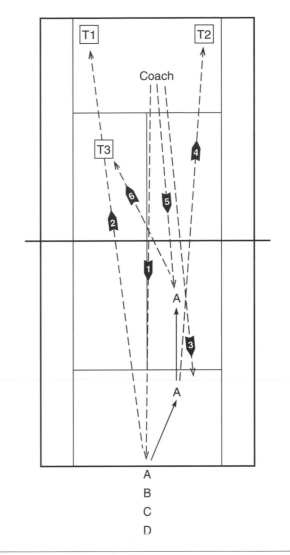

Figure 8.6 Three-ball drill.

1 To eliminate the chance of hitting into the net and to open up wider angles, close in to the net with at least two forward steps so that there is little risk of error as the opponent tries to pass. If she counters with a series of lobs, hang back until she is committed to her shot.

2 On balls below the net level, push the ball back deep down the line and wait for a better opportunity to angle it off. See the Closing to Net drill and Figure 8.7.

3 Quick opponents will often race to cover the open court area. Try hitting behind them once in a while to keep them honest.

4 Once you're at the net, expect to move two steps forward to volley or three steps back to hit an overhead shot. To prepare for the next shot, split-step and get your balance just before your opponent begins the shot, then "explode" forward or backward to the ball. See the Two Steps Up or Three Back drill and Figure 8.8.

Closing to Net Drill

Purpose. To learn to play balls below the net back down the line and those above the net crosscourt for a winner.

Procedure. Feed to player at net. If the ball is above the net, the player closes quickly and angles it off crosscourt. If the ball is below the net, he plays it back down the line and waits for the next ball (see Figure 8.7). After trying a winning volley, the player goes to the end of the line and the next player comes to net.

Coaching points. It's a good idea to start with several low shots to get players used to making a defensive volley. When they do get a high ball, they should pounce on it for the put-away.

Two Steps Up or Three Back Drill

Purpose. To practice moving up or back at the net.

Procedure. Players A, C, E, and G use half the court and players B, D, F, and H use the other half. Be sure players stay on their side of the center line to prevent collisions.

The player at the net puts the ball in play underhand and the baseline player either lobs or drives the ball, trying not to make an error. The net player moves two steps in before each volley or three steps back before each overhead smash, which is directed back to his baseline partner (see Figure 8.8). The ball should stay in play for several hits before the next player, E or F, becomes the net player.

Figure 8.7 Closing to net drill.

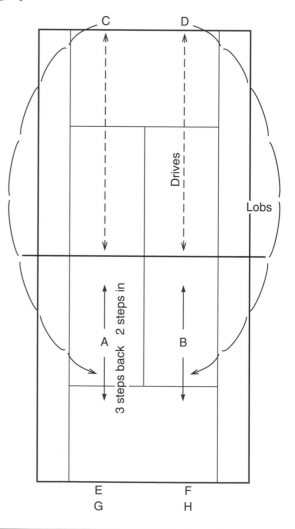

Figure 8.8 Two steps up or three back drill.

Coaching points. Because players defend only half the court, the ball will stay in play. Emphasis should be on quick, explosive steps by the net player to move up or back. Ask net players to watch the baseliner for clues as to whether she will drive or lob.

Principles of Percentage Tennis

There are several more principles of percentage tennis to share with your players that apply to match play. Although there will be exceptions to the rule, each of these principles is sound advice the majority of the time.

Never Change a Winning Game

The adage "never change a winning game, but always change a losing one" is pretty sound conventional wisdom, but there are exceptions. If the score is close well into the match, your players may be better off staying with their strengths and reducing their errors just a bit. Abandoning a sound game plan late in a close match is risky, even if you're a little behind.

Get Your First Serve in

Getting your first serve in is always good advice, especially for players who tend to double-fault under pressure. To gain better percentage, urge your players to add more spin to their first serve rather than reducing the speed.

Use the Elements to Your Advantage

Most tennis players are annoyed by bright sun, wind, heat, humidity, and cold. Train your players not only to tolerate the elements but to use them to frustrate opponents. This means you've got to practice in those conditions and adjust strokes and strategy accordingly. Strokes may have to be shortened on gusty days, and you may need more spin to control the ball in the wind.

Use Your Strengths on Important Points

There's no question that you'd like players to go with winning combinations in a tight match. Drop shots, touch volleys, and cute angles should be outlawed when the score is close. It's simply too risky to rely on a fine touch under pressure.

Last Game Is the Toughest to Win

This is often true, especially when playing an opponent who has been committing unforced errors throughout the match. Suddenly faced with losing, she becomes steady as a rock and refuses to make errors. This calls for practice, determination, and perhaps the element of surprise. Just be sure your players have a plan that makes sense and emphasizes their strengths and the opponents' weaknesses.

Styles of Play

As your players become comfortable with the principles of strategy and can execute the concepts in practice, they should develop an individual style of play based on their particular strengths and weaknesses. Although there will be variations on the theme, styles of play generally fall into one of four categories:

- Counterpuncher
- Aggressive baseliner
- All-court player
- Serve-and-volleyer

Your task as a coach is to help each player choose a style that suits him or her and then plan practice time to develop the skills needed to use that style in match play.

To select a style of play, spend some time with each player to analyze her abilities in three areas:

- Physical abilities
- Racquet skills
- Competitive personality

Most young players will have one or more players on the professional tour whom they admire. Unfortunately, their choice of role models is not always based on style of play. You need to help them choose players who use a style that would be good for them to imitate. Encourage them to watch videotapes of favorite players in action so the visual images become strong and clear.

THE RIGHT STUFF

During a classroom session on a rainy day, I was leading a discussion group of 14- and 15-year-old girls on the importance of role models.

I asked each of them to write the name of her role model on a piece of paper along with the characteristics they admired about the player. Imagine my surprise when every girl but one chose Stefan Edberg as her role model! Obviously they were attracted by his good looks and gentle manner but overlooked his serve-and-volley style of play, as not one of these girls had that particular style.

I learned something from that experience: It's best for players to fully identify with their role models, including how they look on the court and how they respond to the competitive arena. Although these girls enjoyed watching Edberg play, none of them was going to improve her game by emulating his serve-and-volley style.

Let's look at the four styles in terms of the physical abilities, racquet skills, and competitive personality that usually accompany each one. Compare the characteristics of your players to the style they choose to imitate to see if there is a good fit.

The Counterpuncher

This type of player often develops from a retrieving style and makes it a point of honor to return every shot. In junior tennis these players are referred to as "pushers" because they usually hit with little pace and use high, arching moonballs as their bread-and-butter shot. As players mature, they can progress from a pushing style into a legitimate counterpuncher.

The physical characteristics necessary for this style are excellent movement skills and quickness. Physical conditioning is also a key because long points and matches are likely. Defense is the strength of a counterpuncher, so steady groundstrokes, accurate passing shots, and well-controlled lobs are essential skills. Counterpunchers often feel most comfortable playing behind the baseline and have more success on slow-playing courts, particularly clay.

The competitive personality of a counterpuncher is marked by patience, determination, and a "never say die" attitude. These players are fighters who love the battle but typically do not take risks. Role models include: Michael Chang, Sergio Bruguera, Arantxa Sanchez-Vicario, and Amanda Coetzer.

To develop the counterpuncher style, encourage drills that emphasize consistency and concentration on groundstrokes, such as the counterstroking drill discussed below. Ask your players to keep 100 balls in play without an error and then challenge them to break their previous record. Targets on the court should be used to aim for depth and improve accuracy of groundstrokes. You also might stretch a rope above the net 6 to 8 feet from the ground to get them used to aiming high. Naturally, the lob is a key weapon for a counterpuncher, so drills that require lobbing over the outstretched racquet of a net player are helpful, particularly over the backhand side.

Counterstroking

Purpose. To practice defensive play.

Procedure. Two players begin at the baseline, and the counterstroker (A) puts the ball in play with a self-drop and hit from anywhere on the court (see Figure 8.9). The aggressive player (B) looks for the opportunity to take

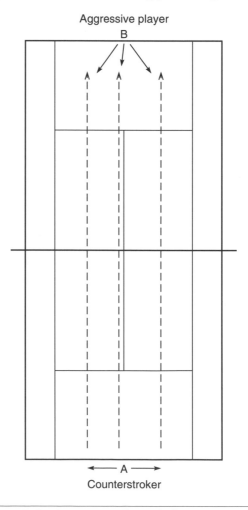

Figure 8.9 Counterstroking drill.

the net via an approach shot or to hit a winner off a short ball. The counterstroker must defend the baseline and cannot approach the net. The winner is the first one to win 21 points.

Coaching points. This is a long, grueling drill that requires patience and concentration. Although this drill may not fit everyone's style, all of your players can benefit from it because there will always be points in a match when they must rely on their defensive skills to get them out of trouble.

Strategies for playing against a counterpuncher require patience in setting up shots because you can expect to see a lot of balls come back over the net. Take advantage of short balls and get to the net so that you can end the point, but vary your approach shots to keep the counterpuncher guessing. You can dictate the play because his style is to react rather than mount an offense himself. Another effective ploy is to draw him in to the net, where he is probably uncertain, and exploit his lack of familiarity and confidence with volleys and overheads. The counterpuncher loves side-to-side running, so challenge him instead with up-and-back movement.

Aggressive Baseliner

Some players will progress from counterpunchers to aggressive baseliners as their skills and strength improve with practice and the natural maturing process. This style requires quickness in setting up for shots and the muscular strength and endurance to hit the ball with pace when there is an opening.

An aggressive baseliner is typically positioned on or just inside the baseline to take advantage of balls that land short and are begging to be attacked. It's not unusual for this player to have a forehand grip more toward a western and a two-handed backhand. Heavy topspin crosscourt drives are the foundation of the aggressive baseliner's game along with the ability to hit winning shots down the line. At least one shot must be a weapon that she can count on in any situation. Her competitive personality includes calculated aggression and a willingness to take some risks. These players delight in going all out for a winning shot, but

only when the odds are in their favor. Current role models in professional tennis include Steffi Graf, Monica Seles, Lindsay Davenport, Jim Courier, Andre Agassi, and Andrei Medvedev.

The aggressive baseliner must develop penetrating baseline groundstrokes that land deep in the court. She should work on precise footwork and steady balance so that she can hit forcing shots off high balls, low balls, short balls, and against all types of spin. A simple but effective drill is to ask the aggressive baseliner to hit 90% of her shots to the opponent's backhand corner. This will improve her ability to exploit an opponent's weak stroke.

Another good drill is to have one player hit crosscourt and the other player down the line for points. First one to earn 15 points wins. Players then switch the direction of their shots for the next game.

Because aggressive baseliners are building at least one shot into a weapon, they must practice that shot thousands of times, until they own it. Most players prefer to develop the forehand, but don't overlook the potential of the backhand, especially two-handed backhands.

Using Your Weapon

Purpose. To open up the court and use your weapon to hit a winning shot.

Procedure. Feed the ball to player A, who hits a forehand deep crosscourt. A second ball from you lands moderately short and A rolls a sharply angled crosscourt with topspin to pull the opponent wide. A second player, B, stationed at the baseline, hits the third ball with her backhand crosscourt to A, who steps in and hits a winning two-handed backhand down the line (see Figure 8.10).

Coaching points. By opening up the court and moving her opponent outside the singles sideline, she has set up her favorite down-the-line backhand. Be sure to emphasize excellent footwork and balance on this shot.

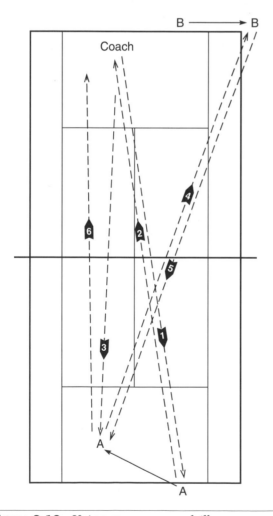

Figure 8.10 Using your weapon drill.

As your player gains confidence, she should take the ball early on the rise to reduce her opponent's recovery time.

Against an aggressive baseliner, the key is to keep the ball away from her big shot by varying the pace and spins of your shots. She likes power, so take the pace off your shots and mix low slices with high-arching moonballs to the center of the court to avoid giving her angles to hit a winner. Because aggressive shot makers usually rely on one shot as a weapon, you may need to hit to her strength first to open up the weaker side. An aggressive baseliner wants to dictate play, so you'll need to mix up the play and seize control of the point as soon as possible.

The All-Court Player

Players with this style are athletic, quick, and have excellent movement skills. The demand for all-court coverage and shot making requires endurance and a high level of fitness.

Racquet skills are weapons of precision for all-court players, who tend toward eastern grips and compact elliptical swing patterns. Because of the variety of shots, they need to learn to become complete players, so it often takes longer for these players to develop. Don't be surprised if your players with this style begin to play their best tennis near the end of their high school years.

All-court players are shot makers who love to make something happen. They shift easily from defense to offense and like the variety of shots. Usually armed with a flexible game plan, all-court players probe until they expose an opponent's weakness. On the professional tour, all-court players tend to compete well no matter what the court surface. Typical role models include: Pete Sampras, Michael Stich, Jana Novotna, and Gabriela Sabatini.

The all-court player's toughest decision is which part of his game to emphasize. Most of the time he'll play offensive tennis and try to take the net on every short ball. Sometimes against particular opponents he may find it more productive to use a game plan that counters his opponent's strengths. Many all-court players do not have one outstanding weapon but balance that by having no obvious weaknesses. They play well from every part of the court.

An excellent game situation for all-court players is to have them play a regular set but reward them with 2 points instead of 1 for every point they win on a volley or overhead smash. This will encourage them to get to the net as quickly as possible to end the point.

The primary focus of drills for the all-court player should be shots from the midcourt. They must develop solid approach shots off both sides and a winning drive for at least one side, as they can often run around to hit their favorite shot on a short ball. Drop shots from both the forehand and backhand are good additions as long as they are not over-used. All of their midcourt shots should be hit with identical racquet and body preparation to disguise their shots. Because all-court players typically want to take the net whenever possible, drills that emphasize midcourt shots (e.g., Weak Serve) are excellent practice and fun to play.

Weak Serve

Purpose. To test the ability to execute midcourt shots and win the point.

Procedure. Two players compete in a regular set with normal scoring except that the server (A) gets only one serve that must be played underhanded out of his hand and below waist level. The receiver (B) must play the ball with his forehand on the deuce court if he is right-handed and with his backhand on the ad court.

The receiver must hit the return and rush the net for the next shot or else lose the point. Naturally, he should try approach shots, winning drives, or drop shots (see Figure 8.11).

Coaching points. This game will quickly reveal weaknesses in the transition game. Players should be expected to lose their serve. Once your players get the idea, they'll love this game. What better way to practice the "chip-and-charge" technique that you want them to use against a weak second serve?

Because they try to play a well-rounded game, all-court players usually have some weakness in shot making. Play to their weaker side and aim for depth on your groundstrokes to prevent them from attacking at net. Try to increase the percentage of first serves in to counter the attack on your weaker second serve, and be sure your own returns have good depth. Use sharply angled ground-

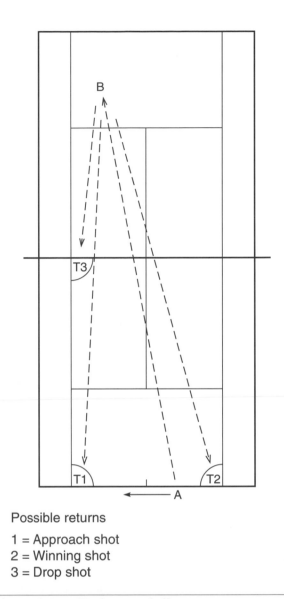

Possible returns

1 = Approach shot
2 = Winning shot
3 = Drop shot

Figure 8.11   Weak serve drill.

strokes to open up the court and then direct the ball to the other side to force the player to cover the entire court.

Serve and Volley

Serve-and-volley players tend to be tall with good reach and agility, powerful overheads, and a soft, deft touch.

Clearly a big serve is crucial to the serve-and-volleyer, as is a punishing overhead smash. Quick hands and penetrating volleys are essential at the net. Because these players are most comfortable at net, they should practice dependable midcourt and approach shots. Shallow or weak second serves should be attacked and followed to the net.

Serve-and-volley players tend toward eastern or even continental grips because grip changes must be very quick and serves, volleys, overheads, and sliced approach shots are often hit with the same grip. These players need to have an aggressive on-court personality and the resolve to make something happen. Points tend to be short and risks high, so there is no room for the faint-hearted. Role models on the professional tour include Martina Navratilova, Lori McNeil, Stefan Edberg, and Boris Becker.

To develop the serve-and-volley style of play, you have to start by creating a serve that is truly a weapon. Players will need to have command over a hard, mostly flat serve that stays low after the bounce, a slice serve to hit the wide angle or curve into the receiver's body, and a dependable spin or kick second serve. Each type of serve is effective if it consistently lands deep in the service box with varied placement.

Convince your players that speed alone will not produce aces or weak returns. Teach them to serve wide to pull the opponent out of the court. Show them the advantage of a serve to the inside corner of the service boxes to reduce the angles of possible returns. Point out that an occasional serve right at the receiver will jam her and often produce a weak return. Of course the most damaging serve is simply one hit to the opponent's weakness.

Eventually you should expect a serve-and-volleyer to have command of 18 different serves, including slice, flat, and kick serves to each of the six target areas shown in Figure 8.12. Make up games and contests between players similar to Around the World in basketball. Each player in rotation tries to hit the 18 different serves consecutively. When someone misses, the next player takes a turn. You might also try playing Horse, another basketball playground game. One player executes a serve and the next player in line must imitate the same type of serve to the same location. If he misses, he has the letter *h*. The first player to spell *horse* loses and drops out of the game.

The bread and butter for a serve-and-volleyer is to execute the serve, follow the path of the ball to the net, split-step to gain balance as the receiver begins his forward

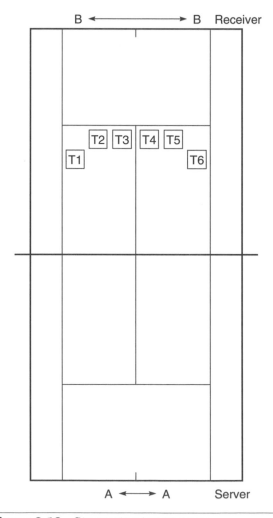

Figure 8.12 Six serving target areas.

swing, and then make the first volley. These three shots require enormous numbers of repetitions. The chances are excellent that if your serve-and-volleyers can perform the serve, split-step, and first volley with consistency and confidence, they'll win their service games decisively.

In your eagerness to work on serving and volleying, don't overlook mastery of the overhead smash. In fact, players who rush the net and close in to angle volleys away are likely to be tested by lobs. No shot in tennis tests the athleticism of your players more, is more fun to hit, and is more demoralizing to miss than the smash. Use the Overhead 10 drill as the basis and vary the difficulty level by requiring placement deep in the court or alternately to the left or right side.

Overhead 10

Purpose. To recover from the net and smash a winning overhead.

Procedure. The player starts at the normal net position halfway between the service line and the net. She runs forward and touches the net with her racquet as the coach or feeder puts a lob over her head. She retreats three steps and jumps, using a scissors kick with her legs to maintain balance, and hits the overhead smash (see Figure 8.13). She recovers immediately and runs forward to touch the net again and repeat the sequence until she has hit 10 smashes.

Coaching points. As players improve their skills, you can increase the difficulty of the lobs. It's also a good idea to have the smash aimed crosscourt to a target to take advantage of the longer angle and reduce the chance for error. This is a great drill for conditioning, team competition, and dealing with pressure. Several sets of this drill are a physical and mental challenge!

Against a serve-and-volleyer, points develop quickly, so you'll need to seize the advantage early in the point. Drive or chip your returns at her feet as she rushes the net and hit the majority of your returns and passing shots down the line to give her less time to cut the ball off. Lob early in the match to slow her closing to the net. If her serve is a real problem for you to return, vary your position at the baseline by moving in and chipping a few returns low, or retreat a few steps to gain time to drive or lob your return.

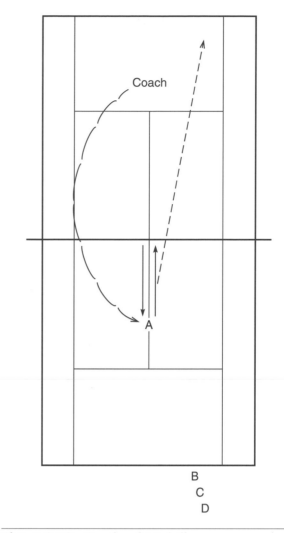

Figure 8.13 Overhead 10 drill.

Practicing the Styles of Play

Players on your team will have different styles of play, so practice sessions must be structured to work on the skills and shot patterns they need to develop. This is where you'll need to be creative in pairing people for drills. During the learning stage, players with the same style of play should be paired together to work on specific skills that define their style. As they gain in skill and confidence, provide them with opportunities to test their style against players with different styles.

The natural next step is to help players analyze how two opposing styles of play relate in match play. They need to learn how to adjust their game plan on the basis of an opponent's style. If all four styles of play are not represented among your team members, recruit some adult players in your community to prepare your team to face a type of game they may see in match play. It's a good idea to include a left-hander, too, so that each of your players has faced one in practice before the season begins.

Summary

The key concepts of singles strategy presented in this chapter are as follows:

- Help your players understand that singles strategy is based on the principles of percentage tennis.
- Teach your players to analyze the strengths and weaknesses of their game and their opponents'.
- Develop a plan for each player to help him develop a style of play that fits his physical ability, racquet skills, and competitive personality.
- Provide opportunities for your players to practice their skills to combat each of the possible styles of play of their opponents.

Chapter 9

Doubles Strategy

From the high school level to professional circles, most successful doubles teams share two components: compatibility and good communication. Compatibility begins with the players' strokes complementing each other's as the team applies sound doubles fundamentals. Communication allows the doubles team to implement tactics as a unit and support one another whether the tactics succeed or not. A good doubles team can be made even greater by playing together for a long time. Covering for each other as a point unfolds becomes automatic for members of a veteran doubles team.

High-Percentage Doubles

Doubles teams give themselves the best chance of success if the stroke production they use during play minimizes unforced errors. Employing high-percentage shots during play allows a team to develop positions of strength on the doubles court. These positions can be capitalized on when the opposition is pulled out of position, allowing for a point-ending groundstroke, or by getting to the net as a team first and winning the point with a volley.

125

First Serve In

In doubles, 75% of the points are won by the serving team when the server gets the first serve in. Teach your players to use a 3/4-speed spin serve as a first delivery when serving, which will allow the server to get a high percentage of first serves in play. A spin serve's chances of landing consistently deep in the box keeps the return of server back, while giving the server more time to move forward to execute a successful first volley.

Teach your players to resist the temptation to hit a big flat first serve in doubles. The server should use his "big" first serve as a change of pace, to occasionally surprise opponents and keep them off balance. Remember that the more first serves your doubles team gets in play, the greater its chances are to hold serve.

Taking the Net First as a Team

Doubles play is most effective when a team takes every opportunity to get to net. Both members of the team should always be looking for ways to close in. Once a team has established net position they are capable of hitting down into their opponent's court, which usually results in a high-percentage winner. Don't let your players fall into the trap of forcing their way in to the net. Instill in your doubles teams the instinct to sense opportunities to close to the net without rushing headlong into disaster by charging the net foolishly at the wrong time.

Play Down the Middle

Doubles is often described as a game of angles. However, the first principle of doubles is to play as many balls as possible into the middle of the court. Teach your players to resist hitting too many balls down the line or at sharp angles. The doubles alleys increase the width of a tennis court, and although there are two players covering this expanded court area, the highest percentage target area is down the middle.

An occasional down-the-line shot can serve as an excellent change of pace to keep the net person from moving into the middle too frequently, but caution your players to use this tactic sparingly, even if their opponents are tempting them to hit up the line. Hitting up the line means your shot crosses the net at its highest point and with the smallest target area to land in.

Trying to create angles by forcing shots crosscourt can present the same pitfalls as up-the-line shots. When your players hit angles, teach them to maintain a safe margin of error by aiming for a target area well inside the doubles sidelines.

Tell your doubles players to patiently work the point. Wait for opportunities to establish a position of strength at the net and put away volleys down the middle. Or move out of position occasionally to execute a winning groundstroke down the middle. Doubles teams who keep most play in the center of the court and resist the temptation to go down the line or create sharp angles give themselves a much better chance of success.

Force Your Opponents to Hit Up

Many high school doubles players react to the threat of an opponent at the net by overhitting their groundstrokes. Remind your players that slow and low is much more effective than hard and high. Establish a tactical priority to try and make opponents hit up so your team can close and hit down. The best way to capitalize is by feeding the opposition low shots at their feet whenever possible, but especially on the return of serve. This tactic can also be employed when volleys are being exchanged. A soft, low volley often produces a high volley that's easy to put away.

Doubles Responsibilities

Each doubles player on court has specific responsibilities to maximize the team's chance for success. Veteran doubles teams not only know what their primary responsibilities are but can anticipate how their partner will react in most situations and respond accordingly. Teach your doubles teams how to react to most situations whether they are the server, server's partner, receiver, or receiver's partner. Once your players have learned their primary responsibilities, focus on communication between partners so the team works as a unit.

Server's Responsibilities

A properly executed doubles serve immediately projects the serving team into a position of strength. Once in this position, exploiting the opponents' tactical or stroke production weakness becomes much easier. Here are the server's responsibilities in doubles:

• Take a service position at the baseline between the center notch and the singles sideline to cover your half of the doubles court.

• Get a high percentage of first serves in play, with depth and spin.

• Vary service placement.

• Move forward to bisect the returner's possible angles.

• Execute a firm, low, and deep first volley.

• Cover the open court if your partner poaches.

• Communicate verbal instructions to your partner as necessary.

Server's Partner's Responsibilities

Communication between the server and the partner before the serve allows the team to work in unison. Once the server hits a successful serve, mobility at the net by the server's partner is key to success. Keep these responsibilities in mind for the server's partner:

• Position yourself between the singles sideline and the center service sideline, about halfway up in the service box.

• Use hand signals for serve placement and to indicate your intention to poach or stay.

• React to any short, soft returns by volleying them down the middle or at the feet of receiver's partner.

• Move closer to the net to poach.

• Remain as active as possible by using head and shoulder fakes to distract the receiver.

Receiver's Responsibilities

A seemingly poor return of serve placed in the court is better than a perfect return that misses by inches. Teach your players to look for offensive opportunities after returning serve. Here are the service receiver's responsibilities:

• Position yourself as close to the service box as possible, while ensuring that you can still return the serve consistently.

• Get as many returns in play as possible—make the other team play.

• Return primarily crosscourt.

• Keep returns low to make the volleyer hit up.

• Move forward whenever possible.

• Chip and charge any short second serve.

• Call serves on balls wide of the service box singles sideline.

• Cover the open court if partner poaches.

Receiver's Partner's Responsibilities

The receiver's partner should attempt whatever will aid the receiver in making a successful return of serve. Here are some tips for that player:

• Position yourself at the service line halfway in from the singles sideline and the service box center line.

• Call all serves for your partner in the area of the service line and the center service line.

• Cut off any floaters within reach at the net.

• Cover the alley, especially after a wide serve.

• Cover the middle when the court is opened up by a weak return by your partner.

Communication between a server's partner and the server can be accomplished verbally before each point or by using hand signals. Common tennis hand signals are described in Table 9.1. The server of course can verbally disagree with any sign by saying no; however, if the server agrees to hand signals given by her partner, she must acknowledge each sign given. If the server disagrees with the signal given, the players should communicate verbally before beginning the point.

Table 9.1 **Common Tennis Hand Signals**	
Hand signal	**Message**
For poaching	
Open hand behind back	Player is poaching
Closed fist behind back	Player is staying
One finger extended down behind back	Player is faking a poach
For service placement	
One finger behind back	Serve out wide
Two fingers behind back	Serve into body
Three fingers behind back	Serve down the middle

Doubles Styles of Play

There are many successful styles of doubles play. When the styles of the two players on a doubles team blend well, the chances for success are much increased. A lot of successful doubles teams are comprised of one player whose style and temperament is steady and another whose style is aggressive. The steady player moves the ball around while the aggressive player looks for a way to end the point. Also, the aggressive player, who may have a more volatile personality, can keep the team emotionally charged while the steadier player keeps the team's feet on the ground. Thus an emotional balance is achieved.

Of course this doesn't mean that two baseliners or extremely aggressive players can't team up in doubles and find success. However, the tactics they employ during match play must accentuate their strengths. If both members of the team are willing to do whatever it takes to make the team a winner, any two styles of play can blend together well.

Parallel Play

A doubles team should attempt to play side by side whenever possible. Parallel play eliminates a gaping hole created when one player is up and the other is in the backcourt. This is why the server or service returner should seize every opportunity to move forward and join his teammate at the net. Not only should the team play shoulder to shoulder, they must move right or left together as they track the ball when in the opponent's court. If a shot is hit to the left corner of the opponent's court, your player on the left side should shuffle in that direction to cover the alley, while his partner moves into the middle to bisect the possible angle of return.

Parallel play should also be employed when the net team is driven away from the net by a defensive lob. Both players should retreat, with the player tracking the lobbed ball retreating the farthest. With both players now at the baseline, no hole is created between the players for the opposition to attack.

Both Players Up

When a doubles team with solid volleys and overheads seizes every opportunity to get to the net, the chances of its winning the point increases to 65%. Once at the net and employing parallel play, a team can isolate an opposing player at the baseline. A triangle can be created so that all volleys are hit back to a single opponent at the baseline until a weak return allows the net team to end the point. This two-on-one concept allows the two players at the net to continue to close toward the net. If both members of the opposition are playing back, their returns will eventually allow the team at net to angle off a winner. If the opposition is playing a one up

and one back, eventually their returns will allow the closing team to volley a winner down the middle or at the net person's feet.

Serve and Volley

The server should deliver a spin serve down the middle (or inside corner) of the opponent's service box as often as possible to cut down on possible angles of return. Depending on the skill level of the opponent, serving wide to their weaker side can also create opportunities to serve and move forward. After serving, the server should move forward until the returner begins preparation to hit her stroke. At this time a split-step is advised so that the server can increase her potential for lateral mobility. A first volley is crucial to the server's chances if she is to join her teammate at the net. The first volley should be hit firmly so that the opponent's net player can't poach and deep enough so that the player at the baseline is pinned there. Once at the net, the server can join her teammate in parallel play.

Chip and Charge

A weak second serve delivered short in the service box is a great opportunity for the receiver to join his teammate at the net. The receiver should move inside the baseline if he

anticipates a weak second serve, slice the return deep into the opponent's court, and move in behind the return. The chip (a sliced return) usually bounces low. The server then faces a low ball, which is usually hit up to the team at the net. The backspin on the ball created by slice slows the ball down, giving the net rusher time to assume a good volley position. But use caution when trying the chip and charge. A lot of high school players rush headlong into trouble because they haven't perfected the slice return of serve. If the return of server uses topspin, the opponent at the baseline will have a good ball to hit back and can often catch the net rusher off balance. So, when employing the chip-and-charge maneuver, always use slice to keep the ball low and give the net rusher time to get to the net.

Playing Against Two-Up Teams

If your doubles teams tend to be defensive or find themselves often retreating from the net, they need to develop some sound strategy to cope with an aggressive team that constantly takes the net. The basic play to move a team away from the net is to employ a defensive lob. But caution your players not to try to lob just barely over the heads of the net team, as this usually results in an easy overhead. Practice hitting high, deep lobs with the primary purpose of moving the offensive team away from the net, which allows your team to move in and take a position of strength.

If the net team plays at the service line without closing in, the best play is a soft ball at the net team's feet, which usually makes them return the ball up into the defensive team's court. This should allow the defensive team to move forward and win the point with a groundstroke. If the net team volleys short, the baseline team can hit a soft dink wide to create an opening that it can exploit then by hitting a winning groundstroke down the middle. Practice these scenarios often so that your doubles teams are prepared to execute them during match play.

One Up and One Back

As mentioned earlier, playing one man up and one man back is dangerous because it exposes a huge hole down the middle where most shots are played. However, if your players' skills are at the advanced beginner level, this formation may be your only choice. Many high school doubles teams lose matches because they are unable to serve and volley. Unsuspecting coaches read about proper doubles techniques and require their players to try to serve and volley even when the players are not ready to do so. If your players lose more points than they win by forcing their way to the net, try playing one up and one back.

Serve and Stay Back

If your players cannot consistently hit a spin serve deep into the service box, or if their first volley is still in the formative stages, they should deliver the serve and stay back. Even if the server has no intention to rush the net immediately, she should be taught to step inside the baseline after serving. By stepping into the court she avails herself the opportunity to move forward. Because this tactic of staying back after serving invites the service returner to move in to the net, the server's subsequent shots must be kept crosscourt and deep. If the returner's partner frequently poaches, try lobbing. This means the returner must retrieve the lob, which creates a hole down the middle that can be exploited by the serving team.

Return and Stay Back

The tactic of returning serve and staying at the baseline can be productive if your doubles teams are strong off the ground but have relatively weak volleys. When the returning team stays back most of the time they are susceptible to angled volleys from a team that closes to the net. Thus, the primary task of returning teams that rely on baseline tactics is to keep the opponents as far away from the net as possible. Soft, low returns at the incoming net rusher's feet often produce a short volley return that can be exploited by the baseline team. Lobbing and angled dinks, as well as strong groundstrokes, are skills required of doubles teams that remain on the baseline. Retrieving lobs and being pulled up and back by the baseline team can be tiring and frustrating to an aggressive doubles opponent. As the match progresses, such tactics can produce unforced errors by the aggressive doubles team as the baseline team patiently remains deep in the court.

Play Down the Middle

The natural weapon against a team that plays one up and one back is to volley down the middle between the two players, which can be done by getting to the net as quickly as possible. Once at the net, either player can cut off crosscourt returns and win the point with an easy volley down the middle. Instruct your net team to position in the middle of possible returns. Bait the baseline player to try and hit a low-percentage shot up the line or a sharp angle crosscourt that might produce an unforced error. The tactic of creating a triangle between the two net players and the baseline player on the opposition's doubles team makes it relatively easy to elicit a soft or high return that can be volleyed at the net person's feet.

Both Players Back

Doubles play will occasionally dictate that both players remain at the baseline—a defensive tactic usually employed when things aren't going your way. However, sometimes this different approach can change the course of a match. An advantage of this tactic is that it can take the pressure off the server or returner who has exposed his partner at the net with weak play. Although you should use this look primarily as a change of pace, if your doubles players are beginners who are uncomfortable at the net, a baseline formation might make the difference between success and failure.

Serve With Partner Back

This formation is most often used by a team with weak serves. Soft serves can expose the server's partner at the net to returns she cannot handle. If your player has a decent first serve but a very weak second delivery, play her partner up at the net on first serve and back her up to the baseline on second serve. With both players at the baseline after the serve is hit, they must move together as a team across the baseline while playing groundstrokes.

Receiving Serve
With Both Players Back

This tactic can be used by any doubles team to give the serving team a different view. However, playing both back to return serve is most often used when the returns of serve have been too high, creating easy volley put-aways for the serving team. With both players back on the returning team, the pressure is taken off the returner whose partner has been a sitting duck at the net. The returner often regains emotional security without the pressure of having to protect his partner at the net with a crosscourt return.

Playing Against Two-Back Teams

When your team encounters a good doubles team that plays both back, the key word is *patience*. Defensive doubles teams are willing to wait for the aggressive team to make an unforced error. Many a high school doubles match has been lost by a team that felt that they used the correct strategy by heedlessly charging the net at every opportunity.

Keep returns low, preferably with slice, so the baseline team has to hit the ball up. Approach the net with caution. If the baseliners lob frequently, stop just inside the service line rather then getting closer to the net. This will allow the net team to turn short lobs into overhead winners. If the baseline team hits powerful groundstrokes, close to the net so that volleys down the middle or angles are easier to achieve. Occasionally hit short drop shots when the baseliners execute soft shots at your feet. This moves the baseline team in, where they are not as comfortable.

The I-Formation

The serving team should use a conventional alignment most of the time. However, when the serving team encounters a returner with a great crosscourt return, the I-formation might be the answer. In the I-formation the net person straddles the center line of the service box and stays as low as possible so the server doesn't hit him. Communication between the doubles partners employing the I-formation is very important. The net person signals which side she will cover and where

she wants the server to deliver the serve. After delivering the serve, the server must cover the area vacated by the net person.

This formation distracts the returner and makes the low-percentage down-the-line return more attractive. It also makes a solid crosscourt return harder to accomplish because the net person may move in that direction and volley the return for a winner.

When playing against the I-formation, keep these simple principles in mind. Return down the middle more often than against a conventional service alignment. The net person who begins the point in the middle will move one way or the other as the serve is delivered, which opens up the middle for your return. If you're distracted by the movement, lob a shot that the server will have to retrieve, negating any advantage the moving net person might have.

Doubles Drills

The following drills will help your doubles teams improve their game.

Half-Court Doubles

Purpose. To practice doubles serves, returns, first volleys, and closing to the net crosscourt.

Procedure. This drill simulates doubles play between two players. Players are positioned at opposite baselines. One is the server and the other the returner. They can only play shots crosscourt as they play out the point (see Figure 9.1).

Coaching points. Instruct the server to serve and volley, as the return of server will try to chip and charge any serves that land short in the service box. This drill eliminates the distractions of all four doubles players being on court and allows two players to concentrate on crosscourt doubles fundamentals without worrying about a poaching net person entering the picture.

The Doubles Drill

Purpose. To develop a better transition game as a doubles team.

Procedure. Two players are a team at net and another two players are a team at the baseline. From the middle of the court behind the net team, you feed the ball short down the middle to the baseline team. As the baseline team comes forward, they return the feed down the middle. The point is played out as all players try to close off the volley (see Figure 9.2) . As soon as the point is finished, the next baseline team is fed another ball and the sequence is repeated.

Coaching points. Returning the short feed low to the team already at the net provides excellent practice for the team moving from the baseline to the net. This also simulates match situations where volleys must be closed off at the net.

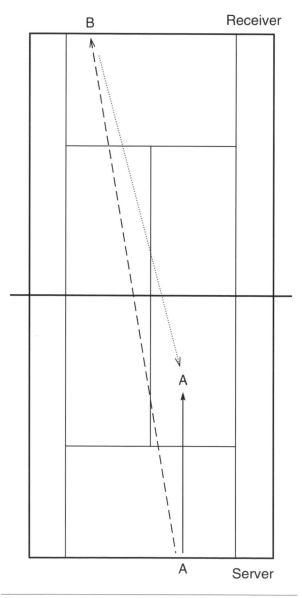

Figure 9.1 Half-court doubles drill.

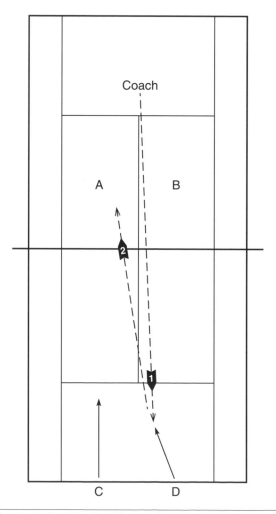

Figure 9.2 *The* doubles drill.

Baseline Doubles

Purpose. To practice transition play for a doubles team moving together from the baseline to the net.

Procedure. All four players that comprise the two doubles teams start at the baseline. One player starts play by feeding a ball out of her hand to the team on the opposite baseline. Players can come forward only when a short ball is hit by the opposing team (see Figure 9.3). Play can be scored to 15 points.

Coaching points. An excellent drill to get doubles teams to come forward together. Emphasize communication by team as they approach. Have the players call the ball by saying "mine."

Doubles Offense-Defense

Purpose. To practice transition play for a doubles team from the baseline to the net.

Procedure. The squad is paired off by teaming the number one player on the ladder with the lowest player on the ladder, and so on until all the players have a partner (e.g., 1-8, 2-7, 3-6, 4-5). Divide the teams evenly on opposite baselines. The coach stands behind teams on the defensive baseline and feeds short balls so that the team on the opposite (offensive) baseline must come forward together and play. The point is played out as the defensive team tries to move the offensive team away from the net and take the net themselves (see Figure 9.4). Points can be scored only by the team that comes forward to play the short feed (offensive team). If the team that began at the baseline wins the point, they switch baseline places with the offensive team they defeated. If the offensive

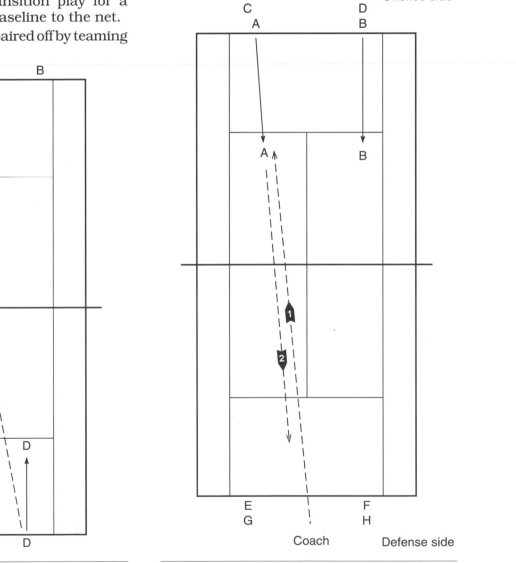

Figure 9.3 Baseline doubles drill.

Figure 9.4 Doubles offense-defense drill.

team wins the point, they score 1 point for their team. The game ends when one team scores 10 points.

Coaching points. This is a great game to conclude practice on days when you're focusing on doubles. Stress to your players the importance of teamwork. Make the higher player on the ladder responsible for communicating positively with her partner no matter what the score of the game might be.

Defensive Lob

Purpose. To practice doubles situations with all four players back.

Procedure. The first doubles pair (A and B) enters the court at the service line and comes forward to the net, which they touch with their racquets. You feed a lob over their heads, which both retreat to retrieve. One of them hits a return lob (see Figure 9.5). The second doubles team, positioned at the opposite baseline, can't come forward unless the lob is short. If the retrieving team wins the point, they exchange places with the team that began at the baseline. The next team enters the court and play continues.

Coaching points. Remind the team retrieving the deep lob to hit a deep lob back to their opponents. Encourage players to come forward as a team if a short lob or groundstroke is hit.

Inside-the-Baseline Doubles

Purpose. To take all shots inside the baseline and not retreat behind the baseline to a position of weakness.

Procedure. Two doubles teams position at opposite baselines. One player begins the exchange by feeding a ball just behind the service line to the opposing team. Players cannot retreat behind the baseline for any reason (see Figure 9.6). The point is played

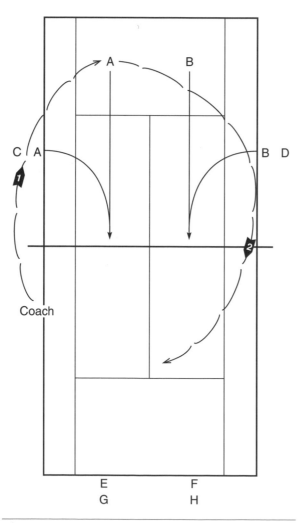

Figure 9.5 Defensive lob drill.

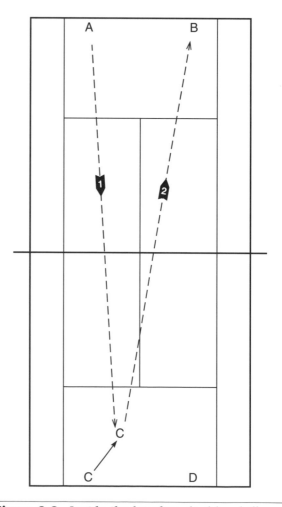

Figure 9.6 Inside-the-baseline doubles drill.

out until an error is made or a short ball allows one team to move forward and end the point with a volley.

Coaching points. This drill makes the doubles teams conscious of holding a position of strength on court and not retreating. Encourage the teams to move forward when possible and practice calling for each shot with a loud *mine*. Calling for doubles shots this way establishes a commitment by the player taking the shot (rather than the more dependent comment of *yours*).

King-/Queen-of-the-Hill Doubles

Purpose. To work toward court 1—where the top doubles team plays—and rebuff all challengers.

Procedure. Action begins on three courts with four games being played, which allows each player to serve one game. If each team wins two games, a tiebreaker is played to determine the winning team on that court. Play stops on each court when a winning team has been determined on court 1. Whichever team on courts 2 and 3 was ahead when play stopped on court 1 is the winner. This prevents slow matches from keeping the other two courts waiting and allows rotation of the teams to occur all at once. The losing team on court 3 stays if no teams are waiting to enter play, or it rotates off the court to the end of the waiting line if there are teams waiting. The winning team on court 3 moves up to court 2. The losing team on court 2 stays on court 2, but the winning team on court 2 moves up to court 1 as the top challenger. If the top challenger beats the kings/queens of the doubles hill, they become the new rulers. The dethroned team moves all the way to the end of the waiting line of teams.

Coaching points. Encourage partners to move right and left retrieving groundstrokes in tandem so that there is no hole down the middle.

Summary

- Compatibility and communication are the ingredients of a good doubles team.
- Employing high-percentage shots during doubles play develops positions of strength on court.
- Get as many first serves in as possible by using a three-quarter speed spin serve.
- The team should move forward toward the net whenever possible.
- A doubles team should play a high percentage of shots down the middle of the doubles court.
- Doubles teams should try to make their opponents hit up as they close toward the net.
- The doubles team, not the two individuals who comprise the team, must be the players' first priority.
- Parallel play by a doubles team eliminates a defensive hole in the middle of the court.
- Instruct your doubles team to place a majority of serves down the middle unless the receiver has a stroke deficiency on either side.
- Teach your doubles teams to slice most approach shots to keep the ball low, and to force the opponents to hit up to the incoming team.
- Primarily use whatever doubles formation that best fits your doubles team's natural style of play.
- The I-formation can be used to take away a receiver's crosscourt return.

Part IV

Coaching Matches

Chapter 10

Preparing for Matches

After several weeks of intense practice on tennis skills, physical training, and mental skills, preparing for matches means helping each player develop a specific game plan. As mentioned in previous chapters, that game plan is built on the principles of percentage tennis and your player's strengths and weaknesses. You've had time to teach and practice the skills and strategies of percentage play as well as evaluate individual strengths and weaknesses. The final component to be completed and added to the equation is a scouting report on the opposition. This information will allow your players to formulate a personal game plan based on

- the principles of percentage tennis,
- your players' strengths and weaknesses, and
- the opponents' strengths and weaknesses.

Preparing for the Opposition

A scouting report can be helpful to your players only if it is accurate, simple to understand, and easily applied to a game plan (see Figure 10.1). Knowledge of what to expect from opponents will help your players relax, reduce anxiety, and focus on the task at hand.

Scouting Report

Scouted player _____ vs. _____ (circle winner)

School _____ Grade _____ School _____ Grade _____

Date _____ Match score _____ Weather conditions _____

Right or left handed? (circle one)

Style of play: (circle one)

   Counterpuncher   Aggressive baseliner   All-court   Serve and volley

Best shot _____ Weakest shot _____

Physical characteristics and fitness _____

Movement skills:

   Side to side _____

   Up and back _____

Mental toughness or weakness _____

Stroke characteristics:

   First serve _____

   Second serve _____

   Forehand _____

   Backhand _____

   Midcourt shots _____

   Volley _____

   Overhead _____

   Passing shots _____

   Lobs _____

   Other _____

General comments: _____

Form completed by _____ Date _____

Figure 10.1   Scouting report.

A poor scouting report, on the other hand, can be damaging to your players' confidence and poise once matches are in progress. Game plans crafted on faulty information are doomed to fail, and confidence will fade quickly. Even good information is of little use if it is too complex and detailed for your player to absorb, understand, and include in tactical play.

You may find that some players perform best knowing nothing about their opponent because of the type of game they play and their lack of experience in using scouting information. A serve-and-volley player, for example, knows that he wants to take charge of the net at every opportunity regardless of the style of his opponent. It may be best to feed just the minimum information to such players early in the season and gradually increase the amount as they gain experience and confidence. By the time you reach championship play, where players often face opponents for the second time of the season, your players may be more ready to apply scouting information.

The Scouting Report

The simple scouting report form shown in Figure 10.1 can be used effectively by you, assistant coaches, or players. Once the form is completed, keep it in the team book and make copies for your players when they are preparing for an opponent.

Some tennis score books include scouting forms along with match result score sheets. You can collect information after every match by asking each of your players to complete the scouting form on their opponent. Your team can then use the information in late-season matches or the next year.

Other Scouting Opportunities

Information on your opponents can be collected by you, your team members, or assistant coaches. You might also seek out knowledgeable tennis friends who can lend a hand by scouting other nearby teams when you have a team match or other conflict.

Try to create an attitude in which everyone associated with your team knows that he or she can make a real contribution to team success by supplying accurate scouting data. Make the team scouting book a treasured resource available to all your players throughout the year. They may find it helpful even for summer play when they face opponents in tournament matches.

Sources of information include scouting reports from the previous year's matches, summer tournament play, early-season matches, and, finally, the scouting your players do in the warm-up period just before a match begins. Each of these times can provide you with helpful data, and it's up to you to be sure that a report is collected at every opportunity.

Previous Year's Matches

Scouting reports from previous year's matches are useful because opposing teams usually have players who compete for several years. The data should be accurate, as it was gathered from your players under your supervision. I've found it helpful sometimes to assign a JV player to each varsity match to chart the complete match and help after the match in filing the scouting report. Besides adding another pair of eyes to watch the opponent, this method really helps your young players learn to analyze opponents early in their career.

The only drawback to information that is a year old is that players may mature physically quite a bit in that time, change their style of play, or convert a weak stroke into a weapon. You should also take into account who they played on your team and whether the contrasting styles of play or competitiveness of the match produced a scouting report that may not apply to this year's match.

Summer Tournament Matches

Summer tournament matches are another source of data, especially if they can add to the information your players provide. For this reason, strive to see any local tournament and take thorough notes. Your players will appreciate your support when they compete out of school.

Again, consider the timeliness of data collected during the summer. Information about players from the previous summer may be outdated by the time you see those players the following spring. If your season is in the fall, of course the previous summer results will be more up-to-date.

Early-Season Matches

Early-season matches are the key time to scout if you play a team a second time or meet them in championship play. You don't have to worry about your report being out-of-date if the information will be used a few weeks later. I like to require each player to give me a written scouting report (like the one shown in Figure 10.1) as a ticket of admission to the next day's practice after a match. This gives players time to reflect on the match and objectively evaluate the opponent. In the rush of postmatch emotion, schoolwork, and rides home, it is often impossible to collect reports. But don't let players slide by—be sure you get their written report before the next practice.

Scouting During the Warm-Up

The warm-up is the final chance for your players to analyze their opponent before play begins. During the ritual 5- to 10-minute warm-up, your players should focus on the key factors they want to know about their opponent. Is he lefty or righty? Which shot is his primary weapon? How is his court movement from side to side and up and back? What kind of spins does he use on various shots? Is there an obvious weakness or tentative shot? What is the likely style of play?

At the conclusion of the warm-up, your players should have a game plan based on all the information collected. If there's time, it's a good idea to check with them briefly, ask one or two probing questions, and give some final reassurances. If you never have this opportunity in matches, you might construct the situation in practice by inviting local adult players, asking them to warm up, and then having a short break to chat with your player about her game plan.

All players should have their game plans about 80% completed before the day of the match. Naturally, the plan will focus primarily on players' own performance and how to best employ their weapons while covering weaknesses. The final 20% of the game plan may need to be finalized after the warm-up, if that's the first opportunity to analyze the opponent's weapons firsthand.

If players in your league compete in both singles and doubles, be sure information is shared with the doubles team after singles play. Emphasize information relevant to doubles play.

Team Scouting

A final source of useful information is the characteristics of teams you notice over the years. Often a coach will insist that her players follow certain strategic principles, especially in doubles play. After your teams have played the same school a few times, you may want to consider these questions:

- Is there a typical style of play?
- Do they attack weak second serves?
- Do they lob well, frequently, or never?
- Do they typically approach to the backhand?
- Do they poach in doubles and use signals?

- Do they serve and volley or play one up and one back?
- Is the net player vulnerable to a lob return of serve?

If you see a pattern of performance and use of certain strategic principles, share this information with your players so they will know what to expect and can prepare counterstrategies.

SHOW THEM THE SKY

After several years of playing one school, our players became friendly with some of their team members during summer tournament play. In casual conversation, their players mentioned that their coach always insisted that his players try one passing shot, and if it was volleyed back, to lob the next shot. His expression was "show those boys some sky." It was sound strategy against net rushers taught to close in to the net after the first volley and their lobs often caught our players by surprise.

The next season, I warned our kids to watch for this strategy and hold their ground after the first volley. Sure enough, on second shots we saw lots of lobs and were in great position to put away overhead smashes.

Readying Your Team

After weeks of preparation, anticipation builds toward the first match of the season. Goals have been set, skills refined, team positions announced, and game plans made. How you handle the practice the day before a match and the prematch gathering can influence your team's performance significantly. I've found that establishing a routine of preparation that addresses all my players' needs relaxes them by reducing their anxiety and nervousness. Once you've established a prematch routine that works, let your older players take the lead and have them help younger players get ready.

Conducting a Prematch Practice

Prematch practices should typically be shorter than normal and high in intensity and quality. No player will be able to learn much the day before a match that he can use under pressure the next day. Your primary goals are to focus players on the next day's matches, allow their bodies to be fresh and rested, build their confidence, provide emergency stroke first aid, and anticipate distractions that might be present the next day.

A word of caution: Never schedule challenge or ladder matches the day before a team match. Your players' energy and emotion will be wasted on competition within your team rather than saved for the opposing team. Now is the time to focus on teamwork, support for teammates, and determination to perform well against another school.

Building Confidence

After the normal warm-up and stretching routine, spend time building confidence by allowing your players to practice their strengths. Let them hit their favorite shots, showing enthusiasm for their success and assuring them that you think they're ready to compete. Resist the temptation to dwell on weaknesses, as this will only reinforce those limitations. Under pressure the next day, any new technique will break down during the match.

Talk with each player about performance goals for the match. Focus on things under his control such as working his way into the point, playing at a controlled pace, coming in to net on short balls, or improved percentage of first serves.

Before practice ends, check that each player has a game plan so there is time to think about it overnight. I've found it helpful to have each player write her plan out on file cards for review that night, the next day, and even during the match when pressure sometimes causes confusion.

Be optimistic and enthusiastic about the upcoming challenge. It's what you've all worked hard for—so enjoy it!

First Aid for Strokes

Over the course of a season some of your players' strokes will break down in match play. Nothing is more damaging to a player's confidence than a serve that suddenly won't go in or an erratic backhand that hits the back fence.

Your first task as a coach is to help players decide if the stroke breakdown is the result of faulty mechanics, poor strategy, or simply the pressure of match play. Once that evaluation is honestly made, you can both agree on a remedy.

If a stroke breaks down because of poor mechanics, you've got to adjust quickly during match play and then plan some individual work in practice. As a general rule, I look first to the preparation for the stroke. Next I check the contact point and hitting area for flaws. Finally, I evaluate the finish of the shot, including balance and recovery. Often a quick reminder to "prepare early," "watch the ball at contact," or "stay balanced" will correct a variety of flaws.

Poor strategy is another culprit of stroke breakdown. Players who try to drive the ball too close to the lines are doomed for streaks of errors. Trying to pass a net player who has closed in tight is foolish when a lob would work better. Likewise, a hard flat first serve that rarely lands in the court should be abandoned for a 3/4-speed serve with good spin and placement.

Pressure and nervousness cause even the best players in the world to choke on shots that are normally routine. While repetition on the practice court will help your players gain confidence in their shots, success under pressure is often a question of improving mental toughness skills (see chapter 3, pp. 31-36). Deep breathing, or centering yourself, a ritual before critical serves and between point behavior and relaxation, and early preparation for groundstrokes are good antidotes to the natural tightness that comes from pressure.

Help your players know what to do when stroke breakdowns occur. If coaching during a match is not allowed in your league, your players can't rely on your help on match days and will have to be their own coach.

Match Play Situations

Every prematch practice should include playing points in a competitive situation. You might try 10-point games where one player serves the entire time until one player earns 10 points, then switch roles. Tiebreaker tournaments are also good, as they review the tiebreak order and add the element of pressure. I also like players to do 10 repetitions of specific shot sequences they favor—for example, serving wide to the deuce court and hitting the second ball deep to the backhand corner.

In general, don't play normal sets and don't emphasize winning and losing during a prematch practice. You want every team player to feel success and confidence. Construct situations that ensure success for each player at some point during the play.

Use your scouting information to devise situations players will likely face the next day. You can even use some other varsity players to imitate the next day's opponent, just as football coaches do. (You might have to give the JV a handicap advantage to make it realistic. For example, if you know one of your players will face a big serve the next day, let the JV player serve from a foot in front of the baseline.)

Preparing for Expected Outcome

You and your players will have a pretty good idea of the expected outcome of each match based on the past year's experience and competitive scores with other teams. Your wise guidance will be helpful to your players whether they expect to win, lose, or play a close match.

Expecting to Win

Overconfidence is the dreaded nightmare of every coach. You've got to focus players' thoughts on specific performance goals for the match and let them know you expect them to achieve their goals. Low emotional intensity is common in this situation, and your players may struggle to raise their emotional intensity to the optimal level for the match. High positive intensity is often described as feelings of fun, challenge, and positive fight.

Here are some suggestions for preparing your team before a match it expects to win:

• Begin raising players' intensity in practice the day before and through team competition and support.

• Suggest thinking about or watching tapes of role models with high intensity like Connors, Seles, Courier, and Muster.

• Practice on-court activation techniques such as jumping up and down, pumping fists, or slapping a thigh.

• Raise the heart rate through other types of physical activity and thinking.

Expecting to Lose

When players expect to lose, they often try to perform at a level beyond their normal capacity, which usually only ensures they will lose quickly. It's natural for players who feel overmatched to hit harder than usual and take greater risks. Their reasoning is that to have a chance to win, they've got to raise their level of play. You've got to convince them that steady, percentage tennis will give them the best chance for success. Make the favored opponent earn the win and know he was in a battle.

Occasionally, players on your team will "tank" in this situation—that is, they don't really try. By withdrawing emotionally from the embarrassment of an expected loss, they protect their egos. Excuses and rationalization are tools of players who tank for ego protection. Urge these players to discuss their feelings with you. Express your understanding and encourage them to give you 100% fighting effort no matter the expected result.

Keep these points in mind when preparing your team for a match against a superior team:

• Talk with your team the day before about giving 100% effort, never giving up, and making their opponents earn each point.

• Emphasize consistency in play and percentage tennis during drills and practice.

• Practice playing points deliberately and controlling the pace of the match by taking time between points to breathe deeply, relax, and focus on the next point.

• Work on body posture and attitude during practice. Help players learn to act confident, poised, and under control regardless of their feelings of inadequacy. Portray the image of a confident fighter determined to put forth a maximum effort.

 MAKE THEM EARN IT

Nothing is more annoying to the favored player than a surprisingly long match, especially if teammates finished earlier. I recall Bill playing an opponent who on paper was simply in a higher class. However, Bill's plan was to dictate the pace of play, take the full time between points and games, and get every ball back he could. His opponent expected an easy match, had little patience that day, and soon threw in the towel. The third set went to Bill 6-1. I'll tell you—he had more than one upset in his career using the same tactic.

Expecting a Close Contest

Matches where the outcome could favor either team are the most satisfying to win and most difficult to lose. Pressure, nerves, and choking are normal for players on both teams. Be honest with your kids about the challenge they face and encourage them to talk about their fears, anxiety, and how they plan to combat those feelings.

Fear of failure tends to produce tense muscles, a faster heart rate, and butterflies in the stomach. Thinking becomes hurried and confused. The deep breathing and muscle relaxation skills you introduced in practice weeks before should be rehearsed in simulated pressure drills during practice the day before. Point out that all tennis players experience choking—but the best competitors learn how to combat it, and they can, too.

Consider these suggestions when readying your team for a tough match:

• Emphasize playing one point at a time and loving the battle. When you feel pressure, smile and enjoy the moment. After all, poor competitors never reach pressure points in tight matches because they give up early without a fight.

• Review the specific performance goals set for each player and focus attention on achieving those goals. Push thoughts of winning and losing from their mind.

• Spend extra time at practice building confidence by hitting favorite shots.

• Promote and encourage a sense of humor and perspective when your players are preparing for the match of their life.

• Sometimes a little friendly competition in table tennis, miniature golf, or video games can help your players relax and take the edge off their nervousness.

• Take care with your prematch routines and rituals that help reduce player anxiety. Many young people turn to music for relaxation. If you expect them to enjoy it, be sure it is music they choose, not you.

Playing Championship Matches

Your months of preparation have set the stage and at last the championship part of the season has arrived. Reassure your players that just like schoolwork, lessons that have been well learned over a period of time will be retained. Trying to cram new strategies or strokes to prepare for season-ending matches is sure to produce confusion, uncertainty, and anxiety.

Players will take comfort in familiar routines and rituals, so you don't want to change their preparation for the final matches. Your challenge together is to encourage the attitude of confident fighters who will give their best effort that day.

 UPSETS DO HAPPEN

A season that stands out in my mind is one in which our team lost five conference matches, all by only 1 team point. Approaching the final conference tournament, we were considered a dangerous team, but not a contender. My players talked endlessly about how close they had been in each of those frustrating losses and things they could have done differently. They realized that for our team to do well in the tournament, every player had to improve his performance just a bit.

In practice that week we planned together one or two new performance goals for each player and shared them as a team. We all bought into the challenge of the mission, and players helped each other practice specific strategies.

An amazing thing resulted. After the first day of the tournament play our team was in first place by 2 points. A sense of destiny began to build, and each success added to the feeling. The final standings after 4 days of play showed our team in first place by 10 points! A championship was ours and a life lesson, too—practice, perseverance, and patience can produce miracles.

Consider these training suggestions as you prepare your team for championship matches:

- Revise or set new performance goals with each player.
- Review your scouting book and use previous match information to construct game plans with each player.
- Spend some practice time on confidence builders and pressure-reducing strategies and behavior.
- Stick to routines and rituals of preparation that have been helpful for the entire season.

Summary

Consider the following points as you prepare your team for matches:

- Develop a simple-to-use scouting form that works for your level of players.
- Collect scouting information from summer play, the previous year's matches, early season matches, and opposing teams' tendencies over the years.
- Translate the scouting information into individual game plans that are realistic for your players.
- Prepare for each regular season match by taking into account the expected outcome.
- Give your players the best chance for good performance in championship play by sticking with routines and strategies that have worked for them during the year.

Chapter 11

Handling Match Play

Sprints have been run, strokes sharpened, and strategy discussed. Finally the day all players and coaches anticipate has arrived—it's time to play a match. Match play is the culmination of all the preparation you and your team have put in, and the degree of thoroughness of this preparation will determine your team's chances for success.

Match play is the time to see where each player stands competitively. No simulated competitive drill or even a ladder match can duplicate the feeling a player experiences during match play. His teammates, friends, family, and spectators are all rooting for him. For an athlete there is no other moment like it!

Choosing a Starting Lineup

Tennis is a little easier than some sports when it comes time to deciding on a starting singles lineup. Using the results of ladder play can make a coach's decision on a lineup almost totally objective. However, there are also subjective criteria that a coach applies to every potential starter before naming him or her to the starting lineup.

Most veteran coaches weigh more factors than just ladder results when choosing a lineup. For example, a letterman's match experience versus a rookie's inexperience must be a consideration. I've found that some players learn how to beat a teammate's

147

game when they play each other repeatedly on the ladder; however, the player who wins on the ladder may not handle interscholastic match pressure as well as the ladder opponent. Results from tournament play in the off-season can give a coach insight into a player's ability to handle match stress. Level of effort during practice and match play must also be considered. The end result should be a lineup that puts the best match player at number one and continues in rank order of proficiency until all the singles slots are filled.

Compared to ranking your singles starters, choosing a doubles lineup can be much more difficult. In some states, singles players aren't allowed to play doubles. In many states, athletes play both singles and doubles. Regardless of your state's rules, when choosing your doubles teams, you must use a different perspective from the one you use when choosing a singles team.

Compatibility, playing style, temperament, and experience are all factors that go into coming up with good teammates for doubles. Doubles players must constantly communicate if they hope to be an effective team. Verbal communication and encouraging their partner are key attributes for good doubles players. Of course playing skills specific to doubles such as quick, soft hands, a consistent first serve, and a great return of serve are also important. I try different combinations early in the season until I settle on doubles pairings that work. The final test a doubles team must pass is making the *team* the top priority, not the individuals. They must believe that it's the team that wins and the team that loses. No finger pointing at each other after a loss.

Communicate with your squad early in the season about how you will select a starting lineup. By knowing up front what it takes to make the lineup, each player will better understand her place on the team. This communication is essential if you want to keep the nonstarting players involved. Whether they are in the starting lineup or not, all players should feel that they fulfill important roles in the team's success.

 **ACCEPTING YOUR ROLE**

In 1988 and 1993, lineup problems presented themselves to me at the conclusion of ladder play. Florida's high school tennis format of five singles and two doubles, with singles players allowed to compete in doubles, can be troublesome if you have a deeply talented team. During both of these years we had six players who deserved a chance to play singles. However, there were only five singles slots available.

In 1988 the sixth player was a senior, James Jamir, who had been sixth in our lineup for 3 years. From his freshman to his junior year he had patiently accepted his role as the first player off the bench. But here he was a senior and faced with being number six again! The solution was to insert him at number two doubles and make him a doubles specialist. James accepted this role and, with his doubles partner, won a district championship, which qualified him for a picture on the Wall of Fame in my office.

During the 1993 campaign, I was faced with a similar situation. This time, however, the sixth player, Matt Barkley, was a sophomore. The 1993 team was so deep that the number six player and the number two player could exchange places with very little noticeable difference in performance. My solution was the same as the one made in 1988, with similar results. Matt and his partner won a district doubles championship and were state runners-up.

The solution to these two lineup problems obviously benefited both players. For the senior, it was a final opportunity to compete in the starting lineup. For the sophomore, it was an opportunity to gain valuable experience. However, during both of these years, two singles players who normally would have played singles and doubles were relegated to singles play only. My task was to convince the team members to accept their role on the team as a singles or doubles player, or even as an alternate. By doing so, the team enjoyed success and every member of the varsity contributed.

Although the ladder results decide the five players in our singles lineup, I reserve the right to determine who competes at which singles slot. As a tennis coach, you are of course thinking that this is tantamount to the sin of "stacking" (the art of lining up your players out of rank order in an effort to create a better chance for success). Every year I listen to inexperienced coaches complain about players who are seemingly out of position on an opponent's team. After playing a team, they think that the number two player on the other team should have played number five. In most cases their suspicions are unfounded. Different playing styles sometimes make the higher ranked player in the lineup look inferior to his lower ranked teammate. Of course in other instances stacking is indeed occurring.

Although most states have written rules prohibiting it, there is no definitive solution to the ethical question of stacking. Each coach has to decide what lineup gives them the best chance for success. However, stacking never contributes to team success. It undermines a team and creates a built-in excuse for a player to lose when competing higher in the lineup than he should be.

When stacking is painfully obvious, deal with the situation in a professional manner and refer the opposing coach to your state's rules. Once the match has been played, however, never allow stacking to become your team's excuse for losing.

STACKING OR NOT?

From 1984 through 1986, I had a player named Paul Williams who was left-handed, extremely quick, and a great competitor. Although Paul's strokes made him look like the number five player in our lineup, I played him at number 2. His unconventional strokes often made opposing coaches slyly comment about the possibility of stacking. Later, in most matches, Paul's ugly strokes and athletic competitiveness left his opponents talking to themselves. Paul's tenacity and unorthodox game would totally disrupt his opponent's game, and after a slow start he would usually come back to win in three sets.

I realized early in Paul's career that he would never possess classic strokes. So we went about building on what he did best—frustrating an opponent. In recalling his high school tennis years, Paul recounts his penchant for match success.

> I was by no means an orthodox player. I had a big left-handed serve and a good volley and backhand. One of my strengths was that I had good foot speed and could put a variety of spins on the ball. Nothing pleased me more than watching my opponent think he was playing a fish early in the match, only to break him down later in the match, and win in three. I appreciated the confidence coach showed in me by playing me high in the lineup.

Paul's teammates playing lower in the lineup could often beat him in ladder matches. They saw his game every day and knew how to play against him. But in interscholastic matches, Paul's game, athletic ability, and mental toughness pushed him higher in our singles lineup and made everyone else more successful.

Determine a lineup that gives every player an opportunity for success. In most cases this can be done by using results of ladder play. But don't hesitate to use other criteria such as mental toughness, experience, and style of play.

If a player makes your lineup but is unsuccessful in interscholastic play, never pull that player from your lineup after a single bad match. Stick with her as long as you can. This will convey to the troubled player that you have confidence in her and that achieving personal performance goals is just as important as winning the match. Once match season begins, I seldom change lineups. However, if players in the middle of the lineup are having problems, I may adjust the rank order of play, which can be accomplished by allowing additional ladder play during practice.

Home Matches

My first objective as a tennis coach on match day is to make the experience special for the competing teams. When our program began, the players competed as they do at most complexes—with no frills. Through the years I have added to our home match atmosphere in several ways. Each addition's objective has been to make the match experience more pleasant and memorable for the players. See which of the following additions could enhance your courts on match day.

On each court is an umpire's chair built by the school's vocational department and maintained by our team. On match day the chair is used by a scorekeeper, whose only job is to keep score during the match. The person does not settle disputes or overrule line calls. Metal scorecards are used on every court so that spectators know each match's current score. A scoreboard with today's matchups also sits in plain view for all to see. As matches are completed, the scorekeepers record match results on the scoreboard next to the players' names. A recent addition is an attractive sign inscribed with previous teams' successes. Included on the sign are the years that previous teams won conference, district, and state championships, and there is room remaining for additions to be made when future teams excel. The sign hangs courtside at every home match. An inscription in the middle reads "Astronaut Tennis, A Tradition of Excellence."

Prematch Routine

Home match preparation for our team begins an hour before the scheduled starting time. During this hour we first practice our ritual of jogging three laps around three courts and stretching as a team. I have found that this ritual has a calming effect for my teams on match day. Consistency gives the players a sense of mental security. Warm-up progresses by pairing the players off so they can hit all the strokes and find a match rhythm. During this 10- to 15-minute warm-up I usually circulate among the players and mention key focal points each player needs to remember once the match begins.

Warm-up concludes before the visiting team arrives. During the next 10 or so minutes each player is allowed to get equipment, water, and other match essentials together. During this time the visiting team usually arrives, and I am exchanging lineups with their coach. If they have arrived early enough, I show them which courts can be used for warm-up. However, it never ceases to amaze me how many teams arrive only minutes before the scheduled match time.

Ten minutes before the scheduled match is to begin, our team walks away from the courts to an adjacent area. The purpose of this exercise is to get the players away from girlfriends, boyfriends, parents, and other well-wishers so they can focus on the task at hand. After giving the lineup sheet to a JV team member to write on the scoreboard, I join the varsity. During this very important time, performance goals for today's match are again emphasized. Prematch preparation is completed with the team joining hands and chanting our team slogan together. We are now properly focused and ready to play. The team, clad in team shorts and game T-shirts, returns to the court area together.

I introduce each member of my team to his opponent on the visiting team. This is an excellent way to show some prematch hospi-

tality to our opponents. Using the score sheet, I read each visiting player's name, followed by his counterpart from our team, and direct them to the proper court. I expect each of my players to extend his hand, establish eye contact with his opponent, and personally welcome him to our courts. Too often opponents don't even acknowledge each other's existence as they walk to the assigned court before a match. The impersonal atmosphere created when two players forego any prematch communication makes controversies that arise during play more difficult to solve. I believe this handshake and welcome is the first positive step toward respect for an opponent. We even practice the firm handshake and eye contact during practices leading up to our first match.

Players not competing or aiding scorekeepers are asked to chart matches. By keeping performance goal charts, each member of your team can be involved in the match. We ask team members to support all players on the court, which means never belittling an inferior opponent or applauding unforced errors by members of the visiting team.

The entire squad remains until the match is complete. It's not uncommon for the varsity to be cheering for a JV player whose match was put on court after varsity singles courts became available. Staying until all

play is complete is simply part of their match. This emphasizes our most important team concept; no player is more important than another. The entire squad from the varsity to our scorekeepers contribute to the team effort. I am always startled when we travel to away matches and a player on the home team who has completed his match before his teammates tells his coach that he's leaving. If you want your tennis program to be team oriented, involve every member of your squad from prematch warm-up until the last ball is hit.

Matches on the Road

Try to keep your prematch routine on the road as similar to a home match as possible. Plan on arriving at the away site early enough to maintain prematch consistency. During the drive to an away match some coaches want their players to focus quietly on their opponents. I recommend letting your players relax during the trip. I let my players listen to music, talk, or do whatever they want during the drive. This keeps them loose and relaxed. When we arrive at the courts and begin the prematch routine—that's when it's time to focus.

Once on court for warm-up, it's not always possible to exactly duplicate our prematch home routine. Such circumstances as administrative problems with leaving school early or lack of lighting at the host school's complex can make it impossible to allow enough time to complete normal warm-up. I will compromise on some aspects of prematch, but I'll never allow my players to take the court without stretching, a prematch talk, and chanting the team slogans. The stretching is always mandatory, but after a car ride it takes on even greater significance. Focusing on the task at hand can be accomplished by a brief prematch talk, during which I try to focus the players on their performance goals for the day. One addition is added to this talk on the road: I remind the players to remain poised and handle any adversity they might encounter with dignity. Finally, the ritual of joining hands and saying the team chant unites players before they take the court.

Tournament Day Routine

During the season you may encounter a situation, such as tournament play or possibly a doubleheader, that requires your team to play more then one match a day. Such a situation calls for careful planning if players are to maintain their competitive edge while waiting to play.

Players should eat 2 hours before play and only enough to maintain their energy level for the match at hand. Overeating or eating too close to their scheduled match time will make them sluggish and ineffective during play. Also remind your players to stay out of the sun while waiting to play. Many a player has stood around at a tournament for hours in the sun only to find herself listless on court when her match is finally played.

Have assistant coaches or parents help you with feeding your athletes at the proper time. Many tournaments, due to facility restrictions, require your players to compete at different sites. This makes assistants and parents even more valuable in coordinating who will stay with which player and how they will be transported to their playing sites. When players are competing at different sites I try to stay with the player who I feel might benefit the most by my presence. Once a match seems to be under control, or my presence can no longer make a difference, I'll move to another site. At our team meeting before play begins, I tell the squad my plans for viewing matches so that no one feels slighted. A game plan is formulated and each player knows that he can accomplish this plan whether I'm watching or not.

Match Time

Some coaches feel that their job ends when the players take the court to play. They bring the team to the match site, tell them to have a good match, and then sit and wait to take scores when the matches are completed. My feeling is that when players take the court, that's when I go to work! I never sit down while our players are competing. If my players are giving their all on court, the least I can do is visibly support them in every way possible. If your state doesn't allow coaching during play, applaud outstanding effort by your players. Present yourself to the players at all times in a positive manner no matter what the circumstances. If audible coaching is allowed in your state, provide your players with technical and emotional support. This is when the players need your presence most, so be there for them.

When a player is having mechanical problems with a stroke, give her one suggestion to correct it. If the problem is with confidence, refocus her attention from negative to positive. Some players just need a little encouragement to let them know that everything is okay as long as they continue to give a good effort.

Players' Conduct

No sport asks more of its competitors than tennis. In most cases there is no third party (umpire) to officiate school matches. Imagine a football game with no referees: A player could score a touchdown only to return to his teammates to be informed that the opposition had spotted his foot out of bounds, so the score was no good.

We ask our players to exhibit exemplary sportsmanship while calling lines on their opponent's shots. Even so, we recognize that problems are going to occur when teenagers are put in this type of competitive situation. How you teach your players to react to line calls during play will determine if they can maintain a proper level of sportsmanship. Teach your players to accept line calls by their opponent. This will allow them to focus on their own play rather then being distracted by arguing or questioning calls. Only if a trend of bad calls by an opponent becomes evident should a player ask for help from a match official.

Purchase a copy of the USTA's *A Friend at Court*, where you'll find the rules of tennis and the code of play. This is the tennis umpire's bible. You might even consider having each player carry a copy of the USTA rules and playing code. Some coaches quiz their players on rules at the beginning of the season. This assures the coach that his or her players know the rules well enough not to be taken advantage of or to take advantage of other players. You may know a rule interpretation that a rival coach is unaware of.

However, your word is not always good enough in the heat of battle. Armed with the USTA rules and any state or regional rule pamphlets, you can prevent some ugly arguments with your coaching counterpart during a match.

Teach your players to play the calls during a match and not judge an opponent for just one bad call. Doing so only results in loss of focus and a ready-made excuse for poor play. If a pattern of close calls becomes apparent and your player asks for help, request that a competent adult officiate. If no one is available, use a player from each team stationed on opposite sides of the court. Only as a last resort should coaches go on court to umpire a match. Although having someone on court to verify calls usually has a calming effect on both players, use help with line calls only as a last resort. Players have to learn to handle adverse situations. It is very rare for one of my players to ask for assistance.

Most states either have a policy on how to handle disputes over line calls or else they resort to the USTA rules. If your state or conference doesn't have a policy to follow in these circumstances, it might be best to address the issue and create one. With a standard operating policy in place, the disagreements can be handled uniformly to minimize controversy.

Your Conduct

No matter what the situation is that requires coaching, remember to always project a positive outlook to your players. If things are going poorly, don't be critical—be a problem solver, not a blamer. Constructive suggestions will help you and your players achieve success. Be a friend and a helper to your players, not a critic.

In times of match stress, you set the tone. Coaches who react negatively to situations that arise during match play are sending all the wrong messages to their players. Over the years I have learned to appear calm, poised, and positive during play. Many a parent has approached me after a difficult match marveling at my composure. This outward appearance of control sends the right signal to your players during times of stress. It's the most important thing you can do for them during play. However, believe me when I tell you that I am churning inside!

When a player is out of line on court, discipline him immediately. Your players should know proper conduct and how you will respond to deviations from it. If you let inappropriate behavior slide even once, it becomes more difficult to correct in the future. If your player's opponent misbehaves, don't try to correct the problem yourself by confronting the player. Instead, inform the player's coach about the infraction and let her or him handle the problem.

Opposing Coach's Conduct

Most coaches are competent and capable of handling match situations. I always assume that my coaching counterparts will handle their players reasonably. They may not handle a situation in the same way that I would, but as long as my players are not put at a disadvantage, I mind my own business. However, with no official present things occasionally get out of hand.

 KEEPING YOUR COOL

In 1985 we were playing our conference rival, Melbourne High, in a very important early season match. Four of the singles matches were complete, each team winning two. The team whose player won the fifth and last singles match would have the upper hand going into doubles play. With the match hanging in the balance, spectators and team members alike crowded around the match in progress. The Melbourne coach, who happened to be coaching his first high school match, and I stood in the background. It was dead even at a set apiece, and two all in the third set.

At this point I was beckoned to the fence by my player on court, who happened to be my son Tom. He informed me that he could no longer play without assistance with the line calls. Such a request was very unlike Tom, who always handled on-court situations himself. This led me to believe that I should comply with his wishes.

One of our former players, who had collegiate experience, was there, so I suggested he be a linesperson. The Melbourne coach refused, saying the player was biased. This being the case, he and I were pressed into duty. We stationed ourselves on opposite sides of the net and informed the players that they were still calling their own lines but that we would overrule any calls made in error.

Just two points later Tom hit a shot inside the line at my feet, which the Melbourne player promptly called out. Shocked by his call, I realized that I would have to overrule. As soon as I informed the Melbourne player that the ball was good, a deafening scream pierced my ears. My coaching counterpart, waving his arms and walking rapidly toward me, let me have it with both barrels. With everyone watching, I was informed that I had just cheated his player out of the match and, worse yet, for my own son's benefit!

We were now nose to nose, as everyone looked on in disbelief. I calmly asked him if this was the message he wanted to send his team. This sent him sputtering angrily back to his post on the opposite side of the net. Tom never lost another game, as his opponent came unglued. We went on to win the deciding doubles match and take a 4-3 victory.

My coaching adversary was instrumental in losing the match for his team. His behavior completely unraveled his player. I tried to maintain my composure for our team's benefit. I was not going to allow our player to be put at a disadvantage in the match. How he handled his players was his own business. His excuse making and total loss of composure under match stress sent all the wrong signals to his players. If you as the coach can't handle match pressure, how can you expect your team to?

Game Plan Adjustments

To make adjustments in a player's game plan, you need to have a plan before play begins. I discuss performance goals and match strategy with each player the day before a match. These same goals and strategy are served up as reminders during warm-up and again at our team gathering just before play begins. Through experience I have discovered that the most efficient way for a player to carry the game plan on court is by using index cards.

 TIPS ON COURT

In recounting their high school playing years, most players have pointed to simple index cards as the most helpful match aid they take on court with them. The following is what is written on a typical card:

Keep pounding away at his backhand, breaking it down. When you get a chance to come in, do so—don't hang back at the baseline after opening up the court with a good shot. Mix in some soft balls and underspin from the baseline to keep him from getting into a rhythm. If he starts producing winners with his big forehand, try to hit with more depth, to force a few errors. Above all, be patient. Your resolve and good conditioning will give you a great chance for success if you keep him out there for a long time today. If your first serve starts missing, remember to check the location of your toss. This is the opportunity you have been waiting for. Go to work and enjoy the competition!

If your state doesn't allow coaching during a match, these cards serve as the perfect on-court game plan for your players. When adjustments to the game plan are necessary, we all hope the players can adjust accordingly themselves. If a player needs help refocusing on important game tactics or fundamentals, tell her to reread your instructions during breaks in play.

Coaching During the Match

If coaching is permitted during crossover games or between points, you can verbally assist your player in making changes to get back on track. Changes in a game plan can be classified under three headings:

- Technical
- Strategical
- Emotional

Whichever area your player needs help with during a match, keep this key coaching tip in mind: Don't give her *too much* information at once. It is impossible to keep a player's attention very long during the stress of match play. Whether you are telling her to get her racquet back early, approach down the middle, or fight harder, don't give her too much. Instead, pick one thing that you feel can help your player immediately. Overloading a player results only in confusing or turning her off completely to your suggestions.

My players enter every match armed with a game plan we have discussed at our team meeting minutes before the beginning of the match. Once the players take the court, I allow them some time to get into the match before talking to them. Slow starters or impatient players need a reminder to play their way into each point by avoiding high-risk

shots at the beginning of a point. At the beginning of a match, I watch each court to get a sense of what is beginning to unfold. As trends develop, I begin working with each player who can benefit from advice. Other players I support verbally but offer no advice. I don't want to overcoach as players are adjusting properly to a match. Instead I simply project a positive image and allow the players to play.

When coaching is necessary, remember to treat each player as an individual. A player's personality determines how you should coach him during a match. Some players will eagerly await your instruction, whereas others will only be distracted by your presence. Know each player's personality well enough to help rather than hinder him during match play.

During the heat of the battle, many coaches get caught up in the moment. Remember to remain composed and think about what you are going to say to your player before opening your mouth. Here are a few tips for various situations:

When players are beating themselves

- Change poor shot selection.
- Increase margin of error over net and keep shots away from lines.
- Maintain better court position.
- Be conscious of balance when setting up for shots.
- Stop the negative talk and gestures.

When players are very nervous

- Let them know everything will be okay no matter what happens.
- Slow down between points and breathe deeply.
- Bounce on toes between strokes if they are sluggish.
- Think positive.
- Play their way into the match—don't panic early.
- Focus on fundamentals (react, bounce, hit).

When players are overconfident

- Refocus on concentration and discipline.
- Respect their opponent's effort no matter what the player's skill level.
- Work on weaker shots in their own game.
- Concentrate on getting off court as quickly as possible.

When players have stroke mechanics problems

- Reread personal stroke production notebook checklist about problem shot.
- Suggest *one* adjustment (balance, grip, swing, contact point, follow-through).
- Concentrate on strokes that are working well rather than dwelling on negative strokes.
- Find a weakness in the opponent's strokes and play to it.

When players are acting inappropriately

- Discipline the player but don't blame or assess punishment.
- Refocus on their game plan.
- Maintain their dignity by showing some sportsmanship.
- Don't use their opponent as an excuse—find a solution to the challenge presented.

Losing Momentum

Other factors also require your attention during match play. At times it appears that your player is cruising along, in total control. Tennis, however, is not a timed sport, which means that momentum will swing from player to player at various times in a match. Subtle changes at crucial times in a match are often missed by teenage players. Watch for the following possible developments and point them out to your player before momentum is lost:

- Changes in tactics by an opponent. These may be very apparent to you but not to a player who is in control of a match.
- Motivation lapse after success. After your player has gained momentum (e.g., by breaking serve), remind her not to let up but to intensify her focus to get off the court as quickly as possible.
- A letdown in concentration. Concentration lapses are common at the end of a hard-fought first set. Remind your players about momentum before they start the new set. If they lost the first set, they need to regain momentum by digging in at the beginning of the new set. If they won the first set, they need to stay focused on keeping the momentum at the beginning of the new set.

Helping Players Think for Themselves

One way I foster independent thinking is by having each player take on court a personal stroke notebook. This notebook, which has been developed during practices, lists each detail of every stroke in the player's repertoire. At practice sessions and individual lessons, the player makes entries into the notebook after we've discussed technique. In addition to the notebook, the player has an index card with a game plan for the current match. If trouble arises, the player can use these aids during the 90-second break on crossover games.

YOU'RE ON YOUR OWN

As coaches, we've all had the type of player who constantly asks us what he or she is doing wrong. Such players generally don't follow suggestions or they try them only briefly before reverting to their usual ways.

In the 1980s I coached such a player. During practice or a match, he would constantly ask me what he was doing wrong, pleading for advice. Then, after I gave him advice, he'd continue to do the same thing as before. Frustrated, I asked the player after a loss, "Why do you want my input if you aren't going to use it?" "I did try it coach," he said. "But it didn't work."

I realized then that this player wanted my input so that he would not have to be mentally responsible if he lost. I reacted by staying away from his court during his next match. After the match, which also turned out to be a loss, the player asked me why I didn't help him. "If you had coached me, I probably wouldn't have lost," he said. My reply was very simple: I told him I knew he had analyzed the situation and made the proper adjustments. But even when the correct adjustments are made, the opponent is sometimes better on a particular day.

The player realized that I was not going to be the scapegoat after a loss. I asked him to use his on-court notebook, which summarizes the mechanics of each stroke in his arsenal, when a breakdown occurred. I told him that during a match the first thing I wanted to hear was how he was dealing with the situation. If I agreed, I would acknowledge as much; if I disagreed, we would arrive at a different solution together.

From that match on, the player never again mindlessly asked me for coaching tips. When I arrived at the fence, I would get a detailed account of what was happening and what he was doing to counteract it. He had begun to think for himself on court. From then on, he and I worked together as a team to find a solution to problems that arose during play. By doing so we could accept the match outcome, knowing that both of us contributed to the end result.

Stay Upbeat

Never get down on a player during a match, either verbally or with your body language. They want the same thing you do. Sometimes when a player repeats a mistake several times, it's hard not to vent your frustrations, but coaching successfully means doing what's best for your athletes in the heat of battle. Screaming at them or communicating your disgust by gesturing is never in your athletes' best interest. Strive to remain positive at all times. You can teach them best how to deal with what their opponent is throwing at them by remaining undaunted against any odds. Remember—you the coach set the tone. Be positive!

Before Doubles

Following a singles match, win or lose, a player should be greeted by her teammates as she comes off the court. This shows her that her effort is appreciated by her teammates.

If your state plays doubles after the completion of singles, give the players 5 or 10 minutes to refocus before starting doubles. Never assume that your teams can begin doubles play without your input. I've found that after a singles match players need to be reminded about doubles principles. Whether you're using the same or different players for singles and doubles, meet briefly with your doubles players to talk principles. In close matches, doubles determine the team winner, so your team can't afford to squander the first few games of their doubles match.

Postgame Procedures

Always conduct a team meeting after the match is completed. This is when I officially ask each player for match scores and record them in my scorebook. As I gather scores, I try to make a positive, encouraging statement to each competitor in front of his teammates.

Different players handle wins and losses differently. The one constant you can give them at the end of every match is praise for effort. Reestablish the personal worth you feel for each player regardless of the outcome of his match.

Save your stroke breakdown analysis for later. Some players want feedback from you as soon as they finish their match, but I've found this to be the worst time to critique their match. Instead, give them some positive reassurance and allow them at least overnight before you analyze the match in detail. During this time they can settle down and think clearly about what occurred during play. They will have the time to detach themselves emotionally from the match and think about it clearly. A time lapse before your critique of the match also develops some independent thinking in your player.

In the next day or two, go over the highs and lows of the match with your player. Review both the positive and negative highlights of the match using objective criteria from shot-charting or videotaping whenever possible. Report facts in a nonemotional way. Once an evaluation has been completed, it is time to begin laying plans to capitalize on success or restore lost confidence. Structure practice goals together and affirm your belief in the player's ability to overcome weaknesses. If overconfidence creeps in after an impressive performance, encourage the player to rededicate effort toward higher goals.

Exchange places with the player by putting yourself in the hot seat, asking her if your coaching was effective or if there are changes you can make before the next match to increase your effectiveness. This will show your players that you are not above criticism, even if you are the head coach. Together formulate a plan for future matches to minimize stroke breakdown.

Winning With Class

After a victory, allow your players to celebrate their accomplishment, but with a sense of humility. As a coach, I always give the players credit for a victory. At a home match we make a point of mingling with the opposition and congratulating them on their effort. After all, it was this effort that makes the victory worth celebrating. After the opposition departs, we hold our meeting, congratulate each other, clasp hands, and chant our team slogan once more. On the road we mingle with the opposition and then move away from the courts to hold our team meeting.

Losing With Dignity

Young people in today's society have a hard time accepting a loss. Thus, some of the greatest coaching lessons you can bestow on your players come after a defeat. If you are humble in victory, you should also teach your players to be gracious after a loss. Begin as you would after a win by congratulating the opponent's effort. Then check with each player to see if he felt he met his performance goals for the match. Remain objective without assigning blame as you talk to your team. When they acknowledge that they worked to meet their performance goals and didn't blame factors beyond their control, such as line calls or wind, for the loss, they are winners regardless of the match outcome.

 TO THE VICTOR

In 1990 we were battling John Fogleman's fine program at Saint Andrew's School of Boca Raton for the National Invitational High School Team Championship held annually in June at Duke University. We were leading the team points total narrowly until the final match of the tournament, when the roof fell in on us and Saint Andrew's edged us out of first place. As you can imagine, our team was devastated. After a short talk, I urged them, as I always do after a loss, to congratulate the victors. The two Florida teams mingled and congratulated one another. Their players consoled ours, as everyone realized what a great event they had just been a part of. Our players knew that they had given their best effort for 3 days. This realization combined with the respect the winners showed us made the loss bitter, but acceptable. Mutual respect between adversaries on the court, win or lose, makes both combatants winners.

Because you always have your players' attention after a loss, this is the coach's best opportunity to get a point across. However, I caution you again to keep your postgame remarks to a minimum. Accept some of the blame for the loss. Don't allow your frustration to make scapegoats of the players. Remember that you and the players all want the same thing. It's best to remain positive and give the team a challenge to look forward to at the next practice.

Athletic accomplishment, kept in perspective, means not getting too high after a victory, or too low after a loss.

Summary

During matches, follow these principles:

- Determine a fair lineup for match play by using results of ladder play as well as effort, experience, mental toughness, and style of play.
- Doubles teams must possess doubles-playing skills and be compatible, communicate well, and win or lose as a team.
- Develop a consistent prematch routine for your team.
- Give *all* the players, not just the varsity, a role to play during a match.
- Remain positive at all times during a match. Be there for your players during match play.
- Teach your players to display an air of confidence on court without being combative with their opponent.
- Discipline unsportsmanlike behavior from your players immediately but allow your coaching counterpart to handle his or her own players' problems.
- Use index cards for players to carry a game plan on court.
- If the game plan needs to be adjusted during play, keep changes as simple as possible.
- Focus doubles teams before they take the court.
- Always conduct a team meeting after a match, and try to say something positive to each player.
- Wait to talk about breakdown during match play until the day after the match.
- Be objective when critiquing the previous day's match play.
- Be humble in victory and gracious in defeat.

Part V

Coaching Evaluation

Chapter 12

Evaluating Your Players' Performance

A straightforward and thorough annual evaluation of each player in your program is key to continued success. Information needed to measure a player's progress should come from your own observations as well as those of the player's teaching pro, if any, and your assistant coaches. Players, especially seniors, can also help you evaluate progress. Decisions on who must be cut and what position in singles and doubles a player should play are much easier to make with input from everyone associated with your program. If everyone can give and receive constructive criticism, your tennis program will flourish.

Summer Evaluation

As a tennis teaching professional, I can be personally involved with my players during the summer months. According to the rules of our state, I can legally work with these players, as well as many other players from schools in our area, through our recreation department programs. This allows me to evaluate the progress of current players, as well as up-and-coming junior high and elementary school players. Be sure to consult your state's rules on out-of-season contact with your players. Many states don't allow contact with players once the season ends.

If your state does allow contact, you should consider involving yourself with the players in your program. Tennis players need to build on-court skills during the summer, and your presence strengthens the rapport with the players that was developed during the tennis season.

Summer offers many possibilities for tennis players to sharpen their skills and develop their games, including summer leagues, tournaments, individual tennis lessons, and summer camps. If players remain active during the summer, you'll have a constant means of evaluating their progress.

Summer Leagues

Junior Team Tennis is recognized nationally through the USTA, and most cities sponsor some type of summer play for juniors. Divisions of play range from 12 and under through 18 and under. Most of our players started their competitive team play through this excellent program. If your town doesn't have a Junior Team Tennis league, contact your USTA sectional office for the information necessary to form a league in your area. Watching young players in league play allows you to evaluate their competitive instincts in a team setting.

 NEW FACES

Before Junior Team Tennis became popular, our players competed in summer leagues throughout the Orlando, Florida, area. The league format allowed boys and girls of various ages to play together on the same team. We would travel the 40 miles to Orlando once a week during the summer to play other teams in the league. During these trips, I had a chance to become acquainted with players who would soon be entering our high school program. Not only could I evaluate each player, but newcomers began bonding with current high school team members. As one of my former players stated: "Summer league was a great opportunity for those who were still in junior high to begin interacting with the people who were already on the high school team." This opportunity made it possible for me to see how these young players handled match pressure in a team setting.

Tournaments

Summer is an excellent time for players to test their skills in tournaments and for you to evaluate their tennis progress. The better players in your program should enter as many USTA sanctioned tournaments as possible. Unranked novice players can find smaller local satellite tournaments to begin testing themselves in matches.

I provide each player in our program with a list of tournaments that will be played during the summer months. Each player can then plan his own schedule around family vacations and other commitments. I try to attend as many of these tournaments as I can to show the players how much importance I place on their participation in these summer tournaments. I can also evaluate each player's progress and use this information to work on a player's weaknesses during upcoming private lessons. Even if you do not teach private lessons, your presence at tournaments will strengthen the bonds between you and your players.

Individual Tennis Lessons

The off-season, especially summertime, is the perfect opportunity to change faulty strokes. If you do not teach yourself, find out which teaching pros in your area are best suited to teach your players. Teaching pros are usually willing to let you be there while they work with your players. If so, use this time to get a professional opinion about each stroke your player must perform to be successful. This information is invaluable for use at practices during the next season.

If you are a teaching pro yourself, you'll find that individual lessons with your players provide immediate feedback. Stroke mechanics, tactical decisions during points, and coping skills under match pressure can be discussed one on one.

Summer Camps

There are many fine summer tennis camps to be found throughout the country. At these camps players can get a perspective on their game from coaches they don't work with every day. I keep a listing of summer camps for my players to look at when they are making decisions about which camp to attend.

When my players return from camp, I always ask them what they learned and if any corrections were made to strokes that we overlooked while they worked at home. I also try to keep in touch with the directors of the camps my players attend. Often I'll ask directors for their analysis of my players' strokes, which gives me another opinion to consider during my evaluation of each player.

Any tennis publication released in the spring will give you the names and addresses of many fine summer tennis camps. Some camps give discounts if your players attend as a team. Use these summer camps as another method of having your players evaluated.

Preseason Evaluation

As the tennis season approaches, I sit down with each player to review the progress made on off-season goals. Ask the player how much she thinks she has progressed. Contribute your own observations based on off-season observations you made at tournaments or lessons.

Have each player complete a form similar to the one presented in Figure 12.1. Ask the players to bring their presummer goal cards with them when you evaluate their off-season progress. These goal cards were the ones you and your player discussed at the end of the previous season.

Once I've met with each player to evaluate summer progress, we make plans to set goals for the upcoming season. Team goals are discussed at the preseason lettermen's meeting. At this time we evaluate where we are as a team, where we want to be at the end of the season, and how we intend to get there. Preseason evaluation ends with each player filling out an information card like the one shown in Figure 12.2.

Evaluating Before Cutting

In our program no player is ever cut. However, I understand that many coaches are unable to keep all the players that try out for their team. Evaluating players before the cut is probably the most difficult task a coach faces. After you finish round-robin play to

Name_____

1. What progress did you make this summer toward your off-season goals?

2. What tournaments did you enter?

3. What summer tennis camp did you attend?

4. Develop some new Now goals for the fall tennis clinics or restate summer goals you haven't achieved yet.

5. What do you see yourself contributing to this year's team?

6. What did you do this summer to strengthen your relationships with your family members?

7. What are your academic goals for this school year?

8. What can I do to help you achieve your family, school, and tennis goals this year?

Figure 12.1 Off-season progress self-evaluation form.

Name_____

Parent's name_____

Address_____

Phone #_____

Year in school_____

1st period class_____

Birthdate_____

Where do you usually play tennis?

_____

Put your complete class schedule on the back and include all teachers' names.

Figure 12.2 Player information card.

determine which new players will make the team, evaluate the intangibles that each player possesses before making the final cut.

Making the Team

The players in my program have played together in the summer and fall, as well as competing as members of the B team before moving up to the varsity. Thus, most players are thoroughly evaluated before they become members of the varsity. If your program does not have this luxury, it's especially important to evaluate each player before cutting anyone.

Basing who will make the team solely on the results of round-robin play will eliminate players who should make your squad. You and your assistants must evaluate each player based on current performance as well as potential and other intangibles. Players with undeveloped tennis skills but who have athleticism, motivation, and a great attitude should be kept on your squad if at all possible. Their athletic ability coupled with a desire to improve will allow you to develop them during the season.

Qualities to Assess Before Cutting

Assess the qualities you are looking for in a player by evaluating him both during match play and in practice. This will allow you to evaluate both stroke production and attitude. Watch the players as they interact with their potential teammates on and off the court. This may give you some indication about whether they are team players. Use all the information you compile to make the best judgment possible before cutting any player. Here are some questions to ask yourself in evaluating each player who tries out for your team:

- What kind of competitor is the player?
- How coachable does the player appear to be?
- How well does the player work with teammates?
- How soft and quick are the player's hands?
- How good is the player's balance?
- How quick is the player?
- How does the player handle adversity on court?
- What kind of student is the player?
- What type of off-court personality does the player have?

Maintaining Contact With Cut Players

Before making the final decision about which players to cut, accumulate information from assistant coaches and teaching pros who work with the players. Use as much data as possible to make a good decision about which athletes should make your squad. This is the toughest decision you will have to make as a coach. Deciding who will play singles and doubles pales in comparison to telling a player that she didn't make the squad.

Talk personally to each player that will be cut. Don't use a posted list of players who made the team as a means of notifying athletes they were cut. Try to make your conversation with the cut players as positive as possible. During this discussion remind each player that there are other avenues available for them to pursue tennis during the year. Refer the players to local teaching pros who can work with them to improve their game. If any leagues or junior clinics are available in your area, keep a list on hand to give to these players.

Invite all cut players back to try out again the following year, unless they're seniors. Remind them that this experience, although disappointing, can be used to better themselves if they keep it in proper perspective. Failure to make the squad should be treated as a learning experience. The player can use it to better himself as a tennis player in the next 12 months or channel his energies into another endeavor he is better suited for.

Evaluating Practice

Being organized at every practice makes evaluating player progress much easier. Use a master plan broken down into monthly activities. Draw daily practice plans from your monthly guide. Set general goals for the team as they progress through the day's practice plan. These goals allow you to evaluate your players' progress on a daily basis.

I keep records of every team I have coached. This data allows me to assess the progress of the current team in relation to similar teams from the past. I can draw on plans made years ago to correct a deficiency in this year's team. Often when I'm reviewing practice plans from the past I'll come across notations in the margins. These notes to myself were written as reminders of solutions I found to problems that plagued my teams. Many times history repeats itself, and current problems often can be solved by applying solutions from the past.

Organization makes for better coaching. Learn from your mistakes so that you will be better able to prevent them when they reoccur later in your career. Practice time can be used more wisely when you don't repeat the same coaching mistakes you made the year before. Keep what works, but don't be afraid to try new techniques. Change is the essence of good coaching.

Observing Practices

The one common denominator all successful teams have is a great work ethic. Don't base your daily evaluation of players during practice solely on the number of errors they make. Look also at the amount of effort your players give as they try to master proper technique. A team's success during match play is directly related to the amount of effort and concentration they produce during practice. The old coaching adage "they'll play at the same level as they practice" holds true almost all the time.

I try to maintain a high level of effort by introducing competitive drills every day in practice. As I said earlier, competitive drills simulate match conditions. Players' efforts will remain high when part of each practice is competitive yet fun.

Use the veterans on your team as a barometer of the team's effort level during different segments of practice. Veterans have been through at least a year of your practices and know what it takes to succeed. Be sure that these veterans are close to giving 100% effort at all times. Younger players on your squad will follow the veterans' lead. This will create a practice atmosphere conducive to learning.

Evaluating Practice With Videotape

One of the best ways to evaluate players in a language they can't dispute is by videotape. Often players who can't visualize corrections in stroke mechanics explained to them verbally view a videotape of their game and gain a different perspective. I have corrected many troublesome strokes by sitting down in front of a TV monitor with a player as she watched herself on tape. For me, videotape has been the most effective teaching tool available.

I videotape each player at least three times during the tennis season. Players bring their own VCR tape to practice on days that we video, which allows them to take the tape home to watch. Once the player has had a chance to view herself on tape, together we evaluate strokes that need attention.

I hold taping sessions three times during the season. The first, which I use to reinforce the verbal evaluation held between myself and each player before the season began, occurs early in the season. Strokes that I mentioned as needing attention are painfully obvious when viewed on tape. The next session is usually held in the middle of the season on a Saturday morning. This video evaluation gives my players a progress report at the halfway point in our season. The last video evaluation takes place at the end of the dual match season before championship play. I try to make this evaluation as positive as possible. I don't want to make changes in strokes at this point in the season. My goal is to focus on stroke production strengths to build self-confidence in each player before the championship season begins.

 BEFORE VIDEOTAPE

In the late 1970s before videotapes were widely available, I had to find other methods of pointing out faulty strokes to the visual learner. In 1980 I had a tenacious player named Mark Heil who could not seem to get enough margin of error over the net on his forehand. Lesson after lesson produced no appreciable improvement. I tried every method of instruction I knew, and I even invented some new ones. Mark and I were both frustrated at not being able to improve this obvious weakness. Finally, as Mark recalls, I came upon a solution to the problem.

> Coach had a photographer take photos in sequence of my forehand. When they were developed it became very obvious to me why this was happening. I had been told how to correct this problem on numerous occasions. I thought I was making the necessary correction, but the stroke never seemed to improve. I could see from the snapshots that I was severely rolling my wrist over when hitting forehands. Instead of brushing up the back of the ball to impart topspin, the way coach wanted me to, I would close my racquet face too much. Using a photographer helped isolate the moment when the racquet made contact with the ball, and I immediately knew what we had been talking about and made the necessary correction.

Use any method available during practice to evaluate a player's progress. Written goals, followed by organized instruction and reinforced with video evaluation, will improve your player's strokes quickly. Attention to detail reinforces to every player that match success comes from giving great effort on the practice court every day.

Evaluating Matches

To evaluate players during match play, you can rely on input from assistants, players charting matches, and personal observations. Once you have compiled the information from match play, you need to put it in a form you can use for evaluation. Accomplish this by giving everyone who evaluates play during matches a specific job.

Assistant Coaches' Evaluation

In years that I've enjoyed the luxury of having volunteer assistant coaches, evaluating match play has become much easier. It is impossible for one person to watch each match on court during play. If you have assistant coaches, use them as extra sets of eyes. Your assistants can report to you during play if a problem arises that requires your coaching attention. After the match is over and the players have gone home, meet with your assistants to debrief each other about how each player performed. During this meeting discuss player evaluations and form a practice plan to correct flaws in players' games that came to light during match play.

 SEEING A FLAW

One season one of our seniors upon whom we were relying to carry us fell into a slump. During his sophomore and junior years, this player had played high in our lineup, but during his senior year he fell to number five singles. His subsequent loss of confidence during match play was evident to everyone. Rival coaches commented on how this player seemed to be only a shell of his former self. I tried my best to help the player shake the mental slump, but to no avail. One of my assistants volunteered to watch each of the player's matches and see if he could find a solution. Shortly before the end of the regular season the player and the assistant coach with whom he had established rapport had a talk without me. The assistant, who had experience coaching other team sports, hit on a solution that worked. The player was refocused and went on to spearhead our drive to a state championship.

As head coaches we sometimes think we have all the answers. However, if we have enough confidence in our assistants to let them coach, the cooperative effort can be beneficial to everyone on the team. Treat your assistants' evaluation of players and situations with respect. Their insight added to your own can sometimes help you and a player to arrive at a solution to a problem that escaped you.

Head Coach's Evaluation

During matches I am keenly aware of the flow of play in as many matches as I feel need my attention. I never sit during matches but walk constantly from court to court, evaluating my team's play. Presenting a positive image and acknowledging good play is my first priority. Imparting coaching suggestions warranted during play is easier when players realize we're working together toward the same goals. In addition, I try to make a note of flaws in tactical, mechanical, or mental aspects of each player's game. I find it's best to write these observations down when they are fresh in mind. Many times I have made observations during play and failed to note them, only to forget them later. Now I carry a notebook with me as I evaluate match play.

Another method of recording thoughts during play is to carry a small audio recorder, which enables you to record your thoughts without taking the time to write them down. No matter how you record your evaluations, do record them. Such notes are invaluable when you and your assistants meet to map a strategy for future practices.

Charting Matches

The fundamental theme of my coaching is focusing a player's attention on performance goals rather than simply winning or losing. Therefore a charting system to evaluate match play is essential feedback to each player. JV players on the team or assistant coaches can accomplish the charting. The system used in our program was developed by a longtime assistant, Richard Dobsha, who developed a general code for charting errors and winners (see Figure 12.3). His system allows all aspects of a match to be evaluated, or just a few.

When JV players chart, give them two or three aspects of match play to watch for that correspond to the player's match card. An example might be charting the number of successful first serves during play. The second performance goal charted could be unforced errors committed from the baseline. The last performance goal might involve the number of times the player took midcourt short balls and came to the net using a slice approach shot.

The speed of doubles play makes it difficult for one evaluator to chart both members of a team. Instead, chart doubles play by making one charter responsible for each member of a doubles team. This allows the evaluator to focus on a single player.

Once the match is completed, the charter calculates numbers for the performance goals and presents the tally sheet to the coach. The performance summaries are discussed by the coaching staff after play (see Figure 12.4), and a strategy to improve weak areas is constructed for future practice sessions.

The evaluation sheets are discussed individually with the players the next day at practice. Nothing can be gained by rehashing match play until the player is receptive to evaluation suggestions. It has been my experience that it's best to wait until the next day to discuss specific evaluations of match play. However, I usually let the player check the charting sheets immediately after play if he wants to get an idea of how he performed in relation to his match cards.

General code for charting errors and winners

F	= Forehand	**V**	= Volley	**P**	= Passing shot
B	= Backhand	**OH**	= Overhead	**Win**	= Winner
1/2	= Half-volley	**SR**	= Service return	**W**	= Wide
D	= Deep	**N**	= Net	**X**	= Point won due to ace
SW	= Service winner	**APP**	= Approach	**U**	= Unforced error
				DF	= Double fault

Figure 12.3

Directions: Use this chart to tally unforced groundstroke errors and groundstroke winners. Log unforced error totals for each stroke in the second row and winner totals in the third row. If the number of unforced errors is higher or equal to winners, then the player should focus on that particular stroke for improvement in practice.

	Forehand	Backhand	Approach	Lob	Half-volley
Unforced errors	20	15	6-F/8-B	4	9
Winners	14	6	5-F/3-B	1	0

Directions: Use this chart to tally unforced volley errors and volley winners. Log unforced error totals for each stroke in the second row and winner totals in third row. Set a number of errors that appears reasonable as a goal for players. If the number exceeds the targeted goal, then work needs to be done on that stroke.

	Forehand volley	Backhand volley	Overhead
Unforced errors	5	3	1
Winners	14	11	4

Directions: Use this chart to tally serves.

Total serves	First serves	% in	DF	Aces	Service win
110	60	54.5	3	5	11

A good percentage of first serves would be in the 60% range. As a rule, double faults should be less than aces and service winners combined.

Code
Total = Total number of serves hit
First serves = First serves that were good
% in = Percentage of first serves in (divide first serves by total serves)
DF = Double faults committed
Aces = Clean aces hit
Service win = Serves that couldn't be put in play by opponent

Figure 12.4   Performance summaries.

The same chart can be used by a more experienced assistant coach to chart every aspect of match play. Referenced comments based on prematch performance goals, such as *player stood flatfooted between shots,* can be noted in the margins of the chart. Another use of this tool is evaluating a future opponent by charting statistics of one of their matches during tournament play. Find a performance chart that you feel comfortable with to evaluate play during singles and doubles. Once you have decided which chart you want to use, devise a coding system to follow play, or use the one in Figure 12.3.

Sample Charting of a Game

Figure 12.5 charts a single game in a match. As you see, the serve is charted in the first row. When charting serves, place a 1 in the box if the first serve is in and a 2 in the box if the second serve is in. DF signifies double fault, and A signifies ace. The server occu-

1	2	DF	A	2	1	1	2
	F-Win		X	FV-Win		OH-Win	B-P
UB-N					FAPP-D		

Figure 12.5   Sample charting of a game.

pies the second row and the receiver the third row. Each column signifies one point played.

1. Figure 12.5 charts your player, whose name is Jim. His opponent is Bob. Jim is serving.

2. Jim hits in his first serve (signified by the 1 in server's first box), but loses the point by hitting an unforced backhand into the net (signified by UB-N). Note that the error committed is listed in the receiver's box, indicating the reason why Jim's opponent, Bob, won the point. Score: Love-15.

3. Point two begins with Jim getting a second serve into play (signified by the 2 in server's second box). The point was finished when Jim hit a forehand winner (signified by the F-Win). Score: 15-15.

4. Jim double-faults the third point away (signified by the DF). Bob won the point due to the double fault. Score: 15-30.

5. Jim serves an ace on the fourth point of the game (signified by the A in the service box and the X in Jim's row). Score: 30-30

6. In the fifth point Jim hits in a second serve and eventually wins the point by hitting a forehand volley winner (FV-Win). Score: 40-30.

7. Jim makes his first serve on the sixth point, which he eventually loses by hitting a forehand approach shot deep (signified by FAPP-D). Score: Deuce.

8. The seventh point is won by Jim, who hits an overhead winner (signified by OH-Win). Score: Jim's advantage.

9. The game ends on the eighth point when Jim's second serve is chipped by Bob, who approaches the net and is passed by a backhand (signified by B-P).

Use Figure 12.6 on next page to chart an entire match.

Summary

Evaluation is the final component of successful coaching. Here's a summary of the key points in the chapter:

- If your state regulations allow contact with your players in the off-season, be sure to involve yourself in their summer tennis activities.
- Provide a list of summer tennis tournaments in your area to every player on your squad and attend as many of these tournaments as you can to evaluate player progress and build rapport.
- Work with your local teaching pro during individual lessons with your players.
- Contact summer tennis camps to inquire about group rates so that you and your squad can attend as a team.
- Conduct a preseason evaluation session with each player.
- Use as much input as possible to fairly evaluate each player who comes out for your squad before cutting anyone.
- Provide each player cut with a means of continuing his or her tennis training through community tennis resources.
- Use records from past years to aid in evaluating problems that arise at practice.
- Base your evaluation of practice on effort, not errors committed by the players.
- Videotape each player at least three times during the season.
- Devise a charting system to use to evaluate match play.

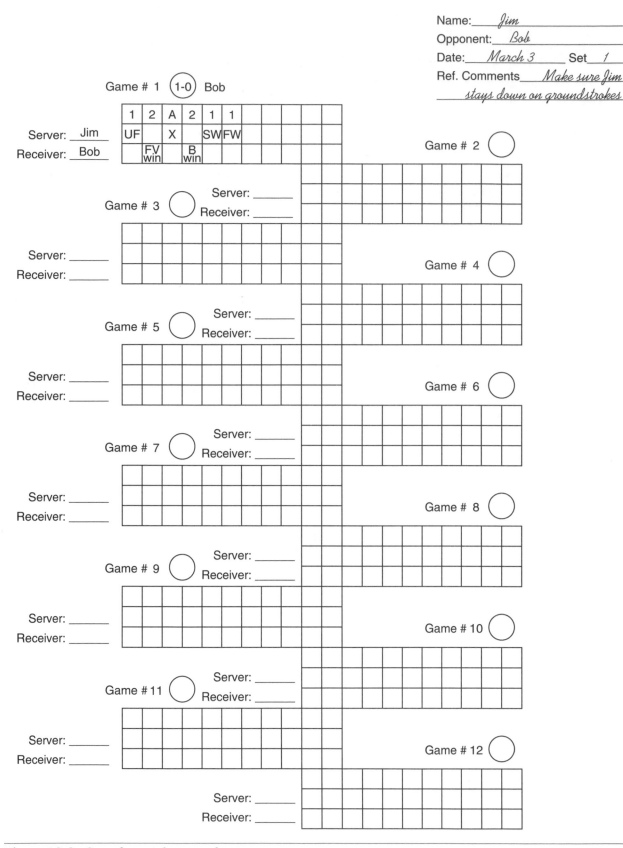

Figure 12.6 Sample match game chart.

Chapter 13

Evaluating
Your Program

When the match season is completed a coach's job doesn't end—it just changes. Every successful coach evaluates and plans in the off-season. I have been asked countless times after a particularly rewarding season how long I would savor the moment. "When I retire from coaching," I always say. Coaching is a year-round endeavor if you hope to be successful. You must review each year, whether it was a good one or bad.

Postseason Evaluation

Develop a system of evaluation that you can use at the end of every year. Reevaluate the goals you set, what you did to try to accomplish them, and where you stood at the end of the year. If the end result was not what you anticipated, then change is warranted. Don't become a coach who coaches 20 years, 1 year at a time, with the same lesson plan.

Review your practice thoroughly. I review the notations I made in the margins of each day's plan. In a separate notebook I write notes to myself about what went particularly well, and what did not. Before the next year begins, I review these notes to restructure my practice plans. Some years I don't find much that needs to be changed before the new season begins. However, I still inject something new into the practice routine every year. This change may be subtle, but the effect is to alleviate practice boredom.

WE WEAR OUR YEARLY PRACTICE SLOGAN

One of the ways I try to make each year different is by having a new slogan or team motto silk-screened on the front of our practice shirts. In 1991, we were coming off a state championship season. We had a veteran team returning, and my biggest concern was that they would rest on their laurels and not work as hard in practice as we had the year before. At our letter winners' meeting we adopted the primary team goal of repeating as state champions. Our slogan became, "Whatever It Takes To Repeat." In reality that meant that from day one a concerted effort was needed on the practice courts from each player. Our 1992 slogan was, "A Healthy Disrespect for the Average," which again reinforced the need for a practice work ethic that would produce above average results. In 1993 the practice theme was evident again when we adopted the slogan, "A Willingness to Prepare."

These slogans are coined to spark a desire to be the best we can be. We decide each new slogan after evaluating the previous year and gauging what type of team we expect at the beginning of the new year. Each team rallies around its slogan and uses it to push each other in daily practice.

Organize your overall evaluation into logical components and gather the information over several weeks before you begin plans for the following year.

If your tennis season was in the spring, school will be ending soon and you need to meet with your players to get their feedback. If you can, squeeze in one-on-one meetings with each player, as they are more likely to be open without the fear of peer reaction. This should be a friendly meeting. Prepare some specific questions to guide the conversation.

A neutral starting point is to review each player's preseason goals and evaluate together her success in reaching them. Give her a chance to react first and restrict yourself to helpful questions and clarifying statements. Ask her how she might adjust her goals now that the season is behind her—this will naturally lead to a discussion of the off-season and the next year.

Each player's plans for the off-season are critical to your team's improvement in the coming year. You may have specific suggestions such as recommending a tennis camp, tournament play, private lessons on stroke technique, or some helpful books or videos on tennis. Offer to help in any way you can throughout the coming weeks and months.

Don't let the season end without some candid discussion of your performance as a coach. You can allay your players' fears of criticizing you by holding a conversation something like this:

Coach: I wondered if you had any suggestions for me in how I can improve my coaching before next season?

Player: Uh . . . not really.

Coach: What one thing did you think I did really well this year?

Player: Well, you sure are organized . . . down to the last detail.

Coach: Yeah, I'm a bit compulsive sometimes. Well, what about one thing I could do better next year?

Player: Maybe you could stay a little calmer during matches. It makes me nervous when you get upset.

Coach: Hummm . . . I see what you mean. I'll think about some ways I can do that. Thanks.

An additional evaluative tool to consider is a postseason form that your players can complete. Figure 13.1 is a sample that you can modify to suit your needs. The anonymity that a written evaluation form offers your players may elicit comments more candid than those you get in one-on-one meetings.

Feedback From Seniors

Your conversation with senior players will be special because they will not be returning for another year. They have also had the opportunity to be part of the program for several years and with their increasing maturity can provide a more objective viewpoint than that of underclassmen.

Some coaches prefer to receive a written evaluation from the outgoing seniors. Let the seniors know that their feedback is important in helping you improve the program and your performance as coach. Since seniors have little to lose from criticism, they can provide the tough comments that you may not like to hear but may find invaluable. Here are the questions I ask my seniors:

1. What were your best experiences in our tennis program during your career?

2. How could I improve practice?

3. What part of practice did you dread?

4. How can we improve leadership from within the players' ranks?

5. How did you manage your time during the tennis season so that your schoolwork didn't suffer?

If you've been able to assist your seniors in choosing a college with a tennis program appropriate for their level of play, use the opportunity to suggest some areas of their game to focus on before they try out in the fall.

Personal Evaluation

Your next task is to begin the process of self-evaluation, which should take several months to complete. The advantage of starting shortly after the season's end is that ideas and feelings are fresh in your mind. As you gather input from other sources, add it to your initial impressions.

Start your self-evaluation with a review of your own goals set before the season began. It's helpful to reflect on both the performance goals you had as a coach and the outcome goals you set for the team.

It may be helpful next to consider your own performance in terms of your communication skills, teaching skills, and organizational and administrative skills.

Evaluating Your Communication Skills

When evaluating your communication skills, refer to the checklist of topics we covered earlier in chapter 2. Consider your success in communicating with players, parents, media, and other team supporters. Rely on your interviews and conversations with each player at season's end for enlightening comments and suggestions for improvement.

 THE GREATEST COACH WHO EVER YELLED

In the early 1970s my players gave me a plaque that read "To the Greatest Coach Who Ever Yelled." It was an expression of my coaching style as well as their feeling about it. And it was with pride that I hung the plaque on my wall.

As I continued through my coaching career, I discovered that yelling did not always bring success and admiration from the team. I had a player who was yelled at all the time, and in a derogatory way. She survived by tuning everyone out who raised his voice at her. She tuned me out, too.

Although that style of coaching worked with some players, I realized it didn't work for everyone. Needless to say, I had to change if I wanted her to be receptive to my advice and criticism. I discovered a more mellow approach to coaching that actually became more pleasurable and successful for me.

Evaluating Your Teaching Skills

I suggest that you review your teaching performance in the following five categories: tennis technique, physical training, strategy, mental toughness, and match play.

The following checklist may help you organize the review of your performance as a

Program Evaluation Form for Players

Please complete each of the following questions, being as honest and constructive as possible. Your input into this tennis program is essential for its future success.

1. In terms of tennis skills and strategies, I learned . . .

   1   2   3   4   5   6   7
   Nothing   A lot

2. My performance of tennis skills and strategies improved . . .

   1   2   3   4   5   6   7
   Not at all   A lot

3. I enjoyed playing tennis this season.

   1   2   3   4   5   6   7
   Not at all   A lot

4. The coaching staff helped me develop as a player.

   1   2   3   4   5   6   7
   Not at all   A lot

5. The coaching staff helped me develop as a person.

   1   2   3   4   5   6   7
   Not at all   A lot

6. Players are treated fairly on the team.

   1   2   3   4   5   6   7
   Not at all   A lot

7. Players on the team respected team rules.

   1   2   3   4   5   6   7
   Not at all   Very true

8. Practices were well organized, challenging, and fun.

   1   2   3   4   5   6   7
   Not at all   Very true

9. The role I played in matches was the best for the program.

   1   2   3   4   5   6   7
   Not at all   Very true

10. I feel more positively about the program now than I did at the beginning of the season.

   1   2   3   4   5   6   7
   Not at all   Very true

The best thing about being a player in this tennis program:
_____

The worst thing about being a player in this tennis program:
_____

Name specific changes you would make to improve or eliminate the worst things about the program:
_____
_____

What can the coaching staff do to make the program better than it was this past season?
_____
_____

Additional comments (use reverse side):

Figure 13.1   Postseason player evaluation form.

coach. Take the time to write out your answers to each question so that you will have a clear plan for improving your coaching skill in the months ahead.

Technique

❏ Did your players improve their technique individually and collectively during the season?

❏ What skills were you most successful in improving? Which were the least successful?

❏ How can you plan an effective off-season for returning players so that their technique will be improved at the beginning of next season?

Physical Training

❏ Were matches won or lost as a direct result of your physical training program?

❏ Was the time spent on training appropriate? Should it be increased or decreased?

❏ Were your players motivated effectively to train throughout the season?

Strategy

❏ Did your players grasp and apply the concepts of percentage tennis?

❏ Did the drills and activities in practice reinforce those concepts as well as possible?

❏ Were your players able to assess their own strengths and weaknesses as well as those of their opponents?

❏ Did each player compete in every match with an identifiable style of play and a well-conceived game plan that fit his style?

Mental Toughness

❏ Did your team respond appropriately and successfully to pressure situations?

❏ Were the principles of good sportsmanship, fair play, and accurate line calls characteristic of your team?

❏ Could you notice improvement during the season in your team's competitive skills? At season's end were they confident and poised during the championships?

Coaching Match Play

❏ Were you effective in helping players prepare for each match?

❏ Did you have success coaching during a match within the rules of your league? What about during the time between singles and doubles?

❏ Did you reserve time after each match as a team and with individuals to assess performance and plan a course of action?

Organization and Administration

The tasks of organization and administration that confront a high school coach can be daunting. Experience in your position is likely the best teacher, but here are a few areas to consider:

1. Did you make effective use of resources at hand such as assistant coaches, team captains, team manager, scorekeepers, volunteers, booster club, and the media?

2. Were you able to delegate tasks effectively, make efficient use of your time, and give attention to the details of organization?

3. What improvements were made to the tennis facilities and equipment this year including courts, nets, water coolers, score-keepers, spectator seating, ball machines, teaching carts, and targets?

4. Was the current budget adequate? What changes in priorities or additions should be made for next year?

5. How appropriate was the schedule of matches in terms of frequency, spacing, and level of difficulty?

6. Generally evaluate the organization of team practices and variations in quality, intensity, and duration throughout the season.

7. Were your team policies and rules effective and infractions handled effectively?

Continuing Education

Your personal assessment should conclude with a plan for continuing education and improvement as a coach. Consider becoming a certified tennis professional of the United States Professional Tennis Association (USPTA) or the United States Professional Tennis Registry (USPTR). Typically, certification requires that you pass a written test on tennis strategy, rules of the game, and coaching strategies along with an on-court practical test of teaching ability and tennis skill.

The USPTA has recently added a membership category that is particularly for high school coaches. It does not require testing and does not result in certification. Call the USPTA at 713-97-USPTA and the USPTR at 803-785-7244.

Other advice to improve your coaching skills includes rereading this book over the winter, attending conferences or workshops in your area, and ordering instructional books and/or videos from the USTA by calling 800-247-8273. You might also consider volunteering as an assistant coach to a local teaching professional or at a tennis camp. Much can be learned by working closely with other coaches.

Building a Dynasty

Every coach dreams of creating a dynasty of successful tennis teams for years to come. The secret to achieving this goal is to mobilize your town or community through forming a Community Tennis Association (CTA). A CTA is a group of individuals who love the game and are willing to volunteer time to promote it in their community for players of all ages, but particularly for kids. Many CTAs raise funds to support affordable tennis instruction year-round, summer tournaments, traveling competitive teams, and special tennis events. The CTA can tap into school funds and build a feeder system for your upcoming high school players.

Enlist the help of local tennis teaching professionals, members of your tennis booster club, and avid players who have a passion for tennis. Together you can turn Anytown, USA, into the tennis capital of the world.

Summary

Here are points to consider as you evaluate your program:

- Develop a personal system of evaluating your program and coaching performance.
- Gather information from players, parents, assistant coaches, and the athletic director.
- Write out your personal evaluation using the questions presented in this chapter.
- Set specific personal goals for the off-season to begin your preparation for the next year.

Off-Season Training for Tournament Play

Stretch before and after each workout.

Day 1   *Drill with partner or on ball machine (2 hours)*
Basics: groundstrokes, crosscourt, midcourt put-aways, down-the-line ap-
*   proach shots*
Strength training

Day 2   *Drill with partner or on ball machine (2 hours)*
Basics (same as day 1)
Distance run (2 miles)

Day 3   *Drill with partner (1 hour)*
Basics (same as day 1)
Play minimum of three sets
Distance run (1 mile)
Strength training

Day 4   *1 hour private lesson with coach*
Groundstroke mechanics: crosscourt from baseline; defensive lob; approach
*   shot; hit out or chip; volley; offensive-defensive*
Work on serve
Half hour hitting
Two to five games to 21 points
Distance run (2 miles)

Day 5   *Play match*
Distance run after match (1 mile)
Strength training

Day 6   *Drill with partner (1 hour)*
              Basics
              Play two different opponents a pro set each
              Distance run (2 miles)
              Sit-ups, push-ups—4 sets (25-15)

Day 7   *1 hour private lesson with coach*
              Same content as day 4 lesson
              Half hour directional hitting (crosscourt and down the line)
              Play match
              Light run (1 mile)

Day 8   *Play three sets*
              Circuit train (index card)
              Strength training

Day 9   *1 hour private lesson with coach*
              Review basics, work on individual weakness, work on strengths, service re-
              *   turn*
              25 serves to each court
              Return serve from partner (25 each court)
              Play match
              Light run (1 mile)

Day 10   *Play match*
              Jump rope 10 to 15 minutes
              Strength training

Day 11   *Play two different opponents a match*
              Circuit train (index card)

Day 12   *1 hour private lesson with coach; emphasis on maintaining a positive attitude*
              *   during play*
              Work on strengths, approach, split-step, volley (offensive-crosscourt,
              *   defensive-down the line), overhead*
              Half hour hitting with partner
              Play match
              No running

Day 13   *Play match*
              Circuit train (index card)
              Strength training

Day 14   *Hit with partner (2 hours)*
              Deep Court game, Crosscourt/Down-the-Line game, Approach If Short Ball
              *   game, One Up, One Back game (play to 10 points)*
              2 mile run

Day 15   *Play match*
              Four quarter-mile repeats (30 seconds between)
              Strength training

Day 16   *1 hour private lesson with coach*
Review "situation shots," serve, service return
Play match
Circuit train (index card)

Day 17   *Play matches with two different opponents*
Four 50-yard sprints (25 seconds between)
Strength training

Day 18   *Drill with partner*
Basics
Play match
Circuit train (index card)

Day 19   *1 hour private lesson with coach*
Review, fine-tune strokes, stress players' strengths
Tell the player to control the ball on their strings and not overhit
1 hour directional hitting with partner, crosscourt and down the line
Jump rope (two 10-minute periods, 3 minutes between)
Strength training

Day 20   *1 hour directional hitting with partner (crosscourt and down the line)*
Serve and service return (served from short court by partner)
Circuit training (index card)

Day 21   *(Light day) Play match*
No running

Day 22   *2 hours hitting (games from day 14)*
Circuit training (index card)
Begin eating for tournament

Day 23   *Play match*
Five 30-yard sprints (20 seconds between)

Day 24   *Half hour directional hitting*
Private lesson with coach
Look at all strokes, be positive, drill strengths
Play match
Five 30-yard sprints (20 seconds between)

Day 25   *Play match*
Five 20-yard sprints (15 seconds between)

Day 26   *Play match*
Six 10-yard sprints (10 seconds between)
Continue eating for tournament and drink more fluids

Day 27   *Light workout with partner and coach*
Two out of three tiebreakers
10 minutes of rope jumping

Day 28   *Travel to tournament, work out on match courts*

Strength Training

Strength—power—speed—flexibility

- *Eat properly*
- *Get enough rest*
- *Lift with a partner*
- *Full range of motion with all lifts*
- *Stress repetition, not amount of weight*
- *Stretch before and after workout*
- *Stop lifting 1 week before a tournament*

Off-season program: 3 days per week (1 day rest minimum between lifting sessions)

1. **Bent-knee sit-up**. *Hook feet under sit-up board strap or have partner hold feet down. Keep knees bent 45 degrees. Fold arms on chest. Lie back until lower back touches. Pull up concentrating on abdominal muscles. Inhale down, exhale up. (1 to 2 sets, 25 to 50 per set)*

2. **Seated barbell twist**. *Place light barbell on shoulders. Sit at end of bench with feet firmly on floor. Twist torso to right, then left, twisting at waist only. Do not move head from side to side. Keep back straight and head up. Inhale to right, exhale to left. Can also be done standing. (1 set, 25 to 50 per side)*

3. **Dumbbell press**. *Lie on bench with feet flat on floor. Hold dumbbell at arm's length with palms facing each other. Lower dumbbells straight down to sides of chest, arms close to sides. Push back to starting position using same path. Arms must be in close at all times. Inhale down, exhale up. (3 sets of 12-10-10)*

4. **Dumbbell pullover**. *Lie on bench, head at end, feet flat on floor. Start with hands flat against inside plate of dumbbell at arm's length above chest. Lower dumbbell in semicircular motion behind head as far as you can without pain. Return dumbbell to starting position, elbows locked. Inhale down, exhale up. Breathe heavily, keep head down, chest high, hips on bench. Can also be done with barbell. (2 sets of 12-10)*

5. **Standing military press**. *Raise barbell to chest, hands shoulder width apart. Lock legs and hips solidly. Keep elbows in slightly under bar. Press bar to arm's length overhead. Lower to upper chest. Be sure bar rests on chest and is not supported by arms between reps. Hold chest high. Inhale up, exhale down. (3 sets of 12-10-10)*

6. **Dumbbell rowing**. *Place dumbbell on floor in front of bench. Put left leg back with knee locked. Bend right knee slightly. Bend over and hold dumbbell with left hand, palm in, about 6 inches off floor. Put right hand on bench with elbow locked. Pull dumbbell straight up to side. Return to starting position using same path. Inhale up, exhale down.*

Reverse position and repeat movement on right side. (3 sets of 12-10-10)

7. **Dips**. *Hold yourself erect on bars. Keep elbows in to sides and lower body by bending shoulders and elbows. Continue down as far as you can. Pause, then press back to arm's length. Do not let body swing back and forth. Inhale down, exhale up. (2 to 3 sets, 15 per set—add weight later)*

8. **Seated dumbbell curl**. *Hold dumbbells. Sit at end of bench with feet firmly on floor. Keep back straight and head up. Start with dumbbells at arm's length, palms in. Begin curl with palms in until past thighs, then turn palms up for remainder of curl to shoulder height. Keep palms up while lowering until past thighs, then turn palms in. Keep upper arms close to sides. Concentrate on biceps while raising and lowering weights. Inhale up, exhale down. (1 to 2 sets, 10 per set)*

9. **Seated palms-down barbell wrist curl**. *Hold barbell with both hands, palms down, hands 16 inches apart. Sit at end of bench with feet on floor about 20 inches apart. Lean forward and place forearms on upper thighs. Place wrists over knees. Lower bar as far as you can, keeping a tight grip. Curl bar as high as you can. Do not let forearms raise up. Inhale up, exhale down. (2 sets, 15 to 20 per set)*

10. **Seated palms-up barbell wrist curl**. *Hold barbell with both hands, palms up, hands 16 inches apart. Sit at end of bench with feet on floor about 20 inches apart. Lean forward and place forearms on upper thighs. Place backs of wrists over knees. Lower bar as far as you can, keeping a tight grip. Curl bar as high as you can. Do not let forearms raise up. Inhale up, exhale down. (1 to 2 sets, 15 per set)*

11. **Jump squat**. *Stand erect with arms crossed over chest. Keep your head up, back straight, feet about 16 inches apart. Squat until upper thighs are parallel, or lower, to floor. Keep head up, back straight, knees slightly out. Jump straight up in the air as high as possible, using thighs like springs. Immediately squat and jump again. Inhale up, exhale down. Can also be done with barbell held on upper back or with dumbbells hanging at sides. (3 sets, 15 to 20 per set)*

12. **Barbell front lunge**. *Place barbell on upper back. Use comfortable hand grip. Keep head up, back straight, feet about 6 inches apart. Step forward as far as possible with left leg until upper left thigh is almost parallel to floor. Keep right leg as straight as possible. Step back to starting position. Inhale out, exhale back. Repeat with right leg. (2 sets, 15 to 20 per set each leg)*

In-season program: 2 days per week with 1 to 2 days rest minimum between lifting sessions. Stop 2 days before matches.

1. **Incline bench**. *Lie on incline bench. Hold dumbbells together at arm's length above shoulders with palms forward. Slowly lower dumbbells to chest until 10 inches from each side of chest. Keep elbows in line with ears and forearms slightly out of vertical position. Return to starting position using same path. Inhale down, exhale up. (2 sets of 12-10)*

2. **Dumbbell pullover**. *Lie on bench, head at end, feet flat on floor. Start with hands flat against inside plate of dumbbell at arm's length above chest. Lower dumbbell in semi-circular motion behind head as far as possible without pain. Return dumbbell to starting position, elbows locked. Inhale down, exhale up. Breathe heavily, keep head down, chest high, hips on bench. Can also be done with barbell or standing medicine ball throw. (1 set, 12 per set)*

3. **Seated side lateral raise**. *Sit at end of bench with feet firmly on floor. Hold dumbbells with palms in and arms straight down at sides. Raise dumbbells in semicircular motion a little above shoulder height. Pause, then lower to starting position using same path. Keep arms straight. Inhale up, exhale down. Can also be done standing. (2 sets of 12-10)*

4. **Medium grip front chin-up**. *Use chinning bar about 6 inches higher off floor than you can reach with arms extended overhead. Hold bar with hands 18 inches to 20 inches apart. Pull up, trying to touch chin to bar. Return to starting position. Try to keep back slightly hyperextended. Do not swing back and forth. Inhale up, exhale down. (Do as many as possible.)*

5. **Seated dumbbell triceps curl**. *Hold dumbbell with both hands and raise overhead to arm's length. Rotate hands while raising dumbbell so top plates of dumbbell rest in palm, thumbs around handle. Sit at end of bench with feet firmly on floor, back straight, and head up. Keep upper arms close to head. Lower dumbbell in semicircular motion behind head until forearms touch biceps. Inhale down, exhale up. (2 sets of 12-10)*

6. **Wrist roll curl**. *Place light weight on end of rope of wrist roller. Stand erect with back straight and head up. Hold wrist roller with both hands, palms down. Extend arms straight out. Roll weight up by curling right hand over and down, then left hand over and down. Keep arms parallel to floor. Continue curling right to left hand until weight touches bar. Lower weight to starting position by reversing movement. (1 set)*

Index

About the Author

The United States Tennis Association (USTA) is the governing body for tennis in the United States. The USTA's membership consists of more than 500,000 individuals and nearly 6,500 organizations, including schools, park and recreation departments or community tennis associations, and tennis clubs.

The USTA is widely known as the owner and operator of the U.S. Open Championships, one of the four Grand Slam tournaments in worldwide tennis competition. The U.S. Open annually attracts more than a half million fans, awards more than $9 million in prize money, and is broadcast on television to 125 countries.

The USTA also sponsors amateur tennis competition for players of all ages and abilities, ranging from events for youngsters 12 and under to national tournaments for those 65 and older. More than 5 million schoolchildren are introduced to tennis each year through USTA school programs, and opportunities for further instruction and play are provided by a menu of USTA entry-level programs.

A full range of player development and sport science programs is offered at Player Development Headquarters in Key Biscayne, FL, at 120 Area Training Centers spread throughout the country, and in communities through local Excellence Training Programs. In addition, the USTA emphasizes coaching education and development through an ambitious offering of coaching seminars, workshops, and conferences. The USTA works closely with the two major coaching certifying organizations—the U.S. Professional Tennis Association (USPTA), and the U.S. Professional Tennis Registry (USPTR)—which together account for more than 18,000 members.

Ron Woods coordinated the project for the USTA and wrote selected chapters of *Coaching Tennis Successfully*. Ron is the director of player development for the USTA and is responsible for planning and implementing programs that help young players achieve their maximum potential, from beginning competitive tennis through the professional ranks. Ron also serves as a senior staff member for USTA committees in charge of player development, sport science, Olympics, junior competition, and collegiate tennis.

Ron is a member of the International Tennis Federation's Coaches Commission and serves on the coaching committee of the United States Olympic Committee. The USPTA honored him as 1982 National Coach of the Year and designated him a Master Professional in 1984. Ron is also an honorary member of the USPTR.

Ron served as a professor of physical education and men's tennis coach at West Chester University in Pennsylvania for 17 years. He earned his PhD from Temple University with an emphasis in sport psychology and motor learning.

About the Contributors

Since **Mike Hoctor** began coaching boys' tennis at Astronaut High (Titusville, FL) in 1972, his teams have won their district championship 13 times and the Cape Coast Conference championship 11 times. They were also Class 3A state champions in 1990, 1992, and 1994 and Class 3A state runners-up 3 times. Mike has been named the Cape Coast Conference Coach of the Year no fewer than 14 times, and in 1994 he became only the second tennis coach to be inducted into the Florida Athletic Coaches Hall of Fame. Mike was also the Chairman of the Florida Athletic Coaches Association from 1988-1994.

Mike is a USPTA-certified teaching professional. In addition to his duties as coach and guidance counselor at Astronaut High, he also enjoys teaching at the public courts in Titusville for the Brevard County Recreation Department.

Becky Desmond has coached the Downingtown (PA) Senior High School girls' tennis team since 1968 and the boys' team since 1983. Her girls' teams have won the Ches-Mont League championship 11 times, while her boys' teams have captured two league crowns. Becky was named coach of the year in 1987 and 1990 by the *West Chester Daily Local News*. In 1983 she was named the USPTA's Middle States Division Coach of the Year and in 1994 she was named the USTA's Middle States Section Coach of the Year.

Becky is the former president of USPTA's Middle States Division. She is on the board of the USTA's Middle States Section and serves on the section's sanction, ranking and endorsement, and membership committees. She has chaired the Ches-Mont and District I (southeastern Pennsylvania) girls' tennis committee for 21 years.

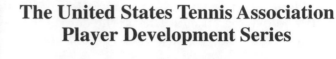
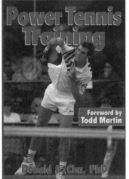
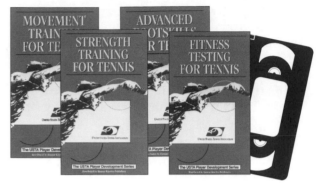

The American Sport Education Program (ASEP) believes that the single most important step in improving amateur sport is to educate coaches. For this reason, ASEP offers its *SportCoach* curriculum at three levels:

- **Volunteer Level**, for coaches who work with youth sport programs
- **Leader Level**, for coaches in interscholastic or club sport
- **Master Level**, for coaches who have completed Leader Level courses and seek further professional development

ASEP's *SportCoach* Curriculum

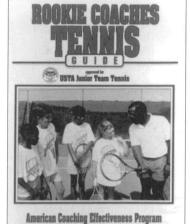

Volunteer Level

One of the *SportCoach* courses for educating youth sport coaches is the Rookie Coaches Course. This course is for anyone who is coaching children's sports for the first time and has no formal training as a coach. The *Rookie Coaches Tennis Guide*, an excellent reference for new tennis coaches, serves as a text for the course.

Leader Level

ASEP's Leader Level *SportCoach* curriculum consists of three courses: the Coaching Principles Course, Sport First Aid Course, and Drugs and Sport Course. These courses teach coaches to form a sportsmanship-based coaching philosophy, communicate better with athletes, plan and teach sport skill progressions, manage risks effectively, provide appropriate first aid for sport injuries, and tackle the problem of drug use among athletes.

Master Level

At the Master Level, coaches can choose from 9 *SportCoach* courses: Sport Psychology, Sport Physiology, Teaching Sport Skills, Sport Injuries, Sport Rehabilitation, Nutrition/Weight Control, Sport Law, Time Management, and Sport Administration.

For more information about ASEP's *SportCoach* curriculum, call the ASEP National Center toll-free at 1-800-747-5698. Let ASEP help you expand your coaching skills and knowledge. Your athletes will be glad you did!

American Sport Education Program

P.O. Box 5076 • Champaign, IL 61825-5076 • Toll-free phone: 1-800-747-5698